IN THE CORNER

Other books by Dave Anderson

Sports of Our Times
Hey, Wait a Minute, I Wrote a Book! (with John Madden)
One Knee Equals Two Feet (with John Madden)
One Size Doesn't Fit All (with John Madden)
Countdown to Super Bowl
Always on the Run (with Larry Csonka and Jim Kiick)
Sugar Ray (with Sugar Ray Robinson)
Shooting for the Gold
Frank: The First Year (with Frank Robinson)
The Yankees
Upset
Return of a Champion: Panche Gonzalez
The Story of Football
The Story of Basketball
Great Quarterbacks of the NFL
Great Pass-Receivers of the NFL
Great Defensive Players of the NFL

IN THE
CORNER

*Great Boxing Trainers
Talk About Their Art*

≡

DAVE ANDERSON

WILLIAM MORROW AND COMPANY, INC.
New York

Recognizing the importance of preserving what has been written, it is the policy of William Morrow and Company, Inc., and its imprints and affiliates to have the books it publishes printed on acid-free paper, and we exert our best efforts to that end.

Library of Congress Cataloging-in-Publication Data

Anderson, Dave.
   In the corner: great boxing trainers talk about their art/
Dave Anderson.
     p. cm.
   Includes index.
   ISBN 0-688-09446-5
   1. Boxing—United States—Trainers—Biography. I. Title.
GV1131.A53 1991
796.8'8'0973—dc20   90-48942
                                                  CIP

Printed in the United States of America

First Edition

1 2 3 4 5 6 7 8 9 10

BOOK DESIGN BY PAUL CHEVANNES

For all the trainers in this book and for all those—Cus D'Amato, George Gainford, Charlie Goldman, Jack Blackburn, Manny Seamon, Dan Florio, Freddie Brown and so many others—who died too soon to be included

Contents

Introduction

===

On my way to Lewiston, Maine, for Muhammad Ali's defense of the heavyweight title against Sonny Liston in 1965, I stopped in Chicopee, Massachusetts, where Ali was training. As a boxer, Ali was at the top of his game. As a showman, he was at the top of his lungs. Then a young sportswriter, I remember Ali shouting, "If I said I would knock out Sonny Liston in one minute and forty-nine seconds of the first round, it would hurt the gate." As it turned out, Ali was declared the winner after one minute and fifty-two seconds. But what I remember most was a quiet moment when Ali's trainer, Angelo Dundee, took me aside.

"When are you driving to Lewiston?"

"Tomorrow morning," I said. "I'll be there around noontime."

"Will you do me a favor? Will you measure the ring for me?"

"Measure the ring?"

"I hear they've got a small ring in the arena. The contract calls for a twenty-foot ring. My guy needs a twenty-foot ring. He needs room to maneuver. In a small ring, Liston's got an edge. Do me a favor. Measure the ring. Then call me."

"I'll measure it," I said.

The next day I walked into St. Dominic's Arena, where the fight would be held the following Monday night. It was empty except for a few workmen in overalls who were hammering together the wooden-board desk tops of the working-press rows. On one of the boards was a steel measuring tape.

"May I borrow that tape?" I asked.

One of the workmen handed it to me. He even held one end of the tape as I measured the ring inside the ropes. Sixteen feet by sixteen feet.

"Thank you," I said.

I phoned Angelo Dundee at the Chicopee motel where he and Ali and the champion's entourage were lodged.

"It's a sixteen-foot ring," I told him.

"Then the fight's off," he said. "If they don't get a twenty-foot ring or move this fight somewhere else, the fight's off. And you can tell Bob Nilon that I said that."

I found Nilon in an empty storefront in Lewiston that was being used as the promoter's ticket headquarters for the fight.

"You've got a problem," I said. "The ring's too small."

I explained that I had measured it myself, that it was only sixteen feet inside the ropes, that Angelo Dundee had told me to tell him that the fight was off unless they brought in a twenty-foot ring.

"Is that so?" Nilon said innocently. "Only sixteen feet."

Typical of the intrigue that always surrounds boxing, Bob Nilon's brother, Jack, was one of Liston's managers. They knew that a small ring would be to Liston's advantage. So a small ring had been borrowed from the nearby Brunswick Naval Air Station gym. But when Angelo Dundee called their bluff and I wrote the story for the *Journal-American,* a bigger ring soon was trucked up from Baltimore.

"It's only nineteen feet, six inches," Angelo told me later. "But that's big enough."

Big enough for Ali to finish Liston within three seconds of his prediction. And big enough for me to appreciate the importance of a trainer. Fighters come and go, but trainers are the constant of boxing. Trainers are its professors. Not just professors of pugilism, but professors of psychology and sometimes of psychiatry. In the gym during the long dreary weeks of preparing a fighter for a fight. In the corner when they must be sixty-second savants.

Trainers toil with young men searching for an escape to a better life, young men who sometimes emerge as champions.

"Tough times make monkeys eat red peppers" is how Ray Arcel describes what boxers endure in order to be champions, in order to be part of some of history's most memorable fights. But that saying also describes what trainers endure in order to help create a champion.

In the tape-recorded conversations with the twelve trainers in this book, you'll find that each trainer is different. Ray Arcel, for example, is scholarly. Angelo Dundee is bubbly. Eddie Futch is fatherly.

The night in Las Vegas in 1983 when Larry Holmes defended the heavyweight title against Marvis Frazier, Eddie Futch knew it was a mismatch. Futch had known Joe Frazier's son from the time Marvis was a little boy.

"I don't want Marvis hurt," Futch told Holmes. "I want you to get him out of there as fast as you can."

Holmes waved for the referee to stop it even before the referee did, after two minutes and fifty-seven seconds.

Of the twelve trainers in this book, only George Benton and Kevin Rooney were highly ranked contenders. Lou Duva, Goody Petronelli, and Jackie McCoy fought as pros. Richie Giachetti, Eddie Futch, and Emanuel Steward were good amateurs. Arcel, Dundee, Gil Clancy, and Bill Slayton learned their trade in dark, dusty gyms by studying older trainers of another era. But all told better stories about their boxers than anyone else in this brutal business. That's why I wanted to put their best stories together. Call it memoirs. Call it an oral history. Whatever you call it, trainers know better than anybody else why the best boxers were the best boxers.

Not that any is up for canonization. They all looked for an edge. Some took an edge, as Lou Duva did the night in Providence when Johnny Bumphus got butted by Marlon Starling in the sixth round.

As an experiment in that televised fight, the scorecards were announced after every round. Knowing that Bumphus was ahead and knowing that the rules called for the boxer leading on the scorecards anytime after the sixth round to be declared the winner in the event of a butt, Duva not only ignored Bumphus's cut, he opened it more.

"My cutman, Ace Marotta, is saying, 'I can handle that cut,' and

I'm saying, 'Stay away from it,' " Duva recalls. "I put my fingernail in there and spread it open just enough so when the doctor got there, he said, 'He can't fight with that. I'm stopping it.' So we win."

In recent years a few trainers have earned millions from big fights. But when those trainers started working with fighters, the money wasn't that big. Whatever big money some have collected in recent years is a reward for what they didn't make years ago.

To a trainer, sculpturing a boxer's skill is much more than draping a towel over a shoulder and carrying a bucket into the ring. It's teaching someone how to fight. Nothing annoys trainers more than a pro football player or a shot-putter who thinks he can become a boxer just by having someone tape his hands.

"You have to be taught how to fight," Gil Clancy says. "It's not a strength sport. It's a skill sport."

It's also a story sport. Perhaps the best story sport of all. These are the stories twelve trainers tell.

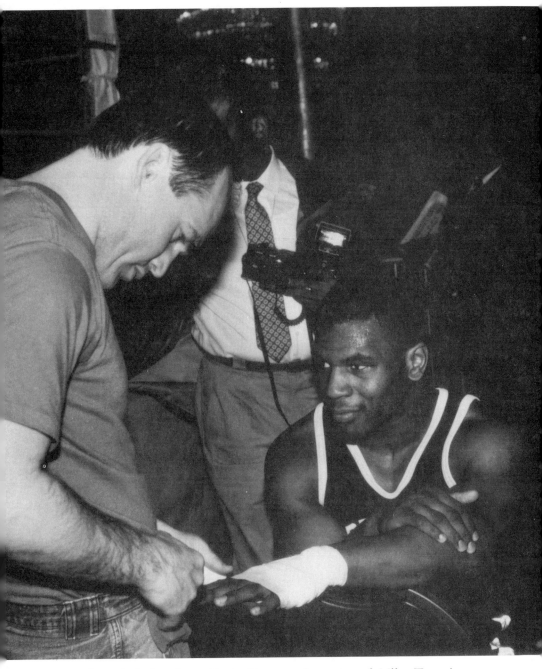

Before their breakup, Kevin Rooney always taped Mike Tyson's
hands.   TOM CASINO

Kevin Rooney:

"Cus Always Talked About Fear"

===

Across the street, alongside a huge photo of this Hudson Valley village's most celebrated resident, a peeling billboard announced, "Catskill, Home of Mike Tyson."

Up a creaking wooden stairway and outside the village offices on the second floor above the police station hangs a painting that should be entitled "The Joy of the Knockout." Tyson, a smile breaking through his mouthpiece, his gloves at his side but slightly in front of him, is turning to walk to a neutral corner after having floored Jesse Ferguson in a 1986 bout.

Up another flight of stairs, across from the village court office, a wooden door opens to what was once a town meeting hall and theater. Now it's a boxing gym.

Newspaper clippings, a yellowed chronicle of Tyson's career, fill the walls. Near the door two red leather heavy bags dangle not far from an exercise bike and some weight-lifting contraptions. Under fluorescent lights is the ring. On the wall to the right is a sign: "Cus D'Amato Catskill Boxing Club." In a far corner is a small plaque with the date of the famous trainer's death, November 4, 1985. Above it are the words "We Mourn His Passing."

One of the mourners, Kevin Rooney, sat at a small table near the ring. Once a welterweight with a 21–4–1 record, he is D'Amato's disciple, the trainer during Tyson's ascent to the heavyweight title.

"Cus used to sit in that metal chair over there by the side of the ring," he was saying now. "I can still hear him saying, 'Move your head after you punch.' He said it to me, he said it to Mike Tyson, he said it to everybody. But he always told me and every other fighter in here, 'In the end, I can only bring you so far. In the end, you got to get in the ring and do it yourself.' I was a fighter, that's why I know."

In a wooden alcove that once served as a stage, two mattresses were strapped to boards. Numbers from 1 to 7 adorned the mattresses at various locations.

"Each number represents a different punch," Rooney explained. "Left hook to the ribs. Right hand to the jaw. Left jab to the head. Right to the body. Left hook to the liver."

Kevin Rooney's voice is out of a Dead End Kids movie. Born in the Bronx on May 4, 1956, he grew up on the Staten Island docks, the fourth of five children. His father was a longshoreman.

"I started hanging out in the Police Athletic League gym," he said. "I went to Curtis High School, didn't graduate, dropped out after my junior year. When I went into the 1975 Golden Gloves as a sub-novice, my friend Brian Hamill was taking pictures for a piece in the *Village Voice* about me. He followed me through the tournament and I won it. Brian knew Cus, so he called up Cus and I came up here in 1975 under Cus's wing."

Now other fighters are under Rooney's wing. Starting in 1985, he organized a boxing program at the Greene Correctional Facility in nearby Coxsackie, New York.

"It's a medium A-security prison, the next one down from a max," he said. "Even when I started making money with Tyson, the program wasn't what I wanted yet, so I stayed with it. Those guys were such bad fighters at first, every day I had to tell them the same thing. But doing that reinforced in my own mind everything Cus had taught me."

D'Amato had sculptured Floyd Patterson into the heavyweight champion and José Torres into the light heavyweight champion.

"I fought Alexis Arguello and Davey Moore," Rooney said. "I sparred with Roberto Duran and Wilfredo Benitez. When I was sparring, Cus always told me to go as hard as I could go. If you train hard, you're going to fight hard. That's how you learn to live with the pressure. Many times your fight is won and lost in the gym. It's not won and lost in the fight. If you're not prepared mentally and physically to fight hard, you're not going to fight hard."

Mike Tyson discovered that in Tokyo when he was dethroned as heavyweight champion by James (Buster) Douglas.

═══

The first time I saw Mike Tyson I was sitting right over there behind that corner of the ring. Bobby Stewart brought him down from the correctional facility where Bobby worked with kids, the Tryon School for Boys up in Johnstown, about seventy-five miles away. Bobby had called Cus and said he's got this kid, he's been showing him a few things, he thinks the kid's got something and he wanted Cus to look at him, so Cus said, "Bring him down." This was in March of 1980 and I'd been told Mike was only thirteen years old. But when he walked in the gym, he looked over 200 pounds, maybe 210. I thought, this is a pretty big kid for thirteen.

Bobby Stewart boxed with Mike that day. I knew Bobby. He weighed about 175 when I boxed with him, and he was about 180 then. I knew he hit hard and he was teeing off on Mike, but Mike was taking the shots. As aggressive as Mike was, basically he took a beating, that's what it came down to. But for his age he was really something.

The more I watched Mike, the more I wondered if he was really thirteen years old. At the time I was working in a juvenile lockup where the bad boys that committed adult crimes served some time before they went to a real prison. I had a few boys over there who were seventeen and they were big, but Mike was just as big and he was supposed to be only thirteen years old. I told Cus, "You better check this kid's age. Maybe he's lying about his age so he won't have to go to the Big House." That's what they call the maximum-security prisons in New York like Sing Sing, Attica, and Greenhaven.

Cus sat right there in that gray metal chair and was very impressed with what he saw of Mike that first day. Bobby Stewart brought Mike down a few more times, then Cus eventually got Mike released to his and Camille Ewald's care over at the house where we all lived together. I was dating my future ex-wife and I was spending some time at her house, so I was back and forth, but I was around Mike a lot.

I thought at first maybe Mike was just trying to get out of the system. Out of jail. Mike knew that if he caused any trouble, he'd have to go right back. He'd been sentenced by the state. He had a school problem, and as his legal guardian Cus had to handle it, but he never had a real problem other than having to adjust to living here in Catskill like all of us city guys did. I was from the city. Tyson was from the city, all the boys who came up here were from the city. When I first came here, people told me, "If you're not born here, you're not really a Catskillian." That's true. I found that's definitely true. Up here they have their own different little ways.

The point is, they never completely accept you. And here was Tyson, a big black kid from Brooklyn who knew if he screwed up, he had to go back to Tryon, back to jail. But then he started to trust Cus and he started to develop as a boxer.

Cus would talk to him about boxing, about everything. I remember Cus telling him, "If you're the heavyweight champion, the money and the women are going to be there. You won't have to worry about money and women." From the first day Cus saw him, Cus thought Mike would be the heavyweight champion. In the gym Mike was a hard worker. He'd come in and stand in front of the mirror and go through the moves with the numbers. Different punches to different areas. Mike was always working, working, working. He had the power. He had the speed. Most people don't realize how fast he is. And he listened to the two things that Cus kept telling him. To move your head after you punch. And to control your emotions.

I'd had those two things drilled into me by Cus when he was my trainer. I was still fighting in 1982 when Cus asked me to help him in the gym. Then he started having me take Mike on trips to amateur fights. I kept fighting myself, but a few months before Cus died in 1985, he told me he didn't want me to fight anymore. He wanted me to concentrate on training Mike.

The thing we always had to work on was Mike's mind. That was the big thing. His mind. To get him to rehearse over and over the defensive moves. To hit and not be hit. And how to do that. To move your head after you punch. To help him do that, I put him through a lot of moves that Cus believed in. Knee bends. Twisting. How to slip and hit. How to bob and weave.

The mind is also how a fighter controls his emotions. Cus was the only boxing man I ever knew to speak about fear, to talk about how every fighter is afraid. He talked about it up until the day he died. You see it all the time right here in the gym. You see a kid hit the heavy bag and he looks like a million dollars. This kid's going to be another Mike Tyson or Ray Leonard the way he looks on that bag. But when he's hitting that bag, that bag don't hit back. So there's no fear. There's nothing inhibiting him because that bag don't hit back. But when you take the same kid and put him in to spar with another kid who hits back, he's terrible.

Or you take what's known as a gym fighter. You put him in to spar in the gym where there's no pressure, where there's nobody looking at him, no paying public, no mediamen critering his performance, he beats the best fighters. But then you put him in a real fight, in an arena with a crowd of five hundred or five thousand people, he folds up. His emotions overcome him. Instead of throwing that jab and moving like he does in the gym, he doesn't do nothing. He takes the shots. He gives up. He gets knocked out.

What it comes down to is knowing how to control your emotions. How to control your fear. How to perform in a disciplined way. To have a clear mind and go out and perform. You hear good athletes in other sports say how they have tunnel vision when they get out there. You hear it from fighters like Mike Tyson and Ray Leonard. But what are they really saying? They're saying that their mind is controlling their emotions. They're concentrating. They know exactly what they want to do. Cus always talked about that, about how to control that fear that's always there. How to step in and do what you have to do no matter how you feel inside.

There was nobody like Cus, nobody. There's a set of moves that Cus put Floyd Patterson through, that he put José Torres through, that he put me through, that he put Mike Tyson through, that he put all his fighters through. The same set of moves I put all my fighters through.

I teach every one of my fighters the same style. Lots of trainers say no, not every fighter can fight the same way. But what I do is teach every fighter the same fundamental moves. Then every fighter incorporates those moves a little differently because of his personality, his emotions, his mind. If you get two guys that do it the same way you're going to have one exciting fight, because they're both going to be going at it. If they're both near-perfect, neither guy is going to be getting hit but there's going to be a lot of action until one guy imposes his will on the other. That's when one guy capitalizes on a little mistake the other guy makes. Once the other guy is hurt, everything goes out the window.

Nobody except Cus ever talked about how boxing boils down to one guy imposing his will on the other guy. But that wins every fight. Imposing your will means you have to be determined to follow the game plan. Whatever it costs, you're going to get the job done.

Cus never sat me down and talked to me about dealing with promoters and big money. He talked to Jimmy Jacobs about that. But he envisioned pay-per-view cable television for fights just like he envisioned closed-circuit television for fights years ago. The big money fighters are making today, it's there because Cus brought the International Boxing Club down in an antitrust suit. He broke the control it had over the boxing game. Until then the IBC made all the money and the fighters made nothing. That's history.

You still have big promoters like Don King and Bob Arum, but there's so much money, they've got to give the fighter a big payday. But without Cus breaking the IBC, who knows how long the IBC would've stayed in control. Maybe somebody else would've done it along the way, but Cus did it. Cus saw it back then. Cus made a stand. Cus did it.

One thing Cus always talked about was the big money a heavyweight champion would make. I remember Cus telling me, "Lots of managers grab the nickels and dimes. They put their fighter in a tough fight because the dime is more than the nickel and they want the dime. But they forget about the dollar up there. My job is to maneuver my fighter to the dollar up there. Once he's ready to win the title, all the money he wants is there. Someday this kid Mike Tyson will take care of all your money problems." Like with everything else, Cus called that one.

The way Cus developed Mike was brilliant. As far back as 1982, when Mike was only sixteen and Larry Holmes was the heavyweight champion, Cus told me, "Mike could beat Holmes right now if he could control his emotions." The thing was, at that age in the amateurs, Mike wasn't ready to control his emotions. His mind.

So from 1982 to 1985, when Mike turned pro, Cus developed Mike to be a pro. Long before the 1984 Olympic Trials began, Cus was told that the Amateur Boxing Federation people didn't want Mike to fight as a super-heavyweight because Tyrell Biggs was going to be the super-heavyweight. Mike had to fight as a heavyweight. Mike always resented Biggs for that, and rightfully so. That's why he gave Biggs a beating in their title bout. Mike went to the Olympic Trials anyway, but he had to kill himself to make the weight, and when Henry Tillman gave him a little trouble, he lost. But early the next year Cus turned Mike pro.

The plan was for Mike to fight as often as possible. To learn his trade. To develop a fighter the way a fighter is supposed to be developed. There's only one way to do that. Put him in the ring as often as possible. Get him better opponents. Move him up the ladder. Once you're ready to go for the title, then you go.

Only a few months after Mike turned pro in 1985, Cus got sick. It happened fast. Just a few days before he went into the hospital in Albany, I asked him what's wrong. He told me, "I'll be all right, don't worry, I'll be all right." Cus had always told me how he had always been able to control sickness with his mind. And he always had, so I believed him. But looking back now, the day I heard him coughing, I wish I had put him in a car and driven him down to the city to Jimmy Jacobs and said, "Here, take care of him." Instead he went into the hospital in Albany, but when Jimmy drove up and saw him, Jimmy brought him down to Mount Sinai Hospital in the city.

I kept calling Jimmy to see what was going on, but all the doctors would say was that Cus had a rare case of pneumonia. I really didn't want to stay up here, but I opened the gym every day because I knew that's what Cus would want.

In the hospital Cus didn't even want Camille to see him. He didn't want no one to see him. One day I went down to see him anyway. I told him, "Don't give up, you got to fight it." When I asked him, "What's the matter?" he looked at me and he shook his head like he didn't know. But he knew something was wrong and it was getting the best of him. He knew he was dying. The doctors just called it a rare case of pneumonia. I keep emphasizing that because if Cus knew what it was, he would've been able to control it with his mind.

You know how doctors are, they come into your room and look you over, they say this is wrong and that's wrong, then they go out. I wonder if any of those doctors took the time to tell Cus exactly what was wrong, that he had this rare case of pneumonia and that it was affecting this or that organ in his body. If somebody explained that to Cus, he would've been able to work on it with his mind. He possibly, probably, would have cured himself. I firmly believe that.

But the story I get, the doctors knew they had to do something to make sure Cus stayed in the hospital, because he wanted to get out. When they sedated him and he went under, he never came out. I don't know if he was in a coma but he didn't know where he was. The day I saw him he was just shaking his head from side to side like you do when you say "No." I looked at him shaking his head and I thought when they gave him that shot, he didn't want that shot, that's why he's shaking his head. That's what I'll always remember. Cus shaking his head.

The same thing happened with my father. Me and my father didn't get along, and as he got older we grew apart. I regret it. I'm a little stubborn. My father was a heavy drinker. In the end he stopped drinking, but he got emphysema. I went home to see him. He was in his bedroom. One lung had collapsed and he was on oxygen. I said, "How you doing, Dad?" But he just looked at me and shook his head. That's the same thing I got from Cus in the hospital. When you think back, I knew my father knew he was dying and I knew Cus knew he was dying. It's a very weird thing.

Now when Cus died, Jimmy Jacobs and Bill Cayton followed Cus's plan to develop Mike to the best of their ability and knowledge. Cus had trained Mike so he was so much better than the guys he fought. Mike was cold and calculating. He was mean. But he was disciplined.

If you've got to put that meanness in a fighter, it's hard. You may never be able to do it. Sometimes there might be layers and layers that you've got to peel away to find that seed of meanness. If the seed isn't there, you're never going to find it. But with Mike that meanness was basically there. He had that aggression, that anger. He nurtured it. He enjoyed it. About three months after Cus died, Mike stopped Jesse Ferguson up in Troy in the sixth round. Mike had decked him in the fifth round with a brutal right uppercut.

Talking to the writers afterwards, Mike said, "I saw the opening for the uppercut. I tried to catch him on the tip of his nose because I try to punch the bone into his brain." Chilling.

To me that was Mike's way of showing off. We don't know what goes on in a fighter's mind in the ring. He may think he's getting laid when he punches a guy out, who the hell knows. But to me, talking about trying to punch the bone of a guy's nose into his brain was Mike's way of bragging. He probably did hear Cus once say something like "If you hit the other guy on the point of the nose, it will move the bone and that hurts." Nothing about driving the bone up into the guy's brain. That was just Mike's way of showing off. But that's what I mean about Mike having that meanness in him that a fighter needs.

Two months later, James [Quick] Tillis gave Mike the most trouble he's ever had as a young pro. At the time, Mike was 19–0. All knockouts. Twelve in the first round. But in Glens Falls that day Tillis showed him a different look. Tillis made him go ten rounds.

Mike won the first four rounds, but he gave away the next four. From the fifth through the eighth, Mike wasn't really doing anything. He was frustrated. He wasn't sure of himself. In the corner before the ninth round I pleaded with him. I told him, "I want you to go out there and fight this round for me. Nobody else but me. Go out there and do something with this guy." He won the ninth, but I knew if Tillis won the tenth round, it's either going to be a draw or we lose. I pleaded with him again. I told him, "Fight this last round for me, do it for me." He said, "Okay, okay," then he went out and dominated the tenth. He won the tenth big. He was moving, he took the shots, and he kept throwing punches. It was close, but Mike got the decision. He won the fight because he was making the guy miss. When it was over, I told him, "Good job." Looking back, if he hadn't won that fight, he wouldn't have traveled the same path to the title.

Mike learned from that Tillis fight. In the Garden less than three weeks later, Mitch Green fought the same type of fight. It went ten rounds but Mike beat the hell out of him. Mike had learned that he could control his emotions, that he could go ten rounds and be effective.

Once a fighter goes ten rounds, he can go a hundred rounds. It's the mind. Mike learned that yes, he could go a hundred rounds if he had to. From then on, he had no competition. Jimmy Jacobs and Bill Cayton got him in the HBO heavyweight tournament because they knew there was nobody in there. And there wasn't. Before he fought Trevor Berbick for the World Boxing Council title later that year at the Las Vegas Hilton, he was very calm, like he knew he was going to win. I kept telling him, "No big production, just another fight." That's how we trained for every fight. Just another fight.

In the dressing room that night I told him, "Do your job. Do what you learned. None of these guys can touch you." By the second round Mike had Berbick flopping around on rubber legs.

Mike had the title now. Or at least a third of it. That was all we needed. And awaaaay we go. But the next fight with James [Bonecrusher] Smith was a bore, a complete bore, a stinker. I figured Smith was going to come out to whack, to go for the knockout. But he didn't. After the first couple rounds, Smith just kept holding Mike, tying him up. Mike got very frustrated. But he took the World Boxing Association title from Smith in a twelve-round decision. And he learned from that fight too. He learned that sometimes the other guy just wants to stink the joint out. Hold, hold, hold.

His next fight, with Pinklon Thomas, was an easy fight. Thomas fought a good fight, but Mike stopped him in six. Easy. Then he brought all that experience from the Smith fight and the Thomas fight to the fight with the International Boxing Federation champion, Tony Tucker, for the undisputed title. Tucker used his guile and experience to go twelve rounds.

In his first undisputed title defense, Mike gave Tyrell Biggs the beating of his life. I knew Mike's resentment from the Olympics was still inside him. In the dressing room in Atlantic City I talked to him about just doing his job. I wanted him to knock Biggs out as quickly as possible, but he dragged it out for seven rounds. Larry Holmes was next, and I knew it would be easy money. I wasn't concerned at all with Holmes, who hadn't fought for nearly two years after losing to Michael Spinks twice. I knew Holmes was going to get the beating he should've got right along. I don't have a high respect for Larry Holmes. I think he had a bad attitude.

As soon as Holmes came out and started dancing around and

the crowd got behind him, I knew that was the finish, because I knew he couldn't do it for more than two or three rounds at the most. When I saw Holmes dancing, I thought it was great because pretty soon I knew he would be a sitting duck. Sure enough, Mike knocked him out in the fourth.

The plan that Jimmy Jacobs and Bill Cayton were following, Cus's plan, was going great. The plan now was to make a lot of money and bring some class back to the heavyweight division. Back to boxing, really, because as the heavyweight division goes, all of boxing goes. And everything was going great until Mike hooked up with Robin Givens and Jimmy got sick.

Going to Tokyo for the Tony Tubbs fight, I was only concerned that we had to make that long trip. But that's when I should've known better. That's when I should've become a penny-pinching sonofabitch. I should've saved all my money and collected my thoughts and talked to Mike more about what was going on. But I was going through my divorce, so I waited for Mike to speak to me. In retrospect, that was a mistake. I should've said more to Mike and Robin and her mother, Ruth Roper. I wasn't crazy about Robin, but I knew Mike was in love with her, and you can't reason with a guy who's in love. So I went about my business. Everything I was doing I was doing for Mike, because I wanted to hold everything together. I wanted the women to accept Bill Cayton, because I knew Bill could make the deals, I knew Bill could get the big money. That's what Mike's missing now. Don King can't get the big money. Bill Cayton can get the big money.

Right after Mike stopped Tubbs in two, Jimmy Jacobs died. Don King started to make his move at Jimmy's funeral. That's when King started building up Mike's ego, started working on the women about Cayton, and the women started polluting Mike's mind. In one sense it showed how weak Mike can be. He's very strong in the ring, but outside the ring he'll listen to any piece of crap.

The women started working on him and working on him and working on him. The women didn't have enough sense to sit back and say, hey, Jacobs and Cayton had taken good care of Mike, they were saving his money but if he wanted to buy a hundred-thousand-dollar car, he could buy it and they would write the check and he'd sign it. Everything was being taken care of. King saw that. King knew Jacobs and Cayton weren't stealing Mike's money, but King wanted to take control. King started working on the women, but I kept trying to hold everything together because I knew that sanity was here in the gym.

In the weeks before the Michael Spinks fight, with all the crap that was going on around him, I kept Mike focused on the fight. I kept emphasizing that he was a professional fighter, that no matter how much crap was going on around him, when he got in the ring, he had to fight.

Even when Spinks's manager, Butch Lewis, tried to break balls in our dressing room, Mike kept focused on the fight. Butch came in to check Mike's gloves. On the left glove I had tied the strings, cut the ends of the strings, and taped over them like everybody does. The inspector had okayed it. But when Butch saw a little lump in the tape, he said, "Take it off." I said, "No way. The inspector's already okayed it." Butch went and got Larry Hazzard, the chairman of the New Jersey commission. Larry looked at it and said, "Just put a little more tape on it to smooth it down." No problem. Butch was just trying to break balls, to upset Mike, to give Spinks a little edge. But just like with all the other crap going on around him, Mike stayed focused on the fight.

Spinks was a good boxer. I thought Spinks would box Mike, but Spinks's emotions overcame him. Almost like when I fought Alex Arguello. I was never a puncher, but I thought, I can take Arguello out and I'm going to prove it. As soon as Spinks came out and planted his feet to trade punches, that's all Mike asks for, because Mike can hit you and you can't hit him. What was it, ninety-one seconds?

That knockout answered all the questions about was I concerned that Eddie Futch was in Spinks's corner. Just like the questions about when Angelo Dundee was in Pinklon Thomas's corner. This is going to be my one arrogant statement concerning other trainers. For all their experience, I know I learned from the best. None of those guys are better than me. Because of Cus, they can't match what I know. I knew all Mike had to do was perform. I wasn't concerned with anything another trainer would teach because I knew my fighter.

But as soon as Mike flattened Spinks in ninety-one seconds, all the crap started all over again. Mike was supposed to be on HBO's replay show of the Spinks fight, but they couldn't find him. I was still in Atlantic City having a good time when they called and asked me where Mike was. "I don't know where he is," I told them.

"After a fight we let him go his own way." They were stuck. They needed somebody, so they asked me to do it, and I said, "Send a limo and I'll be there." The next day I got out of bed and went and did it.

That's the HBO show where I said that Bill Cayton was an honest guy. And from what I know, he was honest, he is honest, and I stand by what I said.

Around that time Robin came out with how there's supposed to be seventy million dollars but there's only fifty million so something must be wrong. I guess Mike believed that crap, but Mike doesn't really understand the money. To tell you the truth, I understand money a little bit but I was a little stupid myself with the money I've blown in casinos. The worst thing that ever happened to me was when I won big money on the craps table in Atlantic City one night. Big money. After that, whenever I was losing, in the back of my mind I kept thinking, I can win big again. But then you keep losing more. You live and learn. If money is your god, you got a little bit of a problem. But that's what the world is run on. All the big businessmen, money is their god. But see, with Cus, the difference is that principle was his god, and I'm the same damn way. Money is money and that's all it is. You're either a stand-up guy or you're not.

Bill Cayton just couldn't handle all the crap Robin and Ruth were throwing at him. Bill was a behind-the-scenes negotiator, he wasn't an out-front personality guy. Bill knew his business, and I still respect him for that. Bill's not a thief.

I don't know what the women found and what they bugged Mike up with. But I do know that when the women first started, Don King was behind the two of them, basically the mother. The women played a con game on Mike, and in the end they got what they wanted, a nice little settlement from the divorce. They're happy.

I only had one run-in with Robin all the time she was around. Mike started training here for his fight with Frank Bruno, but on a Sunday morning, his day off, he knocked himself out driving his car into the big chestnut tree outside Camille's house.

As soon as I heard about it, I went across the river to the hospital in Hudson where Mike was. I asked him, "How you feeling?" He said, "I'm all right." But as a trainer, I wanted to speak to the doctor. I wanted to find out exactly what's wrong with my fighter.

I knew Mike had been out late that Saturday night. My theory was that when he hit the tree, he banged his head and he went to sleep because he'd been out late. I asked the doctor, "If he had a fight next week, could he fight? If he had to spar tomorrow, could he spar?" Not that he had a fight the next week or that I wanted him to spar the next day. But as his trainer, I had to know the medical answers to those questions.

When Robin heard me ask those questions, she started yelling, "All you want to do is have him fight and make money off him." I looked at her and I looked at Mike, who went like this, what are you going to do? I wanted to rap her right in the face, but I walked away. I ignored her.

That night the women had Mike taken by ambulance to the Columbia-Presbyterian Hospital in the city. But when I went down to see him, I couldn't get in. The women had made up a list of people who were allowed to see Mike, and I wasn't on it. I was his trainer and I wasn't allowed to see him. Donald Trump could get in, but I couldn't get in. That's when I should've known what was happening. Trump was the man then. Everyone forgets that. Trump was the man. Trump was making his move like he was trying to steal the fighter. He eventually dropped out of the picture except for trying to get Mike to fight at Trump Plaza in Atlantic City. But at the time Trump was the man.

I've always thought Trump was behind all those big headlines about Mike driving the car into the tree because he was trying to commit suicide. To me, all those headlines was a bunch of bullshit planted by Trump's press agent.

Trump had something to do with bugging up Mike with me and my ten percent. But when I wasn't getting paid anything and doing the job, that was okay, right? Then all of a sudden, when they're making ten million and they have to give me one million, that's too much. Why? What's the difference? I deserve my percentage, whatever it is. I would pay my cutman healthy. Healthy. I'm loyal, that's the way I am. I'll go to my grave that way.

But a trainer should get ten percent. That's the going rate. Cus always told me that's what a trainer is supposed to get. But nowadays they want to pay the trainers less, less, less.

Some trainers accept it. Some promoters and some managers treat the fighters like shit and they treat the trainers worse than the fighters. But let me tell you something, the trainers are the main guys. The main guys. Because the trainer is the guy around the fighter. The trainer's got to get the fighter ready to do combat. To fight. The fighter is the guy, no matter what. In the end the fighter is the guy that does it.

If you get fighters like a Mike Tyson or a Ray Leonard who think that because they're the ones really doing the fighting they don't need nobody, that's just being arrogant. There's always somebody they got to have. Their security blanket. Their trainer.

A good trainer like myself can bring the best out in his fighter. And his fighter can go on and win forever. In my opinion, if I get a guy that listens to me about the style Cus taught me, nobody can beat my guy. It's a scientific method that Cus laid down. If you get a guy who can do it perfect, move your head after you punch and control your emotions, he'll never get hurt and he'll never get beat. Now, that's easier said than done, believe me. But the point is, if you got a good trainer, he's more than worth his money. Even if you got a bad trainer and he's supposed to get ten percent, give it to him. Don't become cheap all of a sudden.

I always thought I had a lifetime pact as Mike's trainer. Not a piece of paper, just handshakes. But to me that was enough. Back in 1986 there were rumors that Jimmy Jacobs wanted to hire Eddie Futch, but when Jimmy was asked about it on television one night, he said, "Kevin Rooney has done a great job for us and Kevin Rooney is going to be the trainer for as long as Mike Tyson fights." That's as lifetime as it can get. Jimmy Jacobs was the man. Jimmy was the manager. The way I understand it, the manager calls the shots. And when we started, Mike told me, "You're my man and we're always going to be together." But then I read in the paper that I was fired.

I didn't want to sue Mike Tyson, but I am the way I am. I'm not going to kiss his ass. I'm not going to kiss King's ass. If you don't want me around no more, if you want to forget the job that Cus started and that I helped finish, if you want to get another trainer, fine. But compensate me.

The fighters, they get that microphone underneath 'em, they think they're the only ones. They forget the trainers. That's bad. Every fighter needs somebody to tell him he's making mistakes. Mike didn't have that without me. He got away with it against Frank Bruno and Truth Williams, but he didn't get away with it against Buster Douglas in Tokyo. That's when Mike needed somebody to tell him what to do. Somebody to wake him up. The guys in his corner, Jay Bright and Aaron Snowell, didn't tell him nothing. Jay Bright was an actor out of work when Mike hired him. Jay boxed a little bit but he don't know anything about how to train a fighter, about what to tell a fighter. You got to know not only what your guy is doing and not doing, you got to know what the other guy is doing and not doing. Jay don't know what to look for. Aaron Snowell is King's man, but Aaron don't know nothing either.

It's not like I'm saying this after Mike got knocked out by Douglas. I was saying it for almost two years. That when Mike got in a tough fight, he'd miss me.

Watching that fight on television, after the third round I heard Snowell tell him, "You're not closing the gap, Mike. You've got to get inside." After the fifth round, he said, "You've got to back this guy up. When you get inside, you got to punch." But there was no urgency in Snowell's voice and no reaction from Mike. He just sat there looking down like he wasn't even listening. Like he didn't respect what he was hearing.

When I was asked later what I would've told Mike, I said, "After the second or third round, I would've yelled, "If you don't start throwing punches, I'm going to stop this fight." That would've got his attention. That would've woken him up. But if I had been over there with him from the beginning, he would've been trained right. He would've been ready. He would've known what the other guy could do and not do.

Before that fight in Tokyo I thought that the only guy who could beat Mike Tyson was Mike Tyson himself, and that's what happened. He wasn't ready to fight. And when he got in a tough fight, he didn't have anybody in his corner who could fire him up, who could tell him what to do.

Too many people were pulling at him. Too many people in his pocket. Don King tried to make it sound like I was taking money from Mike. I wasn't taking money from Mike, but King wanted to get rid of me. King probably told Mike that he didn't have to pay me all that money, that he could get Jay Bright and Aaron Snowell and Rory Holloway and John Horn and he'll save hundreds of thousands of dollars.

Back when Mike and I were together, I found Mike to be a good guy. That's why I'm surprised that he allowed that seed of racism in him to grow. Mike was from a black ghetto in Brooklyn and didn't like whites. Just like if you were from a white ghetto, you didn't like blacks. Mike had that seed of racism in him, and King, who was from a black ghetto in Cleveland, was able to get that seed growing again.

King was a numbers runner. He did time in prison for manslaughter when a guy he got in a fight with hit his head on the sidewalk. He came out of prison talking crap and got into boxing promoting Muhammad Ali's fights. So when King started talking to Mike, it was jailhouse talk that Mike understood. Mike had been locked up at a young age. He would've come out and gone back to jail if he hadn't found Cus when he did. Cus started working on Mike's mind, getting his trust, showing him there's another way of life. But then Cus and Jimmy Jacobs passed away. Mike didn't relate to Bill Cayton, and then Robin and Ruth started working on Mike's mind, started peeling away the good layers that Cus had put there. Now here comes Don King with his jailhouse talk.

I keep hoping Mike will come to his senses, because what he learned from Cus is still there. Cus worked on Mike's mind for Mike's good. Don King worked on Mike's mind for Don King's pocketbook. When I try to look into Mike's future, I see something. I don't want to say I see something bad. Just let's say I see something strange. I don't know what exactly. Just something strange.

Goody Petronelli *(left)* and his brother Pat with Marvelous Marvin Hagler.

Goody Petronelli:

"I Want to Fight That Same Guy"

===

Hanging above the sidewalk outside the thick wooden doors of the old brick building at 24 Ward Street in Brockton, Massachusetts, the small red-white-and-blue sign creaked as it swayed in the soft breeze.

"Petronelli Brothers Athletic Club," it read. "Hours Monday through Friday 7 P.M. to 9 P.M."

Up a steep flight of stairs, a door opened into the bright clean gym. Two boxing rings. Two light bags. Four heavy bags. Mirrors along the far wall. Some red-yellow-and-black boxing showcards. Marvelous Marvin Hagler's private locker room. Another small room with twelve tall beige metal lockers across from a hand-lettered sign: "Individuals Are Expected to Furnish His Own Towel." Several other signs were scattered along the walls of the gym.

"When in Doubt, Jab Out."

"Train Until It Hurts and Then Some."

"Head Down, Hands Up."

"Remember the Key Word Is Work."

"Fit Body = Fit Mind.'

On the wooden floor near the rings, painted white footprints were a reminder that this was once a dance studio. But nobody dances there now, as another sign made clear:

"I Can Only Be Beaten Two Ways, If I Die or If I Quit."

Behind the door of his office at the far corner of the gym, Goody Petronelli, wearing a plaid shirt, black corduroy pants, and white sneakers, walked over to the window, looked past the modern beige newspaper plant of the *Brockton Enterprise,* and pointed toward several old brick buildings.

"The building to the left," he said, "is where our other gym was, where Rocky Marciano trained long before we bought it."

In this shoe-factory city of nearly 100,000 south of Boston, Rocco Marchegiano grew up to be the world heavyweight champion. Guerino Petronelli grew up as Goody "because when I was little I always used to come out of the house with something good to eat, some pastry or a pizza, and the other kids would say, 'Give me something good to eat,' and then it got to be "Here comes Goody.' " In time Goody grew up to be the trainer and comanager with his brother Pat of the world middleweight champion, Marvelous Marvin Hagler.

"Rocky was going to be a partner in our gym with Pat and me after I got out of the Navy," he said. "Driving home from California after my discharge in 1969, I was somewhere in South Dakota when I heard on the radio that Rocky died in a plane crash."

Two of twelve kids of a Brockton contractor, the Petronellis paid for that gym and its expenses out of the profits from their construction business, then moved to the current gym's location. Dozens of professional and amateur fighters have emerged from it. Not only Hagler, but also Hagler's half brother, Robbie Sims, who fought for the middleweight title, and Tony Petronelli, Pat's son, who fought for the junior welterweight title.

"Pat and I are in it because we love the business," Goody said. "We do well at it. But we were in it when we weren't doing well at it. Why didn't we get out of it? Because we love it."

Goody coached boxers in the Navy for over twenty years before his discharge as a master chief petty officer in the medical department. Once a welterweight with a 23–2–1 record, he declined to divulge when he was born.

"I ain't going to tell you my age," he said with a laugh.

Whatever his age, Goody Petronelli is lean and hard. He runs almost every morning. He lives in nearby Bridgewater with his wife, Pat, the mother of their three children. He's made big money as his share of Hagler's purses, but he doesn't flaunt it.

"I've got a 'vette and a Cadillac," he said. "But that's all."

And he hasn't let the money dilute his dedication to boxing and to the kids who walk up the long flight of stairs to this gym five nights a week.

＝＝＝

Where would the fighters be without the trainers? Where were these fighters before the trainers got 'em in a gym? Before the trainers taught 'em how to stand. How to hold their hands. How to punch. How to move.

To begin with, trainers get in the business because they love it. I'm speaking for myself, but I'm sure I'm speaking for a lot of trainers. In my case and in my brother Pat's case, after we opened the gym in 1969, what we did was work all day in construction, wipe the sweat off our hands, then come down to the gym at seven o'clock with the fighters. Not that I expected to get a world's champion like Marvin Hagler. That was far from my mind. I did it to get these kids in from the streets and use my expertise to teach 'em how to fight.

We were over the hill as far as age, so we couldn't fight ourselves anymore. Although with the age of some of the fighters now, you often wonder.

But it was a lot of hard work. The only satisfaction we got was to see these kids develop, get 'em in the amateurs, buy the gauze and tape to wrap their hands, find the transportation to take 'em to the fights. You wouldn't charge 'em a dime. When they won a little trophy, you stuck out your chest a little and you felt, because of me, he won that fight. Or if he got hit unnecessarily, you feel like you let him down. I mean, this is from your heart.

Some people wonder how Rocky Marciano and Marvin Hagler happened to come out of Brockton to be a world's champion. But this is a working-class city. Everybody works in a shoe factory. The kids aren't fed on a silver spoon. Everybody has to earn everything they got. When you come into this gym, you got to go through the school of hard knocks. Then you have to hope you have the right teacher, because the trainer motivates these kids.

Don't forget that boxing is a science. Boxing isn't that guy who walks into the gym and starts slugging like it was a street fight. You don't need a trainer for that. Hopefully, you get the kid in the gym, like Marvin Hagler, that's streetwise, that can fight. He's tough. He can take a shot. When the going gets tough, the tough get going. And if he gets knocked down, when he gets up, that's when the other guy is really in trouble.

The trainer gets the raw talent. The trainer can teach a guy how to fight. But a trainer cannot give a fighter a jaw. They say God created us all equal. He didn't. He gave some of us an iron jaw and He created some with a tinkle in their chin, a glass jaw. You can't develop muscles in your jaw. You either have a good jaw or you don't. One time when Marvin Hagler went for a routine EEG in Hyannis Hospital, the doctor told me that Marvin had an unusually thick skull. Maybe his thick jaw is one reason Marvin always took a good shot. But who knows? Because of all my years in the Navy medical department, I'm familiar with the human anatomy. I've talked to doctors about why some guys have an iron jaw and other guys have a tinkle in their chin. But even doctors don't know for sure.

It might have something to do with the way the jaw is shaped. The guy might have a bad underbite or overbite. Most everybody has a weak side of the jaw and a strong side. Some doctors think removing wisdom teeth weakens the jaw. They recommend leaving wisdom teeth in there unless you get to the point where you have to take 'em out. But you can't explain the jaw. Some guys get hit, bang, out they go like a light.

I've had real good fighters who would've been champions if they didn't have a tinkle in their chin. But because of that tinkle, I told 'em to go get a job. I had a fighter from Canada by the name of Cedric Parsons, who was ranked as a cruiserweight but I always suspected he had a glass jaw. He was always asking me, "How much does this guy weigh?" I'd say, "What do you care? Rocky Marciano weighed 183 pounds and he fought guys 225 pounds." But the way Cedric fought with a peekaboo style, with his hands up alongside his face like Floyd Patterson, he didn't want to get hit on the chin.

One night Cedric fought Henry Tillman in Vegas. He got hit with a right-hand shot in the first round. Nothing drastic. But he went down like a load of bricks. After the fight, I told him, "It's time for you to get a job." He said, "What do you mean?" I said, "Why didn't you tell me?" He said, "Tell you what?" I said, "That you got a glass jaw." He started to say, "Well . . ." but I said, "Don't give me that 'Well . . .' stuff. It's not your fault, but you want to hear it straight, don't you?" He said, "Yeah." I said, "I'm telling it to you straight. Get a job."

Cedric went back to Canada, and when I came home to Brockton, I told my brother Pat that I'd retired Cedric even though he had all the talent in the world. Quick hands. Good range. Moved good. But he had that tinkle in his chin.

When a trainer is starting with a fighter from scratch, if the kid has a good chin and heart or balls or guts, whatever you want to call it, now you can teach him how to fight. Most of the guys I've had, I got from scratch. That's the way I like 'em. If they make any mistakes, I have to take the blame. If they do good, I can take some of the credit. Not knocking Angelo Dundee or Eddie Futch, but they usually get polished fighters. They don't get kids off the street and tell 'em, "This is the way you stand. This is how you hold your hands. This is how you move. This is how you punch." They get guys like Muhammad Ali and Sugar Ray Leonard, or Joe Frazier and Larry Holmes.

When a guy's already polished, you just correct him on this and that. Keep your hands a little higher. Hit to the body. Hit to the head. It's a lot easier. When you've got to teach a kid how to fight from scratch, that's when a trainer really earns his money.

When a kid walks into this gym off the street and tells me he wants to be a fighter, I sit him down and I'll give him all the good reasons why he shouldn't fight. Let's face it. Every time you get hit in the head, whether you want to believe it or not, you get brain damage. It's irreparable. And to be a fighter, you have to give up so much. Up in the morning to do your roadwork. No drugs. No drinking. No going out late at night. You're in the rack early because you got to get at least eight hours' sleep. If you don't get that body in shape, you're going to get your head knocked off. Are you willing to do all this stuff and dedicate yourself to being a fighter? And are you willing to think big?

When I ask a kid why he wants to be a fighter, I'm hoping he tells me, "Because I want to be a champion." If you think big, you'll be big. If you think small, you'll be small.

Some of these kids tell me, "I never fought before, but I can fight. I'm a good football player. I can handle myself all right in the streets." We still don't know whether the kid's going to make it or not, but we put him through a training program. You give him the roadwork, the proper exercises, the bag punching. You teach him the straight punches. Some kids pick it up quicker than others. You can't say in three months he'll be ready to box. It varies with the individual. Now you teach him defense. How to move a little bit. How to step out of the way. Then you teach him offense. Hooks and uppercuts. How to mix 'em up with the straight punches in combinations.

Now he's going to start boxing. Mind you, the kid has looked good hitting the bag. But the bag doesn't hit back. Nobody has hit the kid back yet. And he hasn't even hit anybody else yet.

You try to make sure the kid spars with somebody of equal caliber. Or if the other kid is better, you tell the other kid to lighten up. You don't expect the kid to look as good as he did hitting the bag. The first time he spars, he's sure to get a cut lip or a bloody nose.

When the kid is through sparring, you towel him off and tell him, "See you tomorrow." But you don't see the kid tomorrow. You don't see him no more. Goodbye. He didn't like getting hit.

Now I'll revert to Marvin Hagler, who walked into the gym when he was sixteen years old. His mother took Marvin and his half brother, Robbie Sims, out of Newark after the riots there in 1966, that's how they got to Brockton. I vividly remember Marvin as a little kid coming into the gym and sitting there like a gentleman for two days while I worked with my fighters. I finally said, "Hey, kid, you want to learn how to fight?" He said, "Yeah, man." I said, "Get your gear." But the only gear he had was the sneakers and dungarees he had on. I sat him down like I told you I do with every kid and gave him all the reasons why he shouldn't be a fighter. But he never blinked. And when I asked him why he wanted to be a fighter, he said, "I want to be a champion some-day." I put my arm around him and I said, "When you're a cham-pion, I'll be your trainer." At the same time I was thinking, this kid don't know what he's talking about. But he had a goal. He knew what he wanted and he was willing to work to get it.

One of the first times Marvin sparred, he got a cut lip or a bloody nose, whatever it was. When he left the gym that night, I didn't know if I'd see him again. But the next night, he walked over to me and said, "I want to fight that same guy I fought yesterday." I said, "Why?" He said, "I should've done better." I said, "No, no, Marvin, you did fine." He said, "No, I should've done better." That's when I knew Marvin had a chance.

I don't care if the new kid in the gym gets popped. But if he shows me he's got guts, if he comes back the next night and says, "Where did I make a mistake?" then I know he's got a chance to be a fighter. You expect the kid to make a mistake. But if he doesn't correct it, he makes another mistake. Marvin always corrected his mistakes. I'd tell him something and he'd do it. I never had to yell at him. I could always be cool, calm, and collected with him. When he was learning his punches, he'd see a smile on my face and he'd say, "What's the matter?" I'd say, "You're picking this up a lot quicker than most guys." He'd say, "I've been practicing those combinations in the mirror at home." He used to go home and teach those punches to little Robbie Sims, who was only nine years old then. Marvin got A-pluses all the way through. I'd tell him something and he'd do it. I never had to yell at him. It's like my mother used to say, "People are like the fingers on your hand, they're all different." Now with some guys, I may have to insult them to get their attention. Where another guy, like Marvin, I could look at him and he knew what I was thinking. I wouldn't even have to raise my voice.

When we found out Marvin needed a job, he worked for us on construction. Mixing cement. Carrying bricks. At first he used to call Pat and myself "whiteys." He had a hard-on for whiteys because of the Newark riots he lived through as a kid. If anybody had a right to be prejudiced, he did. He couldn't understand us being so good to him. We'd buy him dinner. We'd do whatever we could for him. But we'd do it for any of our fighters. He was one of us.

We developed a good bond. What we call the Triangle—Marvin, Pat, and me. We could always sit down and talk. We always understood each other. Marvin's been tops. He's the same guy he always was. He never mistrusted anybody. It doesn't happen that way too much anymore. Money changes people. We're still family. But in the boxing business, there's a lot of hustlers around trying

to steal your fighter. Don King tried to get in the act, but Marvin
was always a very loyal guy. King tried to work through Marvin's
mother. Now here was Marvin who should have had a hard-on
for the whiteys surrounding him. The trainer. The manager. The
accountant. The attorney. All white. Not that he had anything
against the blacks, because if we told him we were going with Don
King, he had that much faith in us to stick with us. But of course
we wouldn't go with Don King.

But as good as Marvin was in the amateurs, as good as he was
in winning all the Golden Gloves and Amateur Athletic Union
titles around here, I wasn't convinced that he would make it big
because I could only compare him to the other New England
fighters. Not that New England fighters were bad, but they were
limited. Then in 1973 we had the National AAU championships
in the Boston Garden. Sugar Ray Leonard was there. Leon Spinks
and Michael Spinks were there.

Marvin weighed 157 pounds, but he wanted to fight in the 165-
pound class. At first they didn't want to let him. But he kept saying, "I came here to fight." He just shined. He not only won his
class but he was voted the outstanding fighter in the whole tournament. That's when I told my brother Pat, "We got a future
champion."

The next thing I knew, Marvin walked into the gym one night
with a shaved head. As soon as I saw him, I was surprised, because he had a good head of hair. He said, "How do you like it?"
I said, "It looks good, I guess." I'm from the old school. If you
want to take your head and bang it against that bulkhead, if that
makes you a better fighter, be my guest. If shaving your head
makes you a better fighter, fine, shave your head.

Around that same time Marvin wasn't sure whether he wanted
to fight right-handed or left-handed. He's naturally right-handed.
He writes right-handed. He throws right-handed. But he was more
comfortable fighting left-handed. The trouble was, it's tough for
a southpaw to get fights. Nobody likes to fight a southpaw.

His first pro fight, Marvin fought right-handed and knocked
out Terry Ryan here in Brockton, second round. When it was
over, Sam Silverman, Subway Sam the Boston promoter, told me,
"Turn him back to southpaw. He's more devastating as a southpaw." I said, "Can you get him fights if he's a southpaw?" Sam
said, "I'll get him fights." Sam got him more than two dozen fights

all over New England—Boston, Brockton, New Bedford, and Portland, Maine.

But we knew if Marvin was going to develop into a champion, he had to go outside New England to fight. We went to Seattle and he got a draw with Sugar Ray Seales, but other than that he was 25–0 going into 1976 when we went down to Philadelphia to fight Bobby [Boogaloo] Watts. When we got there I remember the Spectrum promoter, Russell Peltz, telling me, "Guys from Boston can't fight." But I looked Russell right in the eye and I said, "This one can."

Marvin got screwed. He had Watts on the deck but he didn't get the decision. Two months later we went back to Philadelphia to fight Willie [The Worm] Monroe, a real tough fighter.

Before that fight, we were training in Joe Frazier's Gym in Philadelphia when Joe met Marvin for the first time. Joe had watched Marvin work out, and when they shook hands, Joe told him, "You got three strikes against you. One, you're black. Two, you're a southpaw. And three, you're good." Joe always told it like it is. But as good as Marvin was against Willie Monroe, he wasn't good enough to get the decision. Or to be honest, he wasn't well enough. Marvin had been sick. He hadn't been in the gym for about a week and a half. I didn't want him to go through with the fight, but he twisted my head into letting him. So all of a sudden Marvin had lost two of his last three fights. Little did we know that he wouldn't lose another fight for more than eleven years.

Marvin went back to Philadelphia later that year and knocked Cyclone Hart out in the eighth round. Then early in 1977 he fought Willie Monroe again, this time in the Boston Garden. In the last round, the twelfth round, Marvin knocked him out with what I still call the Willie Monroe Punch. Right uppercut and a straight left hand. Cold-cocked him. The Willie Monroe Punch.

After the fight, Willie's trainers, Eddie Futch and George Benton, came into our dressing room to compliment me on the win. Eddie said, "Every time we had Willie do something, Marvin countered with something else." With all of Marvin's knockouts, most people never realized what a versatile fighter he was. He could go right-handed. He could go southpaw. He could box. He could bang. He could do it both ways. Especially back then when he was really hungry and zinging, the whole bit. But after Marvin knocked Willie out, that wasn't enough. He wanted to fight Willie again down in Philadelphia. I didn't really want the match, but we were in a position where we couldn't be choosy.

While we were training I told Marvin, "Don't wait twelve rounds this time. If you get this guy shook, jump on him." The first round, Marvin hit him with a shot and Willie went backwards a little bit, stumbled. But instead of jumping all over him, Marvin stepped back. When he got back to the corner, I said, "What is wrong with you? Why didn't you jump on him?" He said, "I know, man." I said, "Marvin, those opportunities don't come too often." Second round, he got Willie against the ropes, hit him on the chin with a right hook, came back with a left hook, and cold-cocked him. Knocked him out. Retired him. I said, "See, man, you don't have to go twelve rounds."

By then Marvin was ready to fight for the middleweight title. After Carlos Monzon retired and Rodrigo Valdez beat Bennie Briscoe for the vacated title, we tried to get a title shot. Gil Clancy, who was Valdez's trainer, laughs about it now, but he's told me, "No way we were going to fight your man."

The best Marvin could do was win the United States middleweight title from Doug Demmings in Los Angeles in 1977, then he went down to Philadelphia to defend against Bennie Briscoe, another tough fighter. All those Philadelphia fighters were tough. Briscoe, Willie Monroe, Boogaloo Watts. We fought the Iron down there. I called them the Iron because they were as tough as iron. Whenever we fought one of 'em down there, I'd use the others as sparring partners. Lots of times I'd work the opposite corner when Marvin was sparring. Between rounds I'd tell Boogaloo, "Work on that left uppercut. Work on the hook." I knew Marvin's weaknesses, and Marvin would yell over, "I know what you're telling him." But he never complained.

No matter who Marvin ever sparred with, whether it was here in the gym in Brockton or down in Philadelphia with the Iron, he always told me, "Let the guy go all out. Don't hold him back." That's a professional.

For a trainer, the whole idea is to get your fighter peaked at the right time. You don't want to peak him too soon. You don't want to peak him too late. Hopefully you'll get him peaked the night of the fight. But while you're training, all of a sudden you see your fighter is peaking a little bit too soon. Sometimes the fighter himself will see he's a little bit logy. But fighters are stubborn. They won't tell you they're logy. But if a fighter's trainer is on the ball, his trainer can see it. His timing ain't right. Or his zip ain't there. Or he's starting to level off. I've sometimes said, "Tomorrow, Marvin, we're taking tomorrow off." He'd say, "Just roadwork in the morning?" I'd say, "Nothing." He'd say, "Nothing, man?" I'd say, "Nothing. Twenty-four hours. Nothing."

The next day, Marvin would be sharp again. Bop, bop, bop. I'd say, "How come you're a different fighter now?" He'd look over and say, "I hear you, man."

To get back to the Briscoe fight, in the first round Marvin got butted. Got his eye laid open. Worst cut I ever worked on. As soon as the bell rang, I was in the ring. I had one hand behind Marvin's head, the other was pressing a towel on his eye. I told my brother, "Pat, keep everybody away. Keep the referee away. Keep the doctor away." I sat Marvin down and went to work. You got to get all the excess blood out of it. You got to use compresses. You got to use the proper medication. By the time the doctor got past Pat, I'd controlled the blood. When the bell rang, I told Marvin, "Box him. Keep him on the end of your punches. Don't let him get in close." Briscoe kept working on Marvin, kept trying to lace him. Anything to open that cut. But it went ten and Marvin got the decision.

Not being able to get a shot at the title, Marvin could have turned into what I call a gypsy fighter. He could have gone off with another trainer and another manager who promised him a title fight. Most of the time that doesn't work out. But when it happens, I always feel sorry for the original trainer. He develops the fighter into a contender, but all of a sudden the fighter says, "See you later, alligator." The trainer busts his hump for four or five years but then the fighter goes off with another trainer and manager. It happens all the time. But it never happened with Marvin and me and my brother. For all his frustration, Marvin always said, "Don't worry, we'll get the title shot." He always believed in us just like we always believed in him.

Finally, in 1979, when Vito Antuofermo was the middleweight champion, Marvin got a title shot in Vegas. When the fight was over, I'll never forget this, the referee, Mills Lane, turned to Pat and me and said, "Will you please move over a little. When I raise Marvin's hand, I want Marvin and me to be out here together." The referee was ready to raise Marvin's hand, that's how domi-

nant Marvin had been. Then we heard it was a draw. That meant
Antuofermo kept the title. It was very disheartening.

The next year, Antuofermo lost the title to Alan Minter on a
decision in Vegas, then got knocked out by Minter in a return in
London. That put Marvin in line to fight Minter in London for
the title. When we were training, Minter made that statement that
hit the press, that "I'm not going to give my title to any black
man." Marvin came back with the most perfect answer. Marvin
said, "He's not giving me nothing. I'm taking the title from him."
The afternoon of the fight, Marvin and I took a long walk in one
of the London parks. When we stopped to feed the squirrels, I
said, "Marvin, you know what you have to do." He said, "I can't
leave it up to the judges."

Then a few hours before the fight Antuofermo was nice enough
to come over to our hotel and tell Pat and me, "You've got to
warn Marvin about the things these people are going to call him.
You've got to put cotton in his ears." When we got to the Wem-
bley arena, I told Marvin, "It's a long walk to the ring. Some of
these people are going to call you every name in the book. Just
ignore it."

Marvin went out there and destroyed Minter in three rounds.
But it was a crying shame that he couldn't be presented with the
championship belt like the champion is supposed to be. When the
fight ended, people started throwing beer bottles at the ring. We
had to run out of there like thieves, like we did something wrong.
Marvin left his robe there. I left my first-aid kit there. The police
escorted us through a ladies' room into our dressing room. Then
we had to wait until the coast was clear. When we got outside to
our limousine, the windshield had been smashed in. Glass was all
over the seat. When we finally got back to the hotel, we had a nice
party, but Marvin still didn't have his championship belt. He finally got it at a ceremony here in Brockton at Christo's Restaurant.

His first seven title defenses, Marvin had seven knockouts. Then
in 1983, against Roberto Duran in Vegas, he had to go the distance. Marvin won the fight. No question. But it wasn't until the
last few rounds that he really took over. Looking back on it, I
think Marvin gave Duran a little too much respect. Maybe just
Duran being Duran, who the hell knows? Duran was one of his
heroes. He loved Duran. Whatever it was, Marvin just wasn't
perking like he should.

But when Marvin fought Tommy Hearns in 1985, he never

perked better. You're hearing this from the horse's mouth, the way Marvin went out and banged with Hearns right away, that's the way we planned to fight him. In training we said, "He's a big tall guy. He's got a quick left hand. He'll want to keep you at the end of his punches." Fighters have habits. The first three rounds Hearns tries to be very intimidating. He goes out there and he wants to knock your head off. If he can't do it in three rounds, then he starts boxing.

So we told Marvin, "The thing to do with this guy, go out and bang with him. If you get him to bang with you, then we got a good shot. Get in a slugfest with this guy."

Now this was unusual for Marvin, because Marvin can box. But we agreed, Pat and I and Marvin, that this was the way we were going to fight this guy. I knew that if Hearns's trainer, Emanuel Steward, was smart, he'd have Hearns box Marvin, he'd have Hearns keep out of those corners and off the ropes, keep Marvin out there at the end of his punches. If Hearns could do this, he'd have a better shot at Marvin, but he didn't do it. He was too macho. When they went to the center of the ring for the referee's instructions, both were calling each other all kinds of names. That was great. Hearns was too macho. So we sent Marvin in right away. Marvin got him with the first right hook and they got into a banging contest. Hearns fell into our trap. That's exactly the way we wanted to fight him. Exactly the way. Get in tip-top shape and get in a slugfest with him. By the third round, it was all over.

Marvin's cut on the forehead wasn't as bad as some people thought. It hit a little capillary up there, a little bleeder. After the fight, it wasn't bleeding at all. But what happened was, a lot of blood was coming out of it and dripping down his face so it looked worse than it was.

In the corner before the third round I told Marvin, "Don't worry about your cut, I'll take care of it." But when he got out there he got whacked on it a couple times, then the referee stepped in and called the doctor over. Marvin figured he better not take any chances so he really went after Hearns and finished him. What a slugfest. But that's the way we planned it.

Then we had to wait two years before Marvin fought Sugar Ray Leonard, but we had been waiting almost five years going back to 1982 when Leonard needed the operation on the detached retina in his left eye.

If you remember, a few months after that operation, Leonard

invited us down to Baltimore for his big announcement. Marvin, Pat, and myself. We got a special invite. Leonard kept telling us, "Be there." We thought he was going to announce that he would fight Marvin. We were tickled pink. When he got up to speak, he said, "It'll be one of the greatest fights, myself and Marvelous Marvin Hagler." He kept building it up, then he said, "But it's not going to happen." Oooooh, you could have knocked us over with a feather. We wanted that fight so bad. It would've been great if it could've happened back then.

Then when Leonard decided to fight Kevin Howard in 1984, it looked like Marvin was next. We drove over to Worcester that night. I was a nervous wreck. I knew if Howard ever beat Leonard, forget it. As it was, Leonard didn't look good at all. He got knocked down in the fourth round. Even though Leonard won when the referee stopped it in the ninth round, it was a bad fight. Who was Kevin Howard? Leonard was so disgusted, he announced he was retiring again. He knew if he can't look good against Kevin Howard, he didn't have a chance against Marvin. After that, we figured the fight would never happen.

But in 1986, Leonard's attorney, Mike Trainer, called Pat, but nobody knew for sure what was going to happen. Nobody knew where we were going to fight or who was going to promote the fight. Trainer didn't want Bob Arum to promote the fight. Then Marvin decided to retire himself. That's when the air cleared. That's when we started to negotiate. Pat made it clear to Trainer that there'd be no fight unless Arum promoted it. We knew we could make more money with Arum than anybody. We always had a good relationship with Arum that went way back. His money has always been good. You always got what he promised you. So we finally put the fight together for April 6, 1987, at Caesars Palace in Vegas.

We trained in Palm Springs, at the Americana Canyon, and everything went fine. We didn't think it would be too difficult a fight. Marvin had a 62–2–2 record. He hadn't lost in more than eleven years. Not that he was overconfident, but we knew Leonard wouldn't change his style whatsoever. Leonard's Leonard. He fought the way we thought he would. We knew Leonard would flurry and look up at the clock, trying to steal the round. No surprises.

The surprises were the way Marvin fought. He gave away the

first four rounds. He sometimes fought right-handed instead of left-handed. Between rounds he was told to stay southpaw. Especially against Leonard, because he'd be more effective as a southpaw. As a rule, right-handers like Leonard have trouble with southpaws. Marvin was doing better as a southpaw against Leonard with a straight right jab. We kept telling Marvin to put the pressure on, to jump on him. Marvin's got the chin. No way Leonard's going to hurt him. But he was just edging, edging, edging. He got Leonard in trouble in the ninth round but he couldn't finish him off. If he had to fight him again, I'd have to impress on him from training camp on, just hit Leonard on the back, hit him on the head, hit him anywhere. Jump on him. You can't fool around with him. You can't go out there and box him. He's too cute. He knows how to steal the goddam rounds. He's too pretty out there. You've got to rough the bastard up.

Had it been a fifteen-round fight, no question Marvin would've won it. Leonard collapsed after the twelfth round ended. He had nothing left. But he won a split decision.

The judge from Mexico, Jo Jo Guerra, had it way out of line, 118 points to 110. He gave Leonard ten rounds, Marvin two rounds. My brother Pat made the statement "They should put that judge in jail." Another judge, Dave Moretti, a Las Vegas guy, had Leonard ahead by only two points, 115 to 113. In rounds Moretti had it seven to five. But another thing was, the referee, Richard Steele, warned Leonard forty times for holding and for hitting after the bell, but Steele never took a point away from him. If you warn a guy three times and he continues, you've got to take a point away from him. He was warned forty times. Forty times. That's a matter of public record.

If you remember, shortly after that fight, it was investigated by the Nevada Attorney General's Office. Moretti, the judge who had Leonard ahead by two points, and a big gambler out there who also managed fighters, Billy Baxter, were supposed to be in cahoots. They were supposed to be going into business together as fight promoters. Baxter was supposed to have bet something like three hundred thousand dollars on Leonard, who was supposed to have stayed at Baxter's house instead of in a hotel like Marvin did. With all that going on, we thought the commission was going to rule it a no-decision.

After about a month and a half, the Attorney General's Office

announced it had "found no evidence that any illegal activity occurred before, during, or after the controversial bout or that the
outcome of the fight was influenced by any factor other than the
boxer's conduct during the twelve-round fight." But what else could
they say? If the Attorney General's Office found something shady
with the fight, boxing in Vegas would've lost multimillions of dollars. I don't care what they announced, it still stunk like hell. If
you knock Leonard out, you'd be lucky to get a draw.

What a disappointment that was for such a great fighter as Marvin to have a loss like that. Years from now people will look at the
record and say, "Oh, yeah, Leonard beat Marvin Hagler." But
they won't know the details on it.

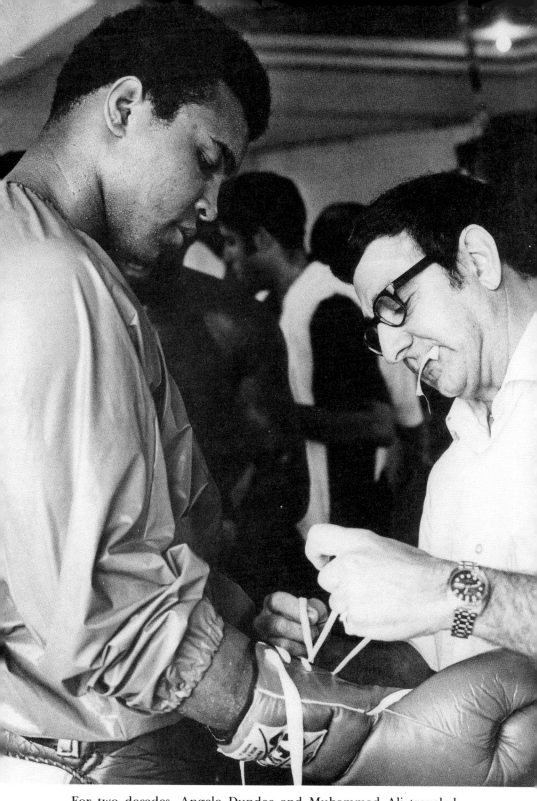

For two decades, Angelo Dundee and Muhammad Ali traveled the world.

Angelo Dundee:

"We Never Saw Muhammad Ali at His Best"

≡

The night before, Angelo Dundee had been in Pikesville, Maryland, working a corner, and now, on his way to a boxing news conference at the Plaza Hotel in midtown New York, he was hurrying through a baggage-claim area in La Guardia Airport when a stranger stared at him.

"Hello, Mr. Dundee," the stranger said.

"How ya doin', my friend," Dundee said.

Of all of today's boxing trainers, Angelo Dundee is the best-known and the most recognizable. For more than twenty years, he was an ambassador of boxing during Muhammad Ali's world travels. He later polished Sugar Ray Leonard into the welterweight and middleweight champion. Over the last four decades, he worked with nine other champions: Carmen Basilio, Willie Pastrano, Ralph Dupas, Luis Rodriguez, Sugar Ramos, José Napoles, Jimmy Ellis, Pinklon Thomas, and Slobodan Kacar.

To him, as to any good trainer, a fighter is always somebody special. Even a fighter who's not his fighter. One night in Nassau, the Bahamas, when Tommy Hearns got butted, Dundee organized the medical treatment.

"Three months earlier I was in Ray Leonard's corner, trying

to beat Tommy Hearns's brains out," Dundee remembered with a laugh. "But that night he got butted I got my friend Dr. Groff to sew him up. Dr. Groff must've put sixty-five, seventy stitches in him. Saved his career. Emanuel Steward and Prentiss Byrd were there with Tommy, but we took care of Tommy in our room, Helen's and mine. In fact, I sent out for beer and sandwiches. Why? Because he's a fighter."

Angelo even met his wife, Helen, the mother of their two children, because of a fighter and another trainer.

"Ray Arcel was working with Jackie Cranford, a big beautiful-looking guy who was fighting Gino Buonvino in the Garden that night," he recalled. "Jackie was lined up to fight Joe Louis next. Jackie was a nervous wreck, so Ray was playing cards with him, trying to calm him down. But that was how I met Helen, who was Jackie's cousin."

Angelo, who was born on August 30, 1921, in Philadelphia, gravitated to boxing through his older brother Chris.

"Chris was managing fighters in New York, so I went up there," he said. "And after Chris moved to Miami to promote fights, I moved to Miami with him. Helen came down to break off with me because her mother told her, 'Go break off with the guy.' Three days later we were married by a Jewish judge. Chris was my best man."

They live in North Miami, Florida, whenever Angelo is not on the move working with "my guy," as he always describes his fighter.

"With some of my guys, I work with them in my gym when I'm home," he said. "With others, I go to where they're training for a fight about a week before and do my shtick."

His shtick is always upbeat, always optimistic. But he has known dark moments. One still haunts him.

"I was in Sugar Ramos's corner the night Davey Moore died," he said of their 1963 featherweight title bout in Los Angeles. "I knew Davey Moore from a kid. You know me, I'm friendly with the enemy. I ain't mad at nobody. When they stopped that fight, I consoled him. He asked me for a return match right there in the ring. Then the newspaper guys were interviewing him later and he said, 'I got a headache. I think I'll lay down.' He never got up. That scared me. That bothered me. Bothered the hell out of me. I almost threw in the towel."

Two decades later, Dundee was watching television when Duk Koo Kim was knocked out by Ray Mancini in their 1982 light-weight title bout.

"Kim's neck hit the bottom rope, that's what killed him," Dundee said. "We've got four ropes, but the bottom rope is the danger rope. They should set the bottom rope back about six inches toward the apron. The bottom rope serves no purpose. You ain't got midgets fighting each other. When a guy goes down, if he hits the ropes and slides down, fine. But if they just hit the bottom rope, they snap their neck. Move it back. I've been trying to get commissions to do something. But nothing happens. You got to do the ultimate to protect."

You do if you're Angelo Dundee, whose business is boxing. Whose life is boxing.

=

In all his fights, I never saw Muhammad Ali in worse shape than in Manila when he came back to the corner after the eleventh round. For the first time in his life it looked like he ran out of gas completely. It looked like exhaustion was setting in. When he sat down, he just plopped. I told him, "Muhammad, now we're going to have to separate the men from the boys. You got to suck it up." He sucked it up.

Those last three rounds were to me a *Rocky* movie. The tide turning. The excitement. Muhammad came back from the bottom of a pit, sucked it up, and did it. And against a tough guy. Joe Frazier was not just another guy. Joe Frazier was a tooouuugh guy.

In the early rounds, Muhammad was handling him. But then Frazier got murderous. I didn't know if Muhammad was going to make it through the eleventh round. When he came back to the corner, I put ice in his cup to get him going, told him he had to suck it up, the whole thing. But great fighters have an innate reservoir, a second gear, where they suck it up and bring themselves back to the point where they defeat the other guy. Human beings aren't supposed to have that second gear. Back in the dressing room after the fight, he just laid there and let Luis Sarria rub him.

When he finally came out to the press conference almost an hour later, one of the newspaper guys asked him what the fight had been like.

Muhammad said, "It was next to death."

Because of the time difference for closed-circuit television, that fight started in Manila about ten o'clock in the morning. After the fight he just hung around the hotel and rested. That night he went to a reception that President Marcos had for him. But he could hardly walk right. His hands hurt. Everything hurt. I heard later that Joe Frazier was singing and dancing that night at a party in his hotel. Muhammad could hardly move, but Muhammad had won the fight by sucking it up when he had to. That's the mark of a great fighter. I think it was Muhammad's greatest moment. And to me, he's the greatest fighter of all time.

The shame is that we never saw Muhammad at his best. He would've been at his peak sometime during the three and a half years he was exiled for refusing induction into the service. People always ask me, "Who would've won, the Muhammad Ali after the exile or the Cassius Clay before the exile?" I say, the Muhammad Ali after the exile. When he came back, he was stronger. The maturity was there.

We'll never have another Muhammad Ali. Forget about it. Before Mike Tyson got licked by Buster Douglas, people were telling me, "Tyson's going to be considered the greatest fighter of all time." I said, "Please, you can't compare anybody to Muhammad." Not only for what he did as a fighter, but from his availability as a superstar to the way he attracted people other than fight fans.

Muhammad changed the concept of boxing. In the old days you couldn't get to the fighter. You had to go through the manager, the trainer, the seconds, the publicity guys. You never got to the star, much less a superstar. Muhammad was the most available superstar there's ever been. I feel good about that because I created that. I made him aware of the people who were coming to see him. The newspaper guys, the magazine guys, the television and radio guys. I told him, "These are your friends. This is what it's all about. They want to talk to you. Always respect that. Because when they stop talking to you, then you're a dead issue."

If Muhammad was going out where he knew there'd be a lot of people, he would sign hundreds of autographs ahead of time so he could pass 'em out. He'd sit in his room signing autographs so he wouldn't disappoint people.

Muhammad loved people. He loved to be around people. He loved to have people around him. That's why his entourage was so big. Me and Sarria and Ferdie Pacheco, the Fight Doctor in Miami, who took care of all my fighters. His brother Rahaman. Drew Brown, Bundini, the one and only. Howard Bingham, his photographer. Gene Kilroy, who put together the Deer Lake camp near Reading, Pennsylvania, who did whatever had to be done. Pat Patterson, his bodyguard. Lana Shabazz, his cook. Wali Muhammad, a big help around the gym. James Anderson, another security guy. Booker Johnson, who came to camp with a Bible and never left. Lloyd Wells, C. B. Atkins, Ralph Thornton, nobody seemed to know what they did but Muhammad liked 'em. And a few days before a fight, his parents and some other friends would always show up. The bigger the fight, the bigger the entourage.

The only time Muhammad ever got p.o.'d at me, we were in Zaire for the George Foreman fight. Some American troops were there, and a major came over with his wife and little girl to where we were training. The little girl, maybe six years old, had a gift for him. I knew if she just gave it to anybody, the gift would never get to Muhammad, so I told her, "You don't have to give Muhammad a gift. He'd be very happy just to see you." So after the little girl went in with her father and mother to see him, he called me in. He said, "This little girl wanted to give me a gift and you said not to give it to me." I said, "No, Muhammad, I told her she didn't have to give you a gift to get to see you." When the little girl was nice enough to give him a gift, he probably just wanted to make a fuss over her.

Muhammad might put on an act that he was upset, but nothing ever really bothered him. Nothing. Not even when his wife, Belinda, walked out on him in Manila after she found out the woman who turned out to be his next wife, Veronica, was there.

As a trainer, I never got involved in Muhammad's marital situations. Or any other fighter's. I just didn't deal with it. For a trainer it's a no-no. In all my encounters with fighters, that's the greatest lesson I learned. I learned it early when my brother Chris let me handle the four-round kids. What happened was, I had this four-round kid training in Stillman's Gym. He came to me one day and said, "That wife of mine, what a pain she is." I said, "You know how women are." End of story, or so I thought. Except he went home that night and told his wife, "Even Angelo thinks you're wrong." I hadn't said nothing except "You know how women are."

Right then I learned my lesson. Whenever a guy comes to me and talks about his wife or girlfriend, I say, "Look, do me a favor, go hit the light bag." I don't live with him and his wife or his girlfriend. I don't know what's going on between them. I don't want to know.

In Manila, the way I heard it, Muhammad's problem started because Veronica was there before Belinda arrived. He took Veronica someplace where Marcos was, and when Marcos told Muhammad, "What a beautiful wife you have," Muhammad didn't correct him. Muhammad just let it go. Some of the Manila newspapers started identifying Veronica as Muhammad's wife. Then when Belinda arrived, she only stayed about twelve hours. She had a big blowup with Muhammad and went home.

All this happened only three or four days before the fight. But like I say, I knew if I got involved with it, I could lose the respect of my fighter. I never mentioned it. I never did anything different in his training to try to distract him or make him forget about it. I didn't have to. He trained like nothing happened. That was always one of the most remarkable things about him. Nothing bothered him. Nothing took away from him training like he should, from him getting ready for the fight.

Looking back, it's easy to say, but if I could pick when Muhammad should have stopped fighting, it would be after Manila. That was such a tough fight. We'd always had conversations about when he should stop. Back when he was a kid in the Fifth Street Gym in Miami, we had a pet joke about an old-time fighter who was skipping rope but his rhythm wasn't fluid. I'd say, "See that guy over there, if you get like that I'm going to tell you, because he's stuttering." Years later we'd be riding in a car somewhere and I'd lean back and say, "Muhammad, you're starting to stutter." He'd say, "Oh, yeah. Oh, yeah." He knew what I was saying. But he didn't want to stop. When Ferdie Pacheco started talking about how Muhammad should stop fighting, I resented it. I don't see anybody playing God in that situation. Muhammad did what he wanted to do.

What he's got now, Parkinson's syndrome, isn't just boxing. It's a world problem. It's a disease they don't have a cure for. And there's another thing that comes into play here. What's affected Muhammad might be insecticide poisoning. The log cabin at our training camp in Deer Lake, Pennsylvania, had creosoted logs, railroad ties. He always had a big fire in the fireplace there and he slept in there by himself. That was his room, that was his hide-away. He may have inhaled those fumes from the creosoted logs. Maybe that's what did it.

His new wife, Lonnie, takes him down to South Carolina to get his blood cleansed every six weeks. She makes sure he takes his medication, which he wasn't taking like he should've. His face is clearer now. I don't think there's anything wrong with his brain, I really don't. But he misses being around boxing. After you've been the world champion, after you've been centerstage for so long, you got to miss it. But he still creates excitement wherever he goes. If he's in Miami, he'll come to the De Leonardis Youth Center in North Miami Beach, where I train fighters now. The last time he worked out for three hours. I wouldn't let him spar, but he still sweats a lot. He still pulls up his rubber shirt and lets the sweat drip out. When I was in Orlando doing a videotape, he had a ball. He and Lonnie and my wife, Helen, went out on the lake in one of those pedal boats. All the way across the lake and back. It was heartwarming. I go back with him so far, way back to when he was just a kid named Cassius Clay in Louisville and I would go there with fighters like Willie Pastrano, Luis Rodriguez, and Ralph Dupas.

In 1959, the year before Cassius won his Olympic gold medal in Rome, Willie Pastrano and I were walking into the downtown gym in Louisville when we heard this kid hitting the heavy bag. Ba-ba-ba-bang. Ba-ba-ba-bang. I found out later that he'd been there an hour waiting for us. As soon as he saw us, he came over to me and said, "I want to work with your guy."

I told him, "No, I don't like amateurs to work with pros." I never messed with amateurs. Maybe it's an old witch's tale with me, but putting professional input into an amateur is a no-no. An amateur has to fight his own way. Hit and don't get hit, a Marquis of Queensberry rules type of thing. If you put a professional out-look on an amateur fighter, maybe he's not going to be the right kind of amateur fighter. I just didn't think it was right for an amateur to work with a pro, that's all. Especially with a guy who'd been a pro for eight years, a future world light heavyweight champion who at the time had won forty-eight of his sixty fights.

So I resisted letting him work with Willie for a few days, but I finally gave in. Maybe just to stop him from pestering me, what-ever it was, I agreed to let him work with Willie.

Lo and behold, as soon as he got in the ring, he did a number on Willie, second to none. He was only seventeen years old but he was so fast. After one round, I told Willie, "You're getting stale. You ain't going to spar no more. This is it." Willie looked at me and said, "Don't bullshit me. The kid kicked my ass. I couldn't hit him. He was too fast for me." But what I didn't know until later was that Cassius also had worked out with Alonzo Johnson, the guy Willie was going to fight. He told Alonzo, "You'll beat that guy." And after he worked out with Willie, he told Willie, "Don't worry, you'll win." But knowing Cassius, he probably thought he was better than both of 'em. For a few rounds, he probably was. Hey, two years later, he beat Alonzo Johnson in a ten-round decision in Louisville.

But after he worked with Willie Pastrano, outside of knowing he won the Olympic light heavyweight gold medal, I pretty much forgot about him until I got a phone call from Bill Faversham, who was the head of the Louisville Sponsoring Group backing Cassius's pro career. When he got home from the Olympics, he went to Archie Moore first, but it didn't work out.

The kid wanted to turn pro right away, but Archie kept telling him he wasn't ready. Archie, meanwhile, was still fighting himself, still traveling. From what I gathered later, they just didn't get along too good. One day Archie wanted him to sweep the floor of the trailer that served as his gym. The way I heard it, the kid told him, "I never swept the floor for my mother. Why am I going to sweep the floor for you?" Anyway, after Bill Faversham called me, he and Worth Bingham, who owned the newspaper and television station in Louisville, came down to interview me.

When they asked me how I was going to handle this kid, I told them, "I'm a patient guy. I don't want to rush him. Let him learn his trade. But it takes time to learn his trade." They seemed to like that.

Around that time, in late October, the kid was about to have his first fight. Tunney Hunsaker in Louisville, six rounds. The businessmen wanted me to come up to work that fight, but I didn't go. I didn't think it was right. I didn't want to walk in like a knight in shining armor. The kid won a decision, then he came down to Miami to go to work in my gym. I put him in a little hotel in downtown Miami, the Charles Hotel, which was near a Famous Chef restaurant where he ate. He knew everybody downtown. At night he'd go over to the Sir John Hotel where all the nightclub stars stayed and tell them what a great fighter he was going to be. He'd tell everybody that. He meant it. He just wanted to be a fighter. In the morning, he'd run from downtown across the causeway to the beach all the way to the old Fifth Street Gym, up a flight of stairs past a shoeshine stand, then he'd run all the way back to his hotel. I'd get phone calls from the police about this big kid running on the causeway. You weren't allowed to run on the causeway with all the cars there.

He was a hard worker in the gym. First guy in, last guy out. When he was through working, he'd sit around talking to anybody who'd listen. Years later Dick Sadler, who was with Archie Moore when he was there, told me, "Working with that kid, you deserve the Purple Heart with nine clusters. That kid drove me crazy."

But all those years he never drove me crazy. Never. We just blended. He was a fun guy, a putter-onner, a mesmerizer, what I call a web-weaver. He'd walk into the gym and tell me, "I'm gonna clean out your gym. Line 'em all up." I'd say, "I only got one guy and he's a middleweight." Fun, we just had fun together.

When he first came down from Louisville, he weighed 182 pounds. You never vision how big a kid's going to be. You never know at what stage of their growth they'll get bigger. But at no time did he ever do anything but work naturally. He'd loosen up three, four rounds. Hit the heavy bag, four, five rounds. Hit the light bag four, five rounds. He hated the light bag because it was so difficult to hit. I had to teach him how to hit the light bag. You don't hit the light bag like you hit the heavy bag. You don't hit the light bag like you fight. You've got to stand straight in front of the light bag and balance yourself, then it's all reflex and timing. And this kid, through doing all these things, got bigger and bigger. Big legs, thick ankles. He always had a great foundation.

But the most important thing was, he really wanted to be a fighter. About a year or two later, he told me, "Ange, you really didn't like me in the beginning, did you?" I said, "What are you talking about?" He said, "That time you sent Alan Harmon to room with me at the hotel, there was only one bed in the room."

Alan Harmon was a heavyweight from Kingston, Jamaica. I figured they'd be sparring with each other, so I had them rooming together. I just assumed there were two beds in the room. But he never said anything about it until later on after Alan left. He tolerated it. That's how much he wanted to be a fighter. Some people think he was a natural, but he still had to be taught. And I taught him everything. When I got him, he was just a kid. When people ask me "What did you do for him?" all I say is, "Look at this kid when he first started and look at him four years later when he was the world heavyweight champion." He got better by degrees. He got more mature. He got solid. He got more fluidness. The bending of the knee, all those little things. If you remember, if you read the clippings from early in this kid's career, nobody thought he would make a fighter. He was too herky-jerky. He carried his hands too low.

One time I even started to believe that maybe they were right. Maybe he was carrying his hands too low. In the corner during the Doug Jones fight in the Garden, I told him, "Get your hands up." He got the hell beat out of him that round. I left him alone about his hands after that. When he kept his hands up, he was never as fluid.

By then we were using the bit about picking the round. People forget that he never guessed it right all the time. But he got it right often enough that it really had impact. Before he fought Archie Moore late in 1962 in Los Angeles, he was shouting, "Moore in four, Moore in four." Sure enough, Moore went in four. When we went to New York for Doug Jones, he predicted the sixth round, but a few days later he said, "Jones is talking too much—I'm cutting it to four." Now we're leaving the ring after getting a close ten-round decision in a tough fight, we're getting booed pretty good, and I tell him, "You said six, you said four. Six and four is ten." He used it and got a laugh with it.

His poems were big. One was "They all must fall in the round I call." Before the Doug Jones fight, John Condon, the Garden publicity man, had him go down to Greenwich Village and read his poems. He mostly did his own poems. I could rhyme pretty good, so I'd help him with that. I helped him with his spelling too.

We did the poems on planes to keep his mind off being scared. He didn't like to fly. The first plane trip I ever took with him, just as we were about to take off, a little kid saw him praying, reached over, and patted him on the shoulder. That's how scared he was, a little kid was patting him on the shoulder. I credit myself for telling him, "Hey, you're a superstar. But if you want to continue being a superstar, you've got to fly whether you like it or not. If you're a superstar, you got to go everywhere."

After the Jones fight, he flew to London for the Henry Cooper fight. That's where I created what's known now as the Dundee Rule where there has to be an extra pair of gloves for each fighter under the ring. What happened was, in the first round my guy's left glove split along the seam between the thumb and the rest of the glove. The split wasn't on top, it wasn't on the hitting area. It was in the seam, the webbing. Not a big split, but enough so you'd notice. In the corner, I told him, "Keep your left hand closed." He'd had a good first round and I didn't want to disrupt the flow of the fight.

During the second and third rounds, the more he snake-licked Cooper with his left jab, the more the split got a little bigger and a little bigger. Between rounds I kept telling him, "Keep your left hand closed, keep it on your lap." It wasn't a crime we were committing. It wasn't something that gave him an advantage. But just before the bell ended the fourth round, my guy gets nailed a left hook and slides down the ropes. My guy likes to say that Cooper caught him while he was looking at Elizabeth Taylor at ringside, but Cooper always had a great left hook. I jump into the ring, drag my guy to his feet, and walk him back to the corner to sit him down and get him together for the next round.

As soon as we get to the corner, I put my finger in the split seam and lifted the leather up. I yell, "Hey, referee, this glove's bad." The referee comes over, I point to the glove, then the referee hurries over where the British commissioners were sitting. I hear them saying, "We must get another glove." They sent somebody all the way back to the dressing room, but he couldn't find another glove. When they told me that, I said, "I guess we'll just have to use the same glove." The glove had never been off my guy's hand. Never. I'd just bought some time. I don't know how much, but it was enough. By now my guy is all pepped up and ready to go.

When they finally rang the bell, he went out there and knocked Cooper out. Fifth round, just like he predicted. But all that stuff about the glove, that's why there's the Dundee Rule now. Another pair of gloves for each fighter under the ring.

By now my guy is the hottest heavyweight contender around, 19–0 with fifteen knockouts. After Sonny Liston knocks Floyd

Patterson out again in the first round, they make them for the title. Not many people thought my guy had a chance, but I kept telling him, "You're gonna lick Liston. You're a better fighter. He's never fought a guy like you." Liston was awesome. He was 35–1 with twenty-five knockouts. But he always had trouble with tall guys. He always had trouble with awkwardness. That was the whole key. His only loss had been to a tall guy, Marty Marshall, an eight-round decision in 1954 in Detroit. That's what I was basing my thinking on. See, certain things bother certain fighters. What bothered Liston was height, awkwardness, and speed, things that prevented him from leaning in with that great left jab he had.

Liston had the best jab in the business. Strong jab. He put it right through you. It wasn't just pop, pop. It was *bang, bang*. It had some speed to it and some distance. He used to really lean in with that jab.

But I figured I knew what Liston was thinking. That this kid can't really fight, that he runs too much. But he didn't know this kid's strength. To me, there was no way this kid could lose to Liston as long as he didn't let Liston jab him. The whole key was for my kid to surround that jab by going to his left, away from Liston's jab. I figured once he surrounded the jab, Liston would lose his mobility. My guy's height was another big factor. At six-four, he had three inches on Liston, who usually fought guys he dwarfed. Even so, Liston was an awesome fighting machine. If he was around today, forget it. He'd clean up. Liston was just what my guy nicknamed him, the big ugly bear. He was more ominous than Mike Tyson, because at six-one, he was taller. Tyson's short-ness is a minus. Everybody he fights is bigger, and if they got the talent to offset his aggression, like Buster Douglas did in Tokyo, then he's got nothing.

But against Liston my guy had another factor going for him. Liston thought he might be a little crazy. One night Liston was at a craps table in the Thunderbird in Las Vegas when my guy taunted him. Another time he drove his red bus to Denver and stood out-side Liston's house at one in the morning yelling at him. I wasn't with him. I never wanted to get into any of those scenes. Drew Brown was with him. Drew Brown was enough.

Drew's nickname was Bundini, which he pronounced Boodini. He was the first member of the entourage. He met my guy in New York and they hit it off. Drew made him laugh. He wanted Drew around. But to tell you the truth, at first I didn't know if I wanted

Drew around. When he told me he was bringing Drew down, I said, "Don't do that, that guy will drive me up a wall." But he said, "Don't worry, I'll make sure he's all right." He wanted Drew around because Drew was fun. And he was right. Drew was fun. I got to really like Drew. He was easy to get along with. He was a very warm guy. He didn't have a mean bone in his body. And he became a very necessary guy with us, with me. He was always part of the scene, beginning with the weigh-in for the Liston fight. The weigh-in we did twice.

When we got to the Miami Beach Convention Hall for the weigh-in, we hung around in my brother Chris's office in the front. Pretty soon there's a lot of people there with us. Sugar Ray Robinson's there. Some guy from Chicago's there with a bunch of pretty girls and banners saying "I'm the Greatest." If you know the Convention Hall, it's a long walk from the front to the freight dock in the back where the weigh-in was. So now we're walking through the halls. My guy and Drew are yelling, "Float like a butterfly, sting like a bee." Drew is holding a bear trap and yelling, "We're gonna get that big ugly bear." We've got thirty, forty people with us walking through the halls. But when we finally get to where the scale was supposed to be, nobody's there. We're an hour early.

We went back to Chris's office, hung around for an hour, and came back. We had no idea it would turn into such a wild scene, but this kid was the greatest producer-director of all time. He's yelling and shouting so much, Liston changed right there. Liston completely changed, because a tough guy is always afraid of a crazy guy. Liston really thought this kid was crazy, yelling "I'm going to get you" and pretending he wanted to fight Liston right there. What nobody noticed was, I'm holding him back with one finger in his chest. One finger.

What I didn't know was that the commission doctor, Alexander Robbins, got so caught up in the scene he thought my kid was scared to death, that maybe the fight should be canceled. He took his blood pressure and it was sky-high, but I said, "Sure it's high, but he was only acting, he was only putting on a show." As soon as the weigh-in was over, I turned to Ferdie Pacheco and said, "You better come with me." We drove over to Muhammad's house, and when we got there, maybe twenty minutes later, he's sitting on the steps, talking to the kids in the neighborhood. Like nothing had ever happened at the weigh-in.

I turned to Ferdie and said, "Take his blood pressure." It was completely normal. I called the Associated Press, the United Press, *The Miami Herald,* the *Miami News,* I called everybody and anybody and told them, "This kid's normal. Everything that happened at the weigh-in was a show." Then my guy went in the house and took a nap.

After what happened at the weigh-in, I figured Liston was a little leery of this kid. So just before we went to the middle of the ring for the referee's instructions, I told my guy, "Stand tall. You're bigger than this sucker. Make sure you look down on this sucker." I wanted him to instill his height in Liston's mind. Liston liked people to think he was even bigger than he was. He would wear big boots to make him taller. He would stuff big towels under his robe. He always had little short guys around him. I've used the same trick. I don't like tall guys around my heavyweights because I want the fighter to project a huge look.

So when we got to the middle of the ring, my guy stood tall, looked down at Liston, and said, "I got you, sucker." Right there, in the middle of the ring before a punch was thrown, that was the beginning of the end for Sonny Liston.

When the bell rang, my guy did just what we planned. Stick, move to the left, stay away from Liston's jab. But after the fourth round he came back to the corner blinking and shaking his head. He was yelling, "Cut the gloves off. Cut the gloves off." He couldn't see. Something had gotten into his eyes. He figured somebody was doing something to him. "Dirty work afoot," he yelled. "Cut the gloves off." I said, "No, no, this is for the world title. Sit down." He sat down. I got the sponge. I washed his eyes out. I put my pinky in there. When my pinky burned, I knew something was in there. Maybe liniment, maybe something that Liston's corner had put on the cut on Liston's cheek after the third round. But he's still blinking, still shaking his head, still yelling, "Dirty work afoot." Now the referee, Barney Felix, is coming toward us. I said, "Get up. Get up. Show this guy you're all right." When he got up, Barney walked away. If he'd come to our corner, he would have heard my guy yelling about dirty work afoot. He might have stopped the fight right then and there. But now I've got my guy on his feet. When the bell rang, I slapped him on the ass and told him, "Run until your eyes clear. Run."

He ran. After about a minute and a half, his eyes did clear. His tear ducts must have cleaned them out. I'll never know what got in his eyes. He was sweating profusely. Maybe when he leaned on Liston, it washed into his eyes. I'll never know. Whatever it was, nature took care of it.

As soon as his eyes cleared, he really did a number on Liston with his quickness and strength. Liston found out how strong this kid was. A couple of times, he kept Liston off with just a straight-arm. He took Liston's mystique away from him. Here's a guy who was supposed to be the toughest kid on the block, who destroyed everybody. But he's getting beat up. In the corner after the seventh round, my back was turned to Liston when all of a sudden Drew Brown jumped up. Drew had seen Liston's corner telling Barney Felix that Liston had a bad shoulder and couldn't continue. That's how I knew my guy was the new heavyweight champion of the world.

Liston was never the same. He knew in his own mind he'd been disrobed, that he'd had his mystique taken away from him. By the time of the rematch in Lewiston, Maine, in 1965, he was thirty-three years old. Age was starting to take a toll on him.

Three days before the rematch, Liston was working out at the Poland Spring House, the resort where he was staying. I went over there and walked in. Nobody stopped me. He looked terrible sparring with Amos [Big Train] Lincoln, then he tried to skip rope and got his feet tangled up. Maybe just to do something, anything, to impress the spectators, Liston let his trainer, Willie Reddish, throw a big leather medicine ball into his stomach. Boooom, boooom, boooom. Some of the people were ooohing and aaahing like this was really terrific, like what great shape he must be in. I turned to the guy next to me and said, "Why don't Willie throw the medicine ball in Sonny's face? That's where my guy is going to hit him."

Little did I know that in the first round my guy would hit him so hard so quick. Some people like to say they never saw the punch, that Liston just fell down from a tap on the head. But there was a punch, a good right hand to the temple my guy threw from up on the balls of his feet. I saw the punch. Lots of people saw the punch. The thing is, Liston never saw the punch.

Liston had thrown a jab and wasn't looking at my guy. That's why he didn't see the punch. But the punch you don't see, that's the one that gets you out of there. When you see shots coming, you brace yourself. You slide over a little bit. You don't take the full effect. But when you don't see the shot coming, that's when you get hit with the full effect. That's what happened when Liston got hit. His whole body picked up, his left leg came up off the canvas. When his left leg went down, his whole body crumbled. As soon as Liston went down, I kept an eye on the knockdown timekeeper, who was to the right of our corner. As the time-keeper was counting, the referee, Jersey Joe Walcott, got con-fused about the count. I could see that the timekeeper had counted to ten so I yelled, "Joe, Joe, the fight's over. Check the time-keeper." In the hue and cry, Joe went over, checked with the time-keeper, ran back to where the fighters were trading shots, waved his arms, and stopped the fight.

By then Nat Fleischer was standing up next to the timekeeper. Nat Fleischer was the editor of *The Ring* magazine. Everybody in boxing knew Nat. So when Nat stood up, people thought he was the timekeeper who told Joe Walcott to stop the fight. But the timekeeper was a little sandy-haired guy sitting next to Nat.

After I jumped into the ring, I walked over to Liston and I said, "Tough night, Sonny." He didn't say anything. He looked right through me. He was out. He was definitely out. When the fight was stopped he was on his feet, throwing shots. But the only rea-son he was on his feet throwing shots was his instincts as a fighter. They're not there, but they're there. I can't explain that with fighters. But it happens. I've seen it dozens of times, maybe hundreds. All those people chanting "Fix, fix, fix" that night weren't able to look in Liston's eyes like I did. But there was another fac-tor, the newspaper stories that the black Muslims who sided with Elijah Muhammad were coming to Lewiston to kill my guy Mu-hammad Ali because he had been converted to the Islamic reli-gion by Malcolm X, who had been assassinated two months earlier. The night of the fight in St. Dominic's Arena in Lewiston the police checked everybody for a weapon. None were found. But who knows how much all that had been playing on Liston's mind?

My guy was sincere about the Islamic religion. When he was getting ready to fight Floyd Patterson in Vegas, in late 1965, Pat-terson made a big thing of calling him Cassius Clay, but my guy kept saying, "He knows my name's Muhammad now. I want him to call me Muhammad."

With most people, my guy never seemed to care what they called him. But when Patterson kept calling him Cassius, he made an issue out of it. That bothered me, but I understood. When his brother Rudy, whose original name was Rudolph Valentino Clay, told me he had changed his name to Rahaman Ali, pronounced Rockman, I said, "I'll call you Rocky." He said, "No, you'll call me Rahaman." I called him Rahaman. No big deal. But in the Patterson fight, especially after Patterson's back went out, I always thought Muhammad let it go twelve rounds just to punish him. He pulled the same baloney with Ernie Terrell early in 1967, fifteen rounds.

When we were in New York to fight Zora Folley a few weeks later, Muhammad trained in the Garden basement. One day he was surrounded by several Black Muslims wearing black suits with white shirts and black bow ties. Wherever Muhammad walked, those guys walked in front of him, clearing the way. It was too much a show of force. By then the Louisville Sponsoring Group's contract had expired and Elijah Muhammad's son, Herbert, was my guy's manager. That night I went to Herbert and told him, "All those guys in black suits are coming on too strong. That's not the kind of image you want to project." Those guys were never obvious again.

By then the Muslim controversy was really building. But my guy was committed to his religion. Nobody was leading him by the nose. He wasn't a guy who was led easily. You've got to remember the intricacies of training this kid. You didn't train him like the usual fighter. He resented direction, so I used misdirection. I cast the illusion of him doing something when he wasn't. To get him to do what he should be doing.

During a workout, I might say, "You're really cooking with that jab. You're really bending your knee and popping it." He'd absorb it and utilize it. The next day, I'd work on the left uppercut or the right cross. Or the slide. Or the technique of don't put your butt on the ropes or your shoulders on the ropes. When you feel the calves of your legs touch the ropes, move. If the guy's coming this way, go that way. If he's coming that way, go this way. When you want to stay off the ropes, as soon as your calves touch the ropes, that's the key. But it's getting the fighter to absorb it. Some guys, you can try and try and try, they're not going to absorb. But you don't get mad. You just keep trying to get the best out of your pupil. You deal with all shapes and sizes. If they're tall, you tell them to stand tall. If they're short, you tell them to dip. That kind of stuff. Some absorb it. Some don't. Muhammad absorbed it. He just didn't know he was absorbing it through misdirection.

Another thing, wherever we trained, I always wanted a lot of big mirrors around. When he was working out, I wanted him looking at himself in all those mirrors and saying, "Hey, look, ain't I the prettiest man you ever saw." Looking at himself in all those mirrors helped him work harder to lose some pounds, to make himself look even prettier.

But the more people got on him for being a Black Muslim, the more he got his back up. As his trainer, I thought it was a plus for him as a boxer. It gave him a purpose. Also the living style. He ate good. He didn't drink, didn't smoke. Not many people would stick to their religion the way he did. Especially when his Army thing developed during Vietnam.

I was in the Army in Europe in World War II. I earned a battle star for kicking parapaks out of a C-47 to soldiers in the snow during the Battle of the Bulge. Compared to what some guys did in combat, that wasn't much, but I'm proud of it. I'm not trying to cop out for Muhammad, but I'm just as proud of what he did. He did what he thought was right. He did what he wanted to do. And let me tell you, he was the leader. He was the first to do it. Nobody had the impact he had. By the time the United States Supreme Court agreed with him in 1971, there was no way he could get back the three and a half years of boxing he lost. He never even sued anybody to get back the money he lost.

The day in 1966 when I heard he was classified 1-A in the draft, he was in Miami in his house. I called him up and told him, "Whatever you do, don't say that you won't go in the Army if you're called for induction. Just say you'll cross that bridge when you get to it." To make sure it sunk in, I drove over to his house. But by the time I got there, some newspaper guys and Bob Halloran were talking to him. The same Bob Halloran who later was in charge of boxing at Caesars Palace and the Mirage in Las Vegas, but then he was a local TV sports announcer in Miami. Bob was badgering him about why should he have to go to Vietnam when other guys didn't. That's when Muhammad said, "I got no quarrel with them Vietcong."

He kept fighting for more than a year, but when he refused to take the step forward for induction in 1967, he was stripped of the heavyweight title. During his exile, if he was in Miami to give a talk at some college, he'd call me up and say, "I want to come work at the gym. Do I have to pay dues?" I'd say, "Muhammad, this is your gym."

At the Fifth Street Gym, dues were twenty dollars a month. But not for him. This was his gym. He had his own little dressing room that was built before he won the title. When he wasn't around, nobody else used it. But when he'd come over to work out during his exile, if Jimmy Ellis was training, I'd have Muhammad spar with him. That way I'd be able to pay Muhammad just like I'd pay any other sparring partner, a hundred dollars a day. It was my pleasure. One time he was in Miami with his wife, Belinda, and they were staying someplace that wasn't too nice. I made them go to the DuPont Plaza and I picked up the tab. It was my pleasure.

I didn't know if Muhammad would ever box again. Then the politicians in Atlanta licensed him to fight Jerry Quarry there in late October of 1970, what turned out to be the first fashion-show fight. People drove up in jazzy cars, the guys wearing big wide-brimmed hats and fur coats over purple suits, yellow suits, baby-blue suits, the women wearing party dresses cut down to here.

But to me, the most important thing was that Muhammad stopped Quarry on cuts. Third round. Hit him with a chopping right hand. If you were susceptible to cuts, Muhammad cut you. My guy was back, but he needed a tough fight and got it. He knocked out Oscar Bonavena in the fifteenth round at the Garden when he sucked it up and got him out of there. Then he signed for Joe Frazier, who was now the heavyweight champion, at the Garden on March 8, 1971. Each got a flat fee of two and a half million, the most anybody ever got for one fight. But when Jerry Perenchio, one of the promoters, started talking at the press conference at Toots Shor's about a gross of twenty million, Muhammad stood up, turned to Frazier, and yelled, "They got us cheap." They did. This was really something special. Each fighter not only could claim the title, but each was undefeated. My guy was 31–0 with twenty-five knockouts. Frazier was 26–0 with twenty-three knockouts.

We were staying near the Garden, at the old New Yorker Hotel only a block away. But after the weigh-in, so many people were outside the Garden waiting to see Muhammad, we were told it'd be safer to stay in the building. We ate in the Penn Plaza Club there, but instead of taking a walk on the street, Muhammad had to walk around counting seats. Drew went to the hotel and got all the gear and brought it back to the dressing room. We were trapped. We just fussed around until it was time for Muhammad to get ready. Not that it bothered him. Like I say, nothing ever bothered this guy.

The plan was to box, box, move. In, out, lateral. Don't lay on the ropes. Pop, pop, lock him up. I honestly think Muhammad had an edge in that fight. I think it's what he didn't do that cost him. Frazier couldn't do nothing early, but then my guy started playing around, patting him on the head, hamming it up by look- ing out at the people at ringside. I told him to stop messing around. But while my guy was playing, Frazier came on strong. In the fifteenth, my guy was looking to throw a right uppercut, his chin was unprotected. He took the best punch of any heavyweight I ever saw, a tremendous left hook. He went down on his back. When he got up as fast as anybody could get up, I never was prouder of him. Taking a shot like that in the fifteenth round and getting up after he'd been down in even worse shape in the eleventh round. I don't know how he survived that eleventh round. He was flopping all over the ring. Some people thought it was an act, that he was playing possum. No, no. When I look at that tape now, I get scared. I don't know how he survived that round. Re- markable.

By the time Frazier's unanimous decision was announced, the right side of my guy's jaw was out to here. Ferdie Pacheco and I took him to a hospital for an X-ray, but the jaw wasn't broke. We went right back to the hotel. To this day, my guy's big thing about that fight is that he didn't have to stay in a hospital, but Frazier did. About a week later Joe checked into a Philadelphia hospital for a few days. Exhaustion.

Muhammad's next fight was with Jimmy Ellis, which meant he wasn't my guy. Except for his very first fight, that was the only time I didn't work his corner his whole career. I explained to Muhammad and to Herbert, "Look, I manage Jimmy Ellis, I got to work with him." Jimmy grew up in Louisville with Muhammad and had once been his sparring partner. But during Muhammad's exile, I managed Jimmy when he won the World Boxing Associ- ation tournament to determine their new heavyweight champion. I knew if I worked with Muhammad against Jimmy, people would say Muhammad was just fighting his old sparring partner. But me working with Jimmy gave the fight some essence. Some people even gave Jimmy a shot. Muhammad stopped him in twelve. Then in his usual wonderful way he said, "Well, Angelo didn't talk too much. I'm going to take him back." He kept busy and he kept winning. Then in March of 1973 he went to San Diego for Ken Norton.

Even though Muhammad didn't start training until late, I figured we'd be there long enough for him to get in shape. But when we got there, the promoter, Lou Lake, took him all over town making appearances. He never did get serious. He never did get into shape. But the mark of the man, he fought twelve rounds with his intelligence and his guts after he got his jaw busted.

When he came back to the corner after the first round, I noticed the dark blood in his mouth. I told him, "I think your jaw's busted. I think I'm going to have to stop this fight." He said, "Don't you stop it. I'll beat this bum. Don't you stop it." I'm not degrading Ken Norton, because he gave Muhammad three tough fights. He had the style to give Muhammad a hard time. He had what I call the stutter-step. He was a big strong guy who offset my guy's smoothness. He knocked him off-kilter. But going twelve rounds with that busted jaw, Muhammad had so much courage. Who knows how it got busted? Sometimes a compacted wisdom tooth will make the jawbone smaller. It's not the force of the blow, it's not enough bone in the jawbone. But when we got to the hospital, he's consoling me. I felt so bad, I was practically crying. But he's saying, "Don't worry, we'll be back."

The rematch in the Forum was up for grabs. Before the last round, I told him, "Close the show." When you close the show, that's the judges' last look, the last emotion. If a fight comes down to the last round, you got to win that round. He won that round. And he got the decision.

Muhammad's career turned right there. If he hadn't won that rematch with Norton, the big promoters might have forgotten about him. But by winning, he set up the second fight with Joe Frazier at the Garden when he did what he was supposed to do in the first fight. Pop, pop, lock him up. Offset his aggression by keeping him off-balance so he wasn't solid on his feet, so he couldn't put the pressure on. In the other corner Eddie Futch kept complaining to the referee, Tony Perez, that Muhammad was holding Frazier behind the head, but Muhammad did it with such class. Any other guy is going to get reprimanded, but Muhammad did it with such class. I also got on his case about how he played around in the first fight. He didn't play around the second fight. When he got the twelve-round split decision, he also got what he was hoping for, a title shot with George Foreman in Zaire for five million each.

When we got there, they put us in a big villa that looked out over the Congo River in a military compound called N'Sele, where the Zaire government housed its diplomatic guests. We were about an hour by car out of Kinshasa, where the fight would be held in a 120,000-seat soccer stadium. We trained in a big auditorium in the compound. Everything was nice except the monkey meat in the dining room. To the Zairois it was a great delicacy, but I never could bring myself to eat it.

Nine days before the September 25 date, Foreman got cut over the right eye while sparring. That put the fight off five weeks until October 30, but I think the delay helped Muhammad get in better shape. We never stopped training. The day we found out the fight was postponed, we went to the gym. That's when I ran into my paisans. During the workout that day, I saw a couple of Italian faces in the crowd. I said, "Hey, paisan." They said, "Hey, paisan." I said, "What are you guys doing here?" They told me they had been hired by the Zaire government to teach the natives how to operate steel mills. They had what they called a "little Italian village" not far from the compound. From then on, Bobby Goodman, who was our publicity man, and I would go over there for spaghetti every so often. Anything to get away from that monkey meat.

The delay didn't help Foreman. He got aggravated. He wanted to go back to the States, but we heard Joseph Mobutu, the Zaire President, wouldn't let him. He moved from his house out near N'Sele into the Intercontinental Hotel in Kinshasa, but that meant he had to come out to N'Sele every day to work out and then go back to town. All this time, Muhammad was getting in better shape. And all this time I kept reminding him, "Don't bend down. This guy is devastating to anybody who bends down." Foreman had a 40–0 record, with thirty-seven knockouts, twenty-four in a row. I wanted my guy to stand tall, use his speed, keep Foreman turning. If you did that, Foreman had to stop and get set and come at you again from a different direction.

Because of the time difference, the fight was scheduled to start about four o'clock in the morning there. That way it would be on closed-circuit television in New York at about ten o'clock the previous evening. The afternoon of the fight, Bobby Goodman and I drove down to the stadium to check the ring. Good thing. The ring was on dirt. It was slanted. And the ropes were too loose. Bobby and I literally set that ring. We got workmen to put wood chocks under one end to level it. Then we started to tighten the ropes. We're breaking our balls when Hank Schwartz, who was in charge of getting the television picture all over the world, walked by. He looked up and said, "How you doing?" and kept walking. I said, "Don't you see what we're doing?" All he cared about was television. But if Bobby and I hadn't gone to check the ring, there would've been no fight to put on television.

As much as we tightened the ropes in the afternoon, we couldn't get 'em tight enough. What made it worse was that it was a high ring. I was scared to death if Muhammad leaned back on the ropes, he would fall out of the ring. So when the bell rang, I kept telling him to stay off the ropes. Whenever he laid on the ropes, I screamed, "Get out of there." But he kept laying on the ropes, covering up and taking punches. He was hoping Foreman would punch himself out.

By the seventh round, Foreman was arm-weary. In the next round, he had nothing left. Muhammad hit him a right hand and it was all over. My guy was the heavyweight champion of the world again. He had won the title with what he called the "rope-a-dope," leaning on the ropes that had me scared to death. The funny thing is, he didn't come up with the term "rope-a-dope" until about six months later, but it caught on quick. When he survived the Thrilla in Manila, he was more popular than ever. But his hands were worse than ever. He'd always had trouble with his hands. I used all kinds of gimmicks to wrap his hands. Sponges. Sometimes I even used Kotex because of its softness.

Muhammad's next fight, with Jean Pierre Coopman in San Juan, his hands were so sore I had to put sponges in both hands. That was an easy fight. Muhammad actually slapped that guy into submission. His hands were so sore he couldn't hit him hard.

But then Muhammad started to have more long tough fights. Fifteen rounds with Jimmy Young, a steady technician, great chin. Jimmy Young retired Foreman the first time a year later, he did the most with the least. Then Muhammad went fifteen rounds with Ken Norton in Yankee Stadium, another fight that went down to the last round. Fifteen rounds with Earnie Shavers, a great

banger. I kept telling him, "Watch him on the break." Shavers hit
him on a break, wobbled him, but he came back with the dipsy-
doodle. Three tough fifteen-round fights. Some people didn't think
Muhammad won 'em all, especially the Norton fight. But the judges
thought he won. Ain't it great to have that allure. It comes
in handy.

When he fought Leon Spinks, that allure wasn't there. He
couldn't get up mentally for a kid with only seven pro fights. Spinks
worried me because he brought back memories of Doug Jones,
the same size guy. Leon had speed, quick hands, but my guy was
thinking, how is a kid with only seven pro fights going to beat
me? But the kid kept coming, coming, coming. Even in the corner, I couldn't tell my guy anything. He kept saying, "I know what
I'm doing." What he was doing was losing a split decision, losing
the title.

For the rematch, I knew Muhammad would be up mentally. I
let the loss of the title take its own effect. He knew Spinks could
fight, he knew the kid was for real. All he had to do was get in
shape, and he did. He was the champ again, for the third time.
The next summer he announced his retirement.

When he came back to fight Larry Holmes the next year, I honestly felt he had a chance. Holmes had been his sparring partner,
he knew Holmes like a book. He got himself into the best shape I
ever saw. He was beautiful. But see, I didn't know he was taking
thyroid pills. I thought he was taking vitamins. Thyroid pills help
you lose weight, but it takes your strength away. The night of the
fight, he had no strength. I finally told him, "If you don't start
throwing punches in this round, I'm going to stop this fight." When
he came back to the corner after the tenth round, I stopped it.
Drew Brown was crying when he grabbed my arm not to call the
referee. But I stopped it. The only time in Muhammad's 56–5
record that he didn't finish what he started.

I thought that was the end of it, but it wasn't. When he took
the fight with Trevor Berbick in the Bahamas more than a year
later, I thought about not going, but I decided that if anything
happened and I wasn't there to help him, I'd never forgive myself. That fight never should have happened. The whole thing
was a joke. They didn't have a boxing bell. They used a cowbell.
They didn't even have any gloves until I asked where the gloves
were. I had some gloves flown over from my Miami office. But

even worse, my guy was fat as a hog. He went ten rounds, but he was so bad, he finally realized he shouldn't fight anymore.

It was a great run. More than twenty years with the greatest fighter of all time. Every little thing with Muhammad was a happening. We went all over the world together. We had so much fun together. He liked to say, "Angelo don't train me. Nobody trains me." To me that was an accolade, because it didn't look like I was training him. But I trained that kid. I was proud of the years I put in with him, especially the early years. I set the foundation for the making of a great fighter. I didn't want no pats on the back, but I was proud of it, I was happy with it. When he was young, a lot of other trainers would come to camp. Cus D'Amato came to camp. Harry Wiley, who trained Sugar Ray Robinson, came to camp. People would say, "Oh-oh, Angelo must be out." But my guy liked boxing people. He was beholden to Cus because Cus once gave him the money to drive home to Louisville when he was a kid. Wiley was connected to Sugar Ray, who was my guy's hero as a kid. But other trainers being around was never no worry on my part. My feeling's always been, if you want me, fine; if you don't want me, fine. With a boxer and a trainer, you got to want each other. It's got to be a compatible situation where you're going to be together and get the best out of each other.

Muhammad made me a better man. It wasn't a one-sided street. I got to be a better man on account of him. I got to be a sharper guy. Nobody ever had the illumination of such a great guy that I had with this guy.

God only knows why we meshed like we did. I think I've just been blessed with the ability to mesh with fighters, with people. Not trying to get sentimental, but growing up in south Philly I think my mother and father, Philomena and Angelo, had a lot to do with it. Mom and Pop had such great input. Pop, go to school. Mom, sweet, nice, soft. I was always nice to people to the best of my ability. I would always have a hello to any neighbor going down the street. Mom wouldn't send me to the store because she knew I'd take too long saying hello to everybody. She'd send Jimmy to the store. Jimmy would run to the store and come right back. I'd stop and talk to everybody.

I always loved my mother and father. But after my wife, Helen, and I took a trip to Italy in 1986, I have even greater respect for my father. For how he got out of Italy from Roggiano Gravina, a little town up in the mountains above Cosenza in the toe of the boot. Helen and I went there. Cobblestone streets. Mercury lights. No television sets.

Pop was a shepherd. He didn't have any money. He didn't have a car. But somehow he got to a port town and got on a boat. He took my mother, he took my grandmother, he took my oldest brother, Joe, who was a baby. How'd he get out of there? He couldn't read, he couldn't write, not even in Italian. When I was little, I had to show him how to write his name. I can imitate Pop's signature to this day because I showed him how to sign his check. He worked on Hog Island, he was a railroad trackman. Pop and Mom had nine kids. Two died at a young age. They raised five boys and two girls in south Philly, which was like a little town. I never had a car. I never had a bike. I had a scooter, a box of wood with two skates under it.

I walked to every school I ever went to. I walked to one grade school two blocks away, another grade school three blocks away. I walked to Southern High and I graduated. Commercial course. I never thought about going to college. Where would the money come from?

Pop came over as Mirenda, then the *d* disappeared someplace. I was Angelo Mirena, Jr. My brother Frank was Mireno. The reason was, when Pop signed his name, sometimes he'd forget to put the little thing to make the *a* so it looked like an *o*. When my brother Joe became a fighter, Italian names weren't popular. He took Dundee, then my brother Chris went by Dundee, and I did too. I never boxed much. Mostly with my brother Jimmy when we were little because Chris sent gloves. Chris had a stable of fighters in Norfolk, Virginia, then he went up to New York, and in 1948 I went up there to work with him. I hung around his office, room 711 in the old Capitol Hotel across Eighth Avenue from the old Garden. In the afternoon I hung around Stillman's Gym watching the famous trainers work with their fighters. And every night but Sunday night I'd go to a fight club. Go with whoever had fighters on the card. St. Nick's, Ridgewood Grove, Sunnyside Gardens, Broadway Arena, Fort Hamilton, Jamaica Arena, Croke Park, Meadowbrook Bowl over in Jersey.

My first night, in Fort Hamilton out where the Verrazano Bridge is now, I was standing around the dressing room when Chickie Ferrara threw me two rolls of gauze and one roll of tape and said,

"Wrap this kid's hands." I said, "I never wrapped hands." So he showed me.

I had the luxury of being around the greatest trainers in the business. Charlie Goldman, Ray Arcel, Whitey Bimstein, Chickie Ferrara, Teddy Bentham, Dick Vick, Al Silvani, little Freddie Fierro from Jersey. I would sit and listen to what they talked about. Like how they had to keep Tony Janiro locked up to keep the broads away. I would get these gems of knowledge. That was my college. The breed then was a different breed. The guys then knew how to do everything. If you looked at Charlie Goldman working on a fighter, he looked like a miniature doctor. He was a little guy who had a little kit of stuff, little bottles. Charlie broke his hand one time. He fixed it with a tube from a tire. Cut it out, put strings on it. Trainers were remarkable.

Ray Arcel was the greatest guy for sending a fighter out of a corner. If his fighter came back all disheveled after a tough round, Ray would have him coming out bright-eyed and bushy-tailed for the next round. Ray always had a little towel in his back pocket. He'd clean him off, wipe his gloves, grease him nice and smooth, push his hair back. Now when the bell rings, his opponent looks over at him and thinks, I thought I was beating this guy.

Ray was great at psychological tricks. I've utilized one of his tricks many times. If the other guy got knocked out and the referee wasn't sure about whether to stop it when he's counting over the guy . . . seven . . . eight . . . Ray would be up on the steps holding his guy's robe out, making believe he's putting it on his guy's shoulders. In those days there was no neutral corner. You use whatever you can to make your fighter win, outside of illegal.

By the time I went down to Miami where Chris was, I'd been around enough that I knew how to handle fighters. How to work a corner. Right after I got there, Carmen Basilio came down for a fight. His managers, Johnny DeJohn and Joe Nitro, were with him, but his trainer was sick or something. They asked me to work the corner. It was supposed to be an easy fight for Carmen with a guy from Cuba named Baby Williams, but it turned out to be a murderous ten-round fight. I wrapped Carmen's hands. I greased him up. I did everything. Back in the dressing room after Carmen won, Joe and Johnny told me they wanted me to work with Carmen from then on. Carmen wanted me too. He told me, "You're the first guy to wrap my hands right." He liked the gauze and tape just barely laid on his hands.

Carmen was always having trouble with his hands. In the dressing room before one of his fights with Johnny Saxton for the welterweight title, a doctor put novocaine in both of Carmen's hands with those old needles with the vials on 'em. They're sophisticated now. They got little thin needles. But then doctors used a big needle with a big vial on it. Screw one vial off. Screw another vial on.

What a tough guy Carmen was. What a tough man. When he fought Robinson the second time, when his left eye was completely closed, I couldn't even put an ice bag on it. The tissues were completely torn. I got heat later that I should've cut it. But it was cut on the upper lid that goes over the lower lid. What an ugly eye. I never seen an eye that ugly in my whole life. He'd had some surgery where they closed off an artery so the blood had no place to go. I told him, "You can't see Robinson's right hands. I'm going to stop this fight." He said, "You stop it, I'll knock you out."

The way it turned out, working with Carmen attracted Muhammad Ali to me. Mike Malitz, who sets up the television for Bob Arum, Mike's father, Lester, was an advertising guy in New York who worked with the Brown and Foreman Distillers, whose boss was part of the Louisville Sponsoring Group. When the Archie Moore thing broke up, they asked Lester Malitz if he knew a good boxing man, and Lester told them about me.

By then I'd been around. I'd learned how to talk to fighters, how to watch fighters. I've had fighters who had to be locked in at night to keep them from chasing broads. Or had to have a sentry outside their room. And sometimes even that didn't help. One night I left my pal Lou Gross in charge of a fighter. Lou wandered away to have a drink and smoke a cigar, and when he got back, he looked in the room and found the fighter on top of a chick. Lou yelled, "Don't come. Don't come."

I always tried to baptize my guys early. It ain't the sexual act. It's the chase. That's what wears you out. It's also the perception. If a fighter is seen in a bar, he's a drunk. If he's seen walking down the street with a broad, he's a womanizer.

One day some guy called me and said, "Hey, Angelo, I saw Willie Pastrano coming out of the Eden Roc last night with a knockout blonde on his arm." I said, "Hey, dummy, that's his wife,

Faye." But years ago I was so dumb I didn't know one of my fighters was popping pills. The guys who hung around him used to call me Square Bear, meaning I didn't know nothing. They'd be hanging around the dressing room snapping their fingers saying "Square Bear." I'd say, "I'll Square Bear you, get the hell out of here." I'd chase 'em out of the room. After a while I caught on to what was going on with the pills. That stuff was new then. Then later on I had to learn how to recognize when a fighter had a drug problem.

I could never understand why a boxer needed drugs to get a high. If you're a boxer, there's no high except winning a fight. That's the high. That's when you get your rocks off.

But the more I learned about boxing, the more I got around. Working with Carmen Basilio helped me get Muhammad, then working with Muhammad helped me get Ray Leonard.

When I first got Ray, right after he won the 1976 Olympics, he was a slapper instead of a puncher. He had quick hands and quick feet, so he got away with it. By the time he fought Wilfredo Benitez for the WBC welterweight title in late 1979, I'd progressively developed him into a professional puncher. Benitez was a great fighter. That was a tough fight until Ray nailed him in close with a left hook. Dropped him. Stopped him in the fifteenth. But when he fought Roberto Duran the first time in 1980, he got outpsyched. Duran abused Ray, and Ray couldn't handle it. Duran would see Ray walking with his wife in the street in Montreal and he'd yell, "I keel your husband. I keel your husband." The night of the fight, Ray wanted to keel him. Ray wanted to fight the guy, not box him. Ray lost.

The second time, in New Orleans, was completely different. I told Ray to ignore him and to box him. This was a Liston situation all over again. Duran got disrobed. Ray took away his machismo, took away his title, took away everything. Duran knew he was going to get knocked out, so he took what he thought was the noble way out. No más. I really think in his mind he thought that was the noble way out.

The next year, when Ray was having trouble with Tommy Hearns in Vegas, I helped him a little. In the corner I was slapping his thighs and giving him hell. I told him. "You're blowing it, son. You've got to pick up your tempo. Don't fight at his tempo. If you don't pick up your tempo, you're going to blow it." He picked up

his tempo and stopped Hearns in the fourteenth for the undisputed welterweight title. The next year he was in Buffalo getting
ready to defend the title against Roger Stafford when he kept
seeing flashes of light in front of his left eye, sometimes a black
or white dot. When he had it checked, he learned he had a detached retina. Maybe it happened in the ring, maybe not. I know
people who got a detached retina just walking around. But when
Ray had to stop boxing, we all got an education on eyeballs. Boxing people got so cognizant of eyeballs, at one commission meeting they had a big plastic eyeball up there for us to see what a
detached retina looks like.

When Ray decided to come back against Kevin Howard in 1984,
it was supposed to be a warm-up fight. He got knocked down, he
got caught off-balance. Getting knocked down was no disgrace.
That can happen to anybody. But the spring wasn't there. When
he decided to retire again, good.

After only that one fight in five years, Ray came back again in
1987 against the guy he'd always wanted to fight, Marvin Hagler,
for the WBC middleweight title. Most people didn't give Ray a
chance, but I had a good feeling about that fight. I must've spent
over a hundred hours studying tapes of Hagler's fights. Looking
for certain things. Guys innately do certain things. Studying those
tapes, I caught Hagler's two-step. He had a two-step sort of rhythm.
One-two. One-two. Once you got rid of the two-step, he was out
of kilter. Another thing, he wasn't the usual type of southpaw. He
turned southpaw. He was really right-handed. He signed autographs right-handed. His strength was in his right hand, not his
left hand. In the clinches, when you move away from a southpaw,
you usually move to your left, away from his left hand, but I wanted
Ray moving right. I didn't respect Hagler's left hand. That was
the little key. But little keys win big fights.

I thought Ray was going to stop Hagler, that's how confident I
was. I thought Hagler was going to run into punches. And he did.
When he gave Ray the first four rounds, I couldn't believe it. I
guess Hagler thought he'd catch Ray sooner or later and knock
him out. But you don't take nobody cheap. You never give nothing away. You don't give a guy the right time.

I had an excellent fighter-trainer relationship with Ray, or so I
thought, but I was very unhappy with the way I was treated financially in the Hagler fight. I had no contract. I made Mike Trainer,
who did Ray's business, aware of it. Letters back and forth. My

lawyer, his lawyer. I even wrote Ray a personal letter that got ignored. Never got an answer. I was hurt, naturally, but I didn't want to make a big thing out of it. So when Ray decided to come back again against Donny Lalonde in 1988, they called me up to go to the press conference in New York. My lawyer called Trainer and left word that Angelo Dundee is not going anywhere until he has a contract and knows what he's getting paid. I never heard from them. Trainer's lawyer would not respond to my lawyer's letters.

I couldn't understand this. I never had a money problem with Muhammad, never. When Herbert Muhammad became the manager after the transition from the Louisville group, Herbert told me, "You'll be with this guy as long as he fights." Muhammad built my first house. Muhammad built my second house. Muhammad built my third house.

I've had fighters make sure I got my money when it came time to get paid. The night Pinklon Thomas lost to Evander Holyfield, when it was over, Pinklon made sure when the purse was divided that I got paid. He said, "I don't care if I get a dime, Angelo's got to get paid." But it didn't work that way with Trainer and Ray.

Trainer's a lawyer himself, but I don't think he likes lawyers. He never had much rapport with any of the lawyers I ever had trying to talk to him. Trainer nailed me through the heart. That was it. But they can't take how I helped Ray beat Hearns in 1981 away from me. And they can't take how I helped Ray beat Hagler away from me.

The way Ray beat Hagler, I'd say that was my best tactical triumph as a trainer. But one of the best accolades I ever got was from a trainer named Bill Gore, who was so tall and skinny he just leaned over the ropes when he worked on his fighter between rounds. I loved to watch Bill Gore work. So now I resurrect Johnny Holman. I get Johnny to the point where people were starting to believe in him. But the night he fought Ezzard Charles in Miami Beach in 1955, he was taking some awful shots in the belly. It looked like Johnny was going to take a walk. But I'd heard him talking about how he wanted to buy a new house with shutters, with a television. So when he took those shots, I got to use my dynamite. I yelled, "This man's taking your house away from you. He's taking those shutters away from you. He's taking that television away from you."

Johnny came back to win a ten-round decision, but I yelled so loud Bill Gore must've heard me in the other corner. Because as we were walking out of the ring, Bill looked right at me and said, "You win it."

That's nice. But the fighter wins the fight. I never won the fight. I'm just there, and whatever little bit I do, I'm happy to do it. I don't ever feel that I won the fight. Let the people say that if they want to, but Angelo won't say it. But the highest accolade I think I ever got was when I heard Eddie Futch on television talking about how he stopped the Thrilla in Manila after the fourteenth round because of Joe Frazier's left eye.

Eddie stopped that fight because Joe couldn't see Muhammad's right hand coming. But then Eddie talked about what bad shape Muhammad had been in after the eleventh round, and Eddie said, "Angelo prevailed upon him to continue." Prevailed upon him. I liked that.

During a workout, George Benton advises Meldrick Taylor, quietly.

George Benton:

"You Can Steal This Fight from Ali"

In the Philadelphia streets George Benton is still remembered as the "uncrowned middleweight champion" of his era. Early in 1955 he was still only twenty-one years old, but he already had a 27–2–1 record with fourteen knockouts. One day as he strolled into Johnny Madison's Gym for his workout his friend Charlie Scott said, "Hey, George, guess who you got turned down by today?"

"Who?"

"You won't believe this, George."

"Who?"

"Sugar Ray Robinson."

"You're crazy."

"Honest to God, George Gainford called Herman Taylor for an opponent," Scott said, referring to Robinson's manager and the Philadelphia promoter of that time. "Herman said, 'Yeah, I got a guy, George Benton.' But when Gainford heard that, he said, 'We don't want him.' "

At the time Robinson had just begun his comeback after more than two years as a nightclub tap dancer.

"You know who Robinson wound up fighting," Benton remembered with a laugh. "Tiger Jones, who he lost to."

George Benton still lives in north Philadelphia, the divorced father of four grown sons, the grandfather of six children. Before a bullet still lodged in his back ended his career, he had a 61–13–1 record that included thirty-six knockouts. Maybe the best middleweight who never fought for the title.

"I was never the house fighter. I was always going against the house instead of with it," he said. "The promoters never had me, so my managers couldn't move me. Herman Diamond couldn't move me. Then he sold a piece of me to Vic Marsillo, who was a mob guy but good people. He couldn't move me either."

But as the trainer known as the Professor, he has helped his fighters move quickly. He has worked with nine champions: Evander Holyfield, Leon Spinks, Pinklon Thomas, Mike McCallum, Pernell Whitaker, Meldrick Taylor, Rocky Lothridge, Johnny Bumphus, and Leo Randolph.

"No matter who your fighter is, he has to fight the other guy the way the other guy fights," he explained. "Styles. Whatever the other guy does, you got to know. Is he going to run from you? Or is he going to come at you? You have to adapt to everything."

From the time he turned pro at sixteen, George Benton was the essence of a Philadelphia fighter, tough and durable. Born on May 15, 1933, the son of a plasterer in a family of eleven kids, he grew up watching Henry Armstrong, Sugar Ray Robinson, and Bob Montgomery, a Philadelphia fighter who won the lightweight title.

" 'Philadelphia fighter' is an expression people use that means you were there to fight," he said. "I was slick but I wasn't slick in a way where you'd call me a fancy Dan or where I couldn't get hit. I was always right there in front of you. If you could hit me, I was there. But not many guys hit me."

He learned how to avoid getting hit from a boxer named Jimmy Collins, whose real name was Marcellus Smith.

"He couldn't break a damn egg, but you couldn't hit him with a handful of rice. He could stand right in front of you and when you punched, he'd disappear. Could he box! I knew I was getting better when one day he told my trainer, Joe Rose, that he didn't want to box with me no more. Joe asked him why not and he said I was getting too big. But it wasn't that I was getting too big. It was that I was on his ass, you know what I mean. And I was only sixteen."

Twenty years later, his career ended suddenly. Walking down a north Philadelphia street he heard a man he knew as "Chinaman" call to him from a doorway.

"He said he wanted to see me, so I walked over to the doorway. He said one of my brothers had done something to him, so he was going to get back at the family. He pulled a thirty-eight and shot me. Just like that. The bullet chipped a piece of my spine. I'm lucky I'm not paralyzed."

Boxing is lucky too.

=====

About a week before Leon Spinks fought Muhammad Ali for the heavyweight title, I told Sam Solomon, "Ali's not a great puncher, he's not a one-punch guy, he's got a tendency to slap. If Leon stays on Ali's ass, Leon can win this fight." You know what Sam told me? He said, "Lay back, George, let me train the fighter." All of a sudden it dawned on me. These sonsabitches don't think this kid can win this fight. Sam and some other people around Leon had been saying, "Well, it's a payday." They didn't think this kid could win the fight but they're going to get a big payday.

Listen, it was a payday for me too. One hundred thousand dollars. But I knew Ali was ready to be taken. He'd just had a hard fifteen-round fight with Earnie Shavers. Before that he went fifteen rounds with Alfredo Evangelista. I knew Leon had a chance.

Three months before, I'd trained Leon for a ten-round decision in Vegas over the Italian boy, Alfio Righetti. So when Leon started getting ready for the Ali fight, Butch Lewis called me. Mitt Barnes was Leon's manager then, a real gentleman, a Teamsters official in St. Louis, where Leon grew up. But they were trying to get rid of Mitt, so Butch called me and said, "George, I've got Leon now and I would like you to help us get him ready." I said, "I'll do it, but I want you to straighten Sam Solomon out. I don't want Sam to think I'm coming in trying to take over his job."

Sam must've been right there, because Butch said, "Here, you talk to Sam." I said, "Sam, you heard what Butch told me, but I don't want to come in and disrupt your camp if you don't want me there. So if you don't want me, tell me now." Sam said, "No, no, I need all the help I can get." His exact words. I said, "Sam, don't say one thing and mean another," and Sam said, "No, I'm happy to have you."

The way I heard it, Leon didn't do nothing until I came to the gym. The kid only had seven pro fights but here he was fighting for the heavyweight title. I don't know what Sam told him, but I know what I told him. I said, "Leon, listen now, Ali's not a guy who's going to try to hurt you. All he wants to do is skip around the ring. But you can steal this fight from him. Jump on him. He ain't got that big shot to hurt you with. So jump on him. If he wants to fight, fight the hell out of him. If he wants to box, don't let him box. Stay right on him. Keep fighting him. Don't give him no air. But the main thing is, don't try to hit him hard. Just hit him. Ali's got a good chin, you're not going to knock him out. Just keep moving your hands."

In his workouts, I got Leon to throw his left jab at his sparring partner's left shoulder. Jab, jab, jab. Hit him on the left shoulder, the deltoid muscle, so that by the late rounds Ali wouldn't have the strength to throw his own jab. Leon was in such good physical condition that he didn't tire in the late rounds the way Ali thought he would.

That's what happened. Leon stayed on top of him. All those wild punches were landing. His left jab was pounding Ali's left shoulder. By using his jab Leon didn't have to throw hooks and he saved his strength. We knew Leon couldn't hit Ali with round-house punches. Ali's always falling back, out of reach. But Leon just stayed on top of him and Ali could never get set. When the fight ended, I thought Leon won, but when they announced the judges' cards, the first one they announced had Ali ahead. I thought, oh my God, they're going to give it to Ali and there's going to be a riot. How am I going to get out of here? But the next two judges gave it to Leon for a split decision.

The winner and new heavyweight champion, Leon Spinks. But as soon as he won that title, I couldn't get next to him. Everybody was pushing me out of the damn way. Leon was Sam Solomon's champ now. You know what I did in the dressing room? I put my clothes on and walked out.

The next morning at Leon's press conference, I got there early. I'd been talking to the writers for about five minutes when Sam walked in. Sam stared at me and told the writers, "There will be no statements until Leon arrives." Next thing I knew, they put the press conference in another room in the Hilton, but I didn't go. That night when I saw Leon in the lobby I told him I wouldn't be with him anymore. I said, "I wish you luck. Stay in school." I meant boxing school. He had to keep learning. He couldn't think he knew everything just because he won the title. It's always tougher to keep the title than to win it.

That was February 1978, and even before Leon started getting ready for the rematch with Ali in September in New Orleans, everybody was climbing all over the kid. By then he was just the WBA champion. He had been stripped of the WBC title because he gave Ali a rematch instead of fighting Ken Norton. I saw the handwriting on the wall. I knew Sam didn't want me around now.

But after Leon got to New Orleans, he himself called me and said, "Man, we want you down here." I figured what the hell, if the kid wants me, I'll try to help him. The day I got to the New Orleans Hilton where everybody was staying, I stopped by the office. I started to go in when this big husky guy in a black suit with a crazy haircut and a lot of gold jewelry stood up and said, "What do you want?" I said, "I train the fighter." He said, "You train what fighter?" I said, "Leon Spinks, man, I train Leon Spinks." He said, "What?" I said, "Look, man, you tell 'em George Benton is here." He said, "Wait here." He went inside and got somebody who came out and said, "C'mon in, George."

In the office, I said, "Who is that guy?" Somebody said, "That's Leon's bodyguard. He calls himself Mr. T." The same Mr. T who's on television now. But he wasn't nothing then. He was just Leon's bodyguard.

I got things squared away with Sam Solomon again. Sam told me he wanted me around, but in the first workout I watched, Leon had forgotten everything he did in the first fight. He'd lost his jab. He wasn't bobbing and weaving. I had only nine days to help him. I gave Leon the same plan he had for the first fight. Jump on Ali, keep landing punches. But he never was in the same shape. One morning we were waiting in the hotel lobby at six o'clock for him to go run. But instead of getting off the elevator from his room upstairs, he walked into the lobby holding a damn umbrella. I looked at him and thought, this guy's been out all night. He didn't train that day. He never really got ready. And the night of the fight, I never saw so much confusion.

When we got to Leon's dressing room in the Superdome, there's at least thirty people jammed in there. Relatives, friends, guys Leon had been in the Marines with. All those people, but nobody had thought to bring Leon's protective cup, his water bottle, and his water bucket. We had to borrow a cup, a water bottle, and a bucket from Mike Rossman after he won the WBA light heavyweight title on the undercard.

The worst thing was the confusion in the corner. Before we left the dressing room, Sam Solomon told me, "We're going to take turns talking to Leon between rounds. Me, you, and his brother Michael. If you want to tell him something and it's not your turn, tell the guy whose turn it is that round." I never heard anything like that before or since. After the fight started, some of his Marine buddies were even yelling to Leon between rounds. By the time it was my turn before the fifth round, Leon had hardly done anything. In the corner I asked him, "What the hell are you doing?" He mumbled something and I said, "You're acting like you're afraid of this guy, but he's afraid of you."

Leon went out and started throwing punches. Ali's eyes popped open this big. Leon won that round. But when I went up to talk to him before the sixth round, nobody let me. That's when I walked. I went back to the dressing room, put my coat on, and went back to the hotel.

Never did see the end of that fight. Never worked with Leon again. Not that I missed him. I've trained plenty of champions, but when Evander Holyfield won the heavyweight title, he was like my first heavyweight champion. With Leon, I couldn't feel it. There today, gone tomorrow. But Holyfield was different. I nurtured this guy. The main thing, we have a good relationship. And this guy deserves it. He does everything I want him to do. Against Buster Douglas, our plan was to resort to a few tricks. Slow that big jab down. Keep hitting him on the left shoulder like Leon did to Ali in their first fight. Douglas was easy to hit with the jab because most tall guys aren't used to being jabbed. I told Holyfield, "Keep sticking and stabbing him. Something might happen." Something did.

I had studied Douglas. I knew he liked to throw a right uppercut, but the uppercut is a stationary punch. You have to be set to throw it. When we trained, I had Holyfield's sparring partners throwing that uppercut. As soon as they dropped their right shoulder, I had Holyfield stepping to the side in a half moon, rocking on his right foot. Then he sprang off that back foot, all 208 pounds of him.

I'm not going to give Douglas a bum rap. When he went down, he was hurt. He was out. Everybody talked about how he was trying to rub his eyes or his nose with his gloves. But if you're asleep and a fly lands on your nose, you're going to scratch it even though you're still asleep. It's like when Douglas had Tyson groping for his mouthpiece in Tokyo. When Douglas went down, his eyes were glassy. He looked like he was smoking reefers. Don't tell me he didn't have heart. He showed me he had heart when he got up in Tokyo after Tyson knocked him down.

But this time Douglas got hit with all of Holyfield's 208 pounds behind the punch. I don't know why some people thought Holyfield wasn't big enough. Any man that's in good condition at 165 pounds can knock a house down. I was a middleweight knocking light heavyweights out. If you hit a man with a perfect punch, he's gone. That was a dead-perfect punch that landed on Douglas's cheekbone, right under the eye. If you hit a man on the cheekbone or on the chin, those are the nerve centers. Say goodnight, baby. I know. I've been training fighters my whole career in boxing. When I was an amateur kid in Philadelphia, when my trainer Joe Rose went away with a fighter, he left me in charge of his other fighters because those other fighters knew I knew what I was doing. I was only twelve, thirteen, fourteen, but even pros would listen to me. I kept tabs on 'em. I told 'em things.

My father was a plasterer. With eleven kids, he never wanted my mother to work a job. He'd tell her, "No need for you to go out there and work, I'm making enough money." Growing up in Philadelphia where I did, you had to learn to be streetwise. In order to survive you had to be very cunning, very keen, very sharp-minded.

On the street, you always had to figure out what the other guy was thinking. You always had to stay ahead of the other guy. You always had to know how to get along with other people's programs, because some guy might be able to take you out. You'd say, this guy can fight. If he jumps on my ass, I'll have to fight him, because I can't let all the other guys think I'm a sissy. So if you didn't want him to jump on your ass, you had to learn how to get along with him. But at the same time you had to show him that you will fight him if you had to. It made you learn how to think.

Anytime I saw a kid who didn't look like he really wanted to fight, I never said this guy ain't got no guts or this guy is going to run, because who the hell was born boxing? Who the hell wants to get hit? Where do you find a guy that's reckless like that? Those that are, most of 'em are a little throwed-off somewhere. If he's reckless in the street, most of the time he's cut up, he's got scars all over him. Or he gets killed.

This was what I carried with me when I was boxing. When I went in the ring, I wasn't scared of nobody. Never. Because if I was, I'd have been knocked out. I was never knocked out in my life. Got stopped twice on cuts, that's all. I was never even on the floor. Never hit the floor. And I fought some of the toughest guys around. I always had confidence in me and I always had confidence in my trainer, Joe Rose, who was almost like a psychologist. I fought out of shape a lot of times. I couldn't always get fights, so I had to take jobs, then I started to get carried away. I started to take out girls a little bit, as we all do. I took some short-notice fights. Can you fight tomorrow night? Yeah, where and who?

One time in the Army I took a fight on a few hours' notice. One of my buddies at Fort Jackson, South Carolina, took me to his friend's house off the base. I was talking to the mother and I told her I was a boxer. I was a top pro then. I'd had thirty-four fights and won 'em all except for two losses and a draw, but I just told her I was a boxer.

She told me about a guy in town who owned a record shop and put on fights, then she took me down to meet him. Only a few days later he called me at the base and asked me if I could sub for a guy named Willie James who had pulled out of his show in Charlotte, North Carolina. When I got there, I used the name Willie James. I'm in the dressing room and some guy is tying my cup on me when the door opens and in walks Angelo Dundee, who knew me from Philly. I put my finger to my lips and went "Shhhh." Angelo's eyes bugged out, but he walked by me without looking at me. When the fight started, I tried to look as bad as I could. The other guy could fight. He knew how to throw punches, but I was slipping and sliding. I wanted to go at least three or four rounds before I took him out. Then the guy did something, so I just slipped his jab and went over the top with a right hand. Bam, down he went. He got up, I held him, and he made it back to his corner. In the second round, he was trying to do something but I slipped his jab, threw a little short left hook. Down he went.

On my way out of the ring, a sportswriter from Philadelphia recognized me. He was there to cover Angelo's fighter, Billy Kilgore, and the next day his paper had a big spread, not a bad spread, but a big spread about me being Willie James. They inserted that fight into my record: August 2, 1956, Henry Ray, Charlotte, N.C., KO 2.

All that experience helps me now. I know every end of it. I know what a fighter's thinking. Like one day Lou Duva asked me, "George, what kind of shape is this guy in?" I said, "He trains one day, then he trains two days later. He ain't in no hell of a shape." Lou said, "Do you think he can fight next Monday?" I said, "Let me find out." I asked him, "You got a six-round fight next Monday if you want it. How do you feel?" He said, "Yeah, I'll take it." But you know he ain't gonna win it. Now when I go in the ring with him, I'll say, "Now look, I know the guy you're fighting, he's a boxer but he ain't in the best of shape and he ain't going to be able to go six rounds. You're going to win the fight because you know how to beat the guy. You're in shape enough to go six rounds. Let him lay back a little like you're trying to catch him. And when you punch, just drop dead weight on him." You'd be surprised what dead-weight punches do to a guy. You're not using any energy but you're landing, you're winning rounds but you haven't done a damn thing. The last few rounds, he's so pumped up, he wins easy.

All those little things, I put them on a guy now. Which I didn't even realize when I was fighting because I didn't think about it. Like when I'd fight a guy, I'd ask five or six boxers I knew, "What can this guy do? How does he fight?" Lots of boxers who want to be macho, they think if they ask questions like that, other boxers will think they're scared. I wasn't scared. I just wanted to know what a guy can do. By the time I got finished talking to five or six boxers, I knew how to beat the other guy's style. See, you beat styles. That's how you win fights. Styles.

You ever see Jimmy Carter, who was once the lightweight champion? Guys used to beat Jimmy Carter because he couldn't fight certain styles. He'd beat great fighters, but some bum would get a decision over him because Jimmy couldn't handle that style.

You take a straight-up guy that's got a good left hand. Jab, jab, jab. You figure most guys that got a good left hand throw a good right hand too. Bop, bop with the jab sets it up good. So you take the left hand away from him. Keep banging him on the left arm, like Leon Spinks did to Ali. After five or six rounds, the other guy can't lift his left arm. Styles.

These are things I picked up over the years from my trainer, Joe Rose, from my own experience as a fighter, and from Eddie Futch when I was a young trainer working with him.

The time I got shot by that guy Chinaman and my career ended, I was the luckiest man in the world. The bullet hit my bowel, then it nicked my spine. The waste from my bowel created an infection in my spine. But when you're laid up for almost a year, it gave me time to think about a lot of things. I saw people in the hospital who couldn't walk, and I thought, there but for the grace of God go I. One day something happened that you might not believe, but it happened. I don't know if I was asleep or what but I heard a voice say, "You were a good fighter and a good hustler but I'm going to take all that away from you. I want to see if you can come back." Just then I looked up and saw this white collar, a young priest who used to come in the gym just to train. Not to fight, just to work out.

I said, "Was that you talking to me, Reverend?" He said, "No, I heard you talking but I wasn't talking." When I told him about the voice I heard, he got down on his knees. I'll never forget that voice as long as I live. That voice was challenging me to make something of myself.

When I got out of the hospital, some white guys who were friends of mine gave me a job writing numbers. I was doing pretty good, but a police captain stopped me one day and said, "I understand you're a nice guy, but I don't want you writing any more numbers in my precinct." I think another numbers guy dropped a dime on me. Dropped a dime in a phone and made a call to get me out of his territory. I started working with some fighters, but then Joe Frazier told me he needed somebody to look after some fighters in his gym while Eddie Futch was away with other fighters.

As soon as Eddie came back, Joe told Eddie that he wanted to keep me around, so I had a steady job in boxing. I was back.

Learning from Eddie how to be a trainer. Not so much the training, but the psychology of it.

You know how fighters like to do shit they ain't supposed to do when they're training. Eddie taught me how to discipline fighters like that. Eddie would tell the fighters in his camp, "I'll meet you outside at five-thirty in the morning for roadwork. Be there." Eddie gets up before anybody. Quarter after five, he's out there waiting. Pretty soon all the fighters but one are out there with him. Eddie waits until twenty-five minutes to six for the one guy who isn't there. But that's all he waits, five minutes, then they're gone. But he leaves me there.

Now it's twenty minutes to six and that one guy comes out dragging ass and says, "Where's Eddie?" I tell him, "Eddie's gone, man. He gave you five minutes, then he left." Eddie doesn't go back and ring your room and tell you to get up. And when he comes back from roadwork with the other fighters, he never says a word to the guy who wasn't there on time.

In the gym that afternoon that guy wouldn't dare go to Eddie, but he'd come to me later and say, "Hey, man, when I came outside to run, nobody's there. How am I going to get in shape?" I'd say, "Don't give me that shit. Eddie was out there fifteen minutes before everybody else and he waited five minutes. What do you want?" Then the guy would go to box three rounds and he'd be tired. Eddie would say, "Go another round." The guy would say, "I'm tired." Eddie would say, "Okay, if you're tired, pack your bag and go on in." Eddie would never blow up. But the next morning that guy was out there for roadwork by five-thirty.

In his quiet way, Eddie told you just what he wanted to tell you. He wouldn't let any of his fighters borrow any money. He told me, "If you loan these guys money, they never pay it back." Even knowing that, I loaned a sparring partner forty dollars one time and I forgot all about it. The next time we were in camp I loaned him fifty dollars and after I did, I remembered he hadn't paid me the forty.

Eddie just knows how to do it. He'll tell a fighter what he wants done, and if the fighter doesn't do it, Eddie will quietly say, "After the fifth round, then you will know what I was talking about." No argument. Eddie knows that if a fighter doesn't want to do what he tells him, he's not going to jam it down his throat. It's as simple as that. That's why I don't hang with my fighters when I'm fin-

ished with 'em in the gym. They don't see me until the next day
unless I cook for them. I cook just about anything, but I don't fry
no foods and I very seldom mess with pork. I'm not against pork.
But most of our guys are trying to make weight, and pork doesn't
help you make weight. When a fighter's got to make weight, he
should eat roast chicken, turkey, fish, green vegetables. When my
fighters find out I'm cooking, they break the doors down.

I really think diet has a lot to do with how fighters develop.
Puerto Rican and Mexican fighters, most of them are brawlers
and good punchers. You know why? Beans and rice and tortillas,
that's why. They eat food that's strictly from the earth. Beans,
rice, flour, corn.

It's a funny thing, you eat better when you're poor than you do
when you're rich. The more money you make, the more you start
eating fancy food. When I was a kid, I was eating collard greens.
Now I never eat collard greens. But they're better for you than
fancy food.

I've had some good fighters. Pernell Whitaker, Meldrick Taylor, these kids can fight. I thought Tyrell Biggs would be a good
fighter. He had the tools but not the desire. He did everything
good for four or five rounds. Even when he got up from his
knockdown by Mike Tyson, he was still doing it right. But the
desire wasn't there.

You train everybody different for each opponent. Some trainers just get a fighter in shape and tell him to hook, jab, duck. But
you've got to know what the other fighter can do. That's how you
beat styles. You can't go out there and fight every fight the same,
because the styles aren't the same.

That's what makes Evander Holyfield a good fighter. He's fought
all styles. He's easy for me to train, because first of all, him and
me get along good. He respects me and I respect him. He knows
I know what I'm doing. But he's not a hard guy to train. His
personality, the way he's been brought up, he'll listen. I've got
some kids, after a while, they think they did it all by themselves.
Evander's not like that.

When he turned pro after the 1984 Olympics, Evander couldn't
go three rounds. I don't know what it was. He just couldn't do a
fast three rounds. He'd get tired as hell. He was pitiful. He'd be
boxing and he'd look over at me like a little puppy and I'd say,
"Baby, you got to go the rounds."

Evander had a six-round fight coming up in the Garden, his first pro fight, but I told Lou Duva, "This kid's gas is bad. He's no six-round fighter." So we had to con him into thinking he could go six rounds. After he boxed three rounds and got out of the ring and went to the bag, I'd cut his rounds on the bag by a minute. Some days he thought he was boxing three minutes a round when he was only boxing two minutes. So when he went to boxing four rounds, I'd say, "One more minute." That way he went to rounds of four minutes, at least in his head, and I'd tell him, "You know, you boxed four minutes in that round." We just kept conning him and conning him until we got him up to where he thought he could go six rounds. And he did. Then he just kept getting better and better.

Back before Buster Douglas knocked out Mike Tyson to win the heavyweight title, Evander was scheduled to fight Tyson and the writers started to ask me how Evander would fight him. I knew it would be a tough fight, but I also knew what Evander would have to do.

Tyson is a very, very durable sonofabitch. He's like a tank. I didn't want Evander backing into the ropes. I didn't want Evander tying him up by grabbing and holding. Evander had to tie him up slick. To me, Evander has two things that let him do all right with Tyson. Number one, he'll be in real good shape. Number two, he won't be scared of him. Evander's got icewater in his veins. He's cool and calm. He's not a great big guy but he's strong. Heavyweights don't have to be no great big man. All a heavyweight's got to be is over 200 pounds. Any guy that weighs 210 is big enough.

Joe Louis, his best day, he was 205, and he was knocking out giants. Look at Rocky Marciano, he was under 190 in all his title fights. Floyd Patterson never got to 200, but he had that hand speed. He'd hit you bing, bing, bing, you'd never see his punches coming.

Patterson punched fast like Tyson, but Patterson was more my size. In fact, when Patterson first turned pro, they tried to make me and him in the Eastern Parkway in Brooklyn, but Cus D'Amato wouldn't take it. I was 165 pounds, but Cus wouldn't take no live bodies. When Cus took you as an opponent, you had to be fresh out of the graveyard. Cus wasn't a trainer who taught punches and strategy. Cus taught thoughts. Cus's whole life was boxing. And as I watched Tyson, I realized he was a student of boxing just like I am. Most people think this guy is just a fighter, but he's not just a fighter. He's smart as hell. He's a thinker.

If you hit Marciano, he'd just go crazy and throw punches. Wing 'em, wing 'em, wing 'em. But if you hit Tyson, he won't do that. If you hit Tyson, he'll try not to get hit again. So if you give him a helluva fight, you'll slow him down like Buster Douglas did and he'll start boxing. Marciano, he wasn't crazy, but when he got hit he just didn't know but one way. React. But for all his strength, Tyson is a thinker. If you hit him, he's going to try something else. I always watched him, because sooner or later I knew I'd have somebody in there fighting him.

COURTESY CAROUSEL PHOTOGRAPHY

Jack McCoy *(left)* with Carlos Palomino and promoter Aileen Eaton.

Jackie McCoy:

"The Kind of Boxer You Dream of Getting"

Outside the wide glass wall, soft sunshine glistened off the palm trees above the greenish water in the swimming pool. Inside his El Toro, California, home, the boxing manager and trainer known as Jackie McCoy was laughing.

"My real name is Warren Spaw," he was saying. "That's the name on this house, that's the name on everything. We used to have a thing out front that said 'The Spaws,' but anybody who saw that kept going, so we took it down. When I started fighting as a kid in the amateurs, I had seen a movie with Robert Taylor, *The Crowd Roars*, I thought his name in the movie was Jackie McCoy, so I took that name. I found out later it was Johnny McCoy, I didn't even get the name right. Jim Murray once did a column on me in the *Los Angeles Times* and wrote 'He's not even the real McCoy.' "

But for nearly half a century, Jackie has been the real McCoy as the trainer of six world champions, notably Carlos Palomino.

"What ancestry Spaw is, I couldn't tell you. When I was a kid, some of my aunts who used to keep up with the history of the family told me that I was Scotch-Irish, that some settlers came over from Ireland and then they brought a shipload of French women over. My father fought under the name of Jack Spaw, but sometimes it got changed to Jack Spar."

Near the fireplace, Jack Spaw, in boxing trunks and poised to throw a punch, surveyed the living room from a framed photo.

"Spaw is the name on my driver's license," he said, his voice as solid as his waistline. "That's the name on my paycheck on the docks."

Every weekday morning he's up at five o'clock. By seven he has shaped up and is on the job somewhere in Los Angeles harbor.

"It used to be hard work," he said, "but now most of the freight is in containers. You pull the trucks around, they take the loads off the trucks, then they set 'em where the cranes can pick 'em up and put 'em on the ships. There's not much manual labor anymore."

After work, he stops at the Westminster Gym, not far from Anaheim, to supervise his fighters for a couple of hours. Then it's home to his wife, Shirley, and their two daughters, Julie and Angela.

"We also have a son, Jack, who's up in San Francisco now. I've got an older son, John, from my first marriage, but Shirley raised him from the time he was about two years old."

Boxing trophies from his own career are perched near the fireplace. Slightly faded red-yellow-and-black showcards advertising his fights cover the walls of a nearby hallway.

"That one there, the one in Vegas, the Last Frontier Arena, they had rodeos there when they didn't have fights," he was saying now. "That was an amateur thing in 1941."

Jackie McCoy, born on October 4, 1923, was wearing a short-sleeved shirt that displayed his tattoos; a heart, boxing gloves, the word "Ireland," an eagle with an anchor.

"I got the eagle with the anchor in Hawaii when I was in the Navy. The others I got when I was a kid in a tattoo shop in downtown Los Angeles, Fourth and Main. I think they were fifty cents each. My mother wasn't too happy. And when our son John came home with a couple of tattoos when he was a teenager, I had a fit. I think he would've become a fighter if I'd let him. I took him to some amateur fights and he said, 'Why don't you let me have a couple of fights? I know I can lick some of those guys.' I said, 'Those guys aren't as easy as you think they are.' Shirley even said, 'Let him have a few fights.' But I told her,

'You can't let him have a few fights, because if he likes it and he wins, there's no possible way you're going to stop him.' I discouraged him. He drifted into other things. Now he's trying to be a rock star. He'd probably be better off trying to be a fighter."

Jackie McCoy laughed. But now he stopped laughing. He had begun to talk boxing.

===

When we went to London for Carlos Palomino's shot at the welterweight title in 1976, the papers were saying he'd last four rounds, maybe five. Carlos was a ten-to-one underdog, nobody thought he had any kind of chance. All the papers talked about was what a great fighter John Stracey was and how he wanted Carlos Monzon next. The promoter, Mickey Duff, even told me, "I think Palomino is very ordinary, to be honest with you." Mickey's a sharp guy. Obviously it was a big advantage for Mickey as a promoter if Stracey kept the title. But when Mickey told me that I didn't say a word.

Just before the fight started, Mickey's walking around inside the ring wearing a tuxedo. I walked over to him and said, "Hey, Mickey, we didn't come here for a payday, because we're not getting one." We were getting ten thousand dollars, which even then was real small. Then I told him, "We came over here to take the title, and that's exactly what we're going to do." Mickey looked at me and said, "Oh, my God!"

Afterwards, I asked Mickey, 'How come you acted so scared when I talked to you in the ring?" And he said, "Because you usually don't talk like that." I don't, but I did that time because I just knew we were going to win. When I first started working with Carlos, he had an AAU style. Stood straight up, jab, straight right hand. But he developed a great hook to the liver. Early on against Stracey he started digging that hook in the body. In the twelfth that's what he knocked Stracey out with. The second time Stracey went down he was in agony.

From personal experience there isn't any punch that hurts like a hook to the liver. You're in agony. I don't know what it is with your liver but when you're hit there, it's just something you have to experience to know the agony.

The hook to the liver is like any left hook. You start with the weight on your left foot and when the punch lands, your weight should be on your right foot. Usually when a guy has his right arm against his side, they usually have it up just a little bit high. If you land your hook just under his right elbow, it usually hits in the liver area. Even if you don't land it the first couple of times, somewhere along the line you're going to land that shot.

You see very few good fighters that don't have that hook to the liver. José Torres was devastating with that punch. He won the light heavyweight title from Willie Pastrano with a left hook to the liver that just caved him in.

Carlos did the same thing to Stracey, then Carlos came back to L.A. and beat the number-one contender, Armando Muniz. Then they made him with Davey Boy Green, another Englishman who was undefeated and had moved up to the number-one contender. Carlos went over to London and knocked Green out too, so he was really accepted by the English fans. After that fight Mickey Duff told me that if Carlos wanted to live in England, he'd make more money outside the ring than in it. The people there loved Carlos because he was such a classy guy. So modest. Somebody over there said he was as honest as a preacher, as handsome as a movie actor, and as articulate as—I forget what.

Carlos was super-dedicated. You have to have ability and good reflexes, but the biggest thing Carlos had going for him was great determination. If he got cut, he wouldn't pay any attention to it. If he got knocked down, he got right up as if nothing happened. He had a great mental attitude.

Carlos made eight title defenses. I made more money with him than I made with any other fighter. When he fought Wilfredo Benitez in San Juan in 1979, at the time that was the biggest purse any welterweight ever got, four hundred and fifty thousand dollars plus fifteen thousand in training expenses. That was like a fortune in those days.

Before the Benitez fight, I told Carlos I was already talking to Angelo Dundee about the possibility of his fighting Sugar Ray Leonard and I said, "I'll make you a promise, Carlos—if you beat Benitez, when you fight Leonard we'll make this money look like peanuts." It was a close fight, but Benitez got a split decision. It

wasn't really a robbery. It was a fight you could've given to Palomino, but I didn't feel it was a robbery. There aren't that many
robberies in boxing, and when there is one, it's mostly an honest
mistake. People think that referees are paid off, but the biggest
robberies are in hometowns where every time the hometown guy
throws a punch, everybody cheers. I think it's human nature. The
officials want to make people happy, so they give it to the hometown kid.

I've seen some terrible decisions in other countries. Much more
than you see here. Mando Ramos fought Pedro Carrasco in 1971
for the vacant WBC lightweight title in Madrid, which is where
Carrasco was from. Mando dropped him three or four times. The
last time Carrasco went down, they stopped the fight and they
said Mando pushed him down. I said, "If Mando pushed him
down, why don't he get up?"

They disqualified Mando for pushing. They fought two more
times. Mando beat him in L.A., then they went back to Madrid
and Mando beat him over there. Mando had more ability than
any fighter I've ever been around, but he never did reach his
potential. He could've been a super fighter. It's amazing he won
the lightweight title twice, because he admits himself now that he
used every drug known to man plus alcohol since he was about
twelve years old. He used to clean up his mother's Mexican restaurant, and any alcohol he could find, he'd put that away.

When Mando was fighting, I had no idea of the extent that he
used drugs. I thought maybe once in a while, but I didn't think
he used heroin. I'd never have any fighter who I thought was on
drugs.

Mando works on the docks now. He's married. He hasn't had
any drugs or alcohol for ten years. I see him all the time. I was
training his son for a little while and Mando told him, "Hey listen,
you become a fighter, you're liable to wind up with a nose like
mine." The kid said, "I don't care about that." Mando told him,
"You're liable to get scars over your eyes." The kid said, "I don't
care about that." But then Mando told him, "Well, you're liable to
start talking like me." The kid said, "No more boxing."

I had Mando's older brother, Junior, his real name was Manuel.
He was undefeated in about ten fights, then he went to prison.
When he came out, he was about thirty and tried to make a come-
back. He had one fight in Vegas and got stopped. He just ran out

of gas. Shortly after that, Mando came to the dispatch hall on the docks and told me his brother had died of an overdose. I think Mando and Raul Rojas were with him. The way I heard it, Mando told Raul, "I can't wake Manuel up." Raul said, "You're not going to wake him up. He's gone."

When his father brought Mando to me, I said, "I've had enough of your family. I don't want any more problems." His father said, "No, this kid's not like that, he's different." Mando was always one of the most personable guys you'd ever want to be around. You just loved the guy. After he won the title, he stayed at our house in Torrance and came down with the mumps. Our older daughter, Julie, she was maybe three years old then, and they were sitting at the breakfast table and she said, "You're a sweetheart, Mando." She loved him. Everybody did.

Mando had so much talent. When he was sixteen, seventeen years old, he was so good, I couldn't keep from chuckling when I'd watch him work out. I'd just be so happy with the way he looked, I'd tell myself, this kid is the kind of boxer you dream all your life of getting. Raul Rojas was the world featherweight champion at the time, but I'd put Mando in with him in the Hoover Gym and here was this kid sixteen, seventeen years old in a brutal life-and-death struggle with the world featherweight champion.

Back in 1968 I had Mando and Raul both fighting for world titles at the L.A. Coliseum. Mando was challenging for the lightweight title against Carlos Teo Cruz of the Dominican Republic and Raul was defending the featherweight title against Shozo Saijyo of Japan. We made a deal with a guy in Santa Ana who ran the Saddleback Inn to train there. They set up a nice training area out in the patio, the food was taken care of, we had a real good deal. And there was a nice park nearby to run in. Everything was great. But one morning I went to get the two of them up to run and neither one had come in from the night before.

I went running anyway with the sparring partners, but when I was running, I thought, is this stupid? Here I am running and those two guys haven't even come in from last night.

I took the sparring partners back to the motel, then I left and went home. Later in the day Mando called me and said, "How come you left?" I was so mad, I said, "Listen, you jerk, you think I'm going to be hanging around when you guys are out screwing around." They were both uncontrollable screwups.

Fairly predictably, they both got licked on that card. Raul lost the featherweight title. Mando, even in the shape he was in, came on the last five rounds and took Cruz apart, but he was so far behind he wound up losing. When they fought a rematch early in 1969, he knocked out Cruz in the eleventh for the title. He was only twenty years old.

Mando had such ability, it was worth almost anything to try and keep him under control when he trained. Sometimes we stayed in a motel in Santa Monica. When we first went there, I told him, "Mando, we're going to stay in the same room. The only time you're going to be out of my sight is when you're in the bathroom. Even then I'm going to be outside the door." He just laughed.

Mando went along with that for a couple of fights. He was in tremendous shape and he looked great. But when we went there after that, there was always something. His grandmother was sick. His aunt was sick. He'd disappear and I'd have to wait for him to show up again. One time when I paid the bill, they had charged me for an extra room. I asked him, "What's this extra room?" But he just laughed. I guess he'd get girls and slip away for an hour.

Mando had such great stamina, but all of that went at an early age. I used to run a lot with my fighters, and he was one of the best fighters I ever ran with. He could really run. I'd start out with him and he'd leave me standing still. But at the end, he got so bad we were running once in Vegas and he crossed over to the other side of the street. I said, "Hey, Mando, what're you doing?" He said, "I'm not going to let anybody see an old man outrun me."

Don Jordan was another messup. He had great ability but he drank like a fish. One time in South America he passed out in the hall outside where we were staying. I couldn't carry him. I had to grab him by the feet and drag him into the room.

Not only did Jordan drink but he was a chain cigarette smoker. Not many fighters do that. This guy never stopped smoking. But somehow he won the welterweight title. After he stopped boxing, he went to work on the docks. When I introduced him to Mando Ramos, I said, "You two guys really have a lot in common. You both should be rich but you're both down here working on the docks." Then I said, "I should be rich too, but we're all down here working on the docks."

I don't know what it is about fighters. Some television people who once were doing a documentary on boxing told me their the-

ory was that anyone who becomes a fighter is self-destructive because the average person wouldn't get too enthused about getting
punched in the face. That theory made a lot of sense to me. You
can't argue with that theory too much.

I was a fighter myself. The picture right over there on the wall
is my father. He had somewhere around three hundred fights.
He fought Young Corbett, Sammy Mandell, a lot of those old-time
guys. Some were world champs. I had sixty-three pro fights, around
the same number of amateur fights. I've lived all my life in the
Los Angeles area, and when I was real small, we lived at Sixty-
fifth and Main. If I lived there now I'd be the only white guy in
the neighborhood. Even in those days it wasn't Beverly Hills. But
when my father was boxing, I used to go to the gym with him and
watch him spar. But the main thing, when I was older, I used to
read his scrapbook. I thought it'd be great to be a fighter like that.

After my father stopped boxing, he went into the Merchant
Marine and spent most of his life at sea. He was gone two-thirds
of the time. I didn't have any brothers or sisters. I was the only
child. I guess my parents got discouraged after they saw me. But
when I was about twelve in junior high school, there was a guy
about two years older who was boxing amateur, Frank Rath. He
was my idol. I started going to fights with him and his father.

Frank was a guy that walked right in and took a lot of punishment. He didn't have many pro fights, maybe four or five. Him
and I drifted apart, but I still had boxing in my mind when I went
to the Main Street Gym. There were two black guys in charge
there, Charlie Williams and Duke Holloway. One day when I was
fourteen I asked Charlie Williams if I could spar with somebody.
I did okay, so he said, "Hey, champ, how'd you like to fight tonight?" I said, "You mean a real fight?" He said, "Yeah, we're
having fights out at San Bernardino. You get three dollars."

They took me to San Bernardino and got me a fight. In California at that time you were supposed to be eighteen to box. I was
only fourteen and I looked like I was twelve but I had some cal-
luses on my hands from working out on the parallel bars at school.
When the commissioner questioned my age, Charlie Williams told
him, "No, no, look at his hands. He's in a CCC camp at Pismo
Beach." The commissioner bought it. Before I went down the aisle,
I was thinking, if I get out of this alive, they'll never get me in
here again. But I would up winning the fight. I had the other kid

down a couple of times. Anyhow, that was the start of a boxing career of sorts.

My mother had been dead set against me boxing. My father was a super guy. He didn't have a mean bone in his body, but he had a cauliflower ear. He got pretty well banged up. So my mother didn't want me boxing.

I told my father that I was boxing and he started laughing. He just told me, "If your mother finds out, don't tell her I know about it." I didn't dare tell my mother. When I went out, I told her I was setting pins in a bowling alley. But after about eight fights, somebody mailed my amateur license to the house and she found it. The next day she went to the commission and told them she'd put everybody there in jail if they let me fight again. But when I was seventeen, she said, "If you want to fight now, I'll okay it." As an amateur I had fifty-something fights and never lost. As a pro I had sixty-three fights and lost eleven.

I was a journeyman featherweight, but I fought some good fighters. Manuel Ortiz, who had been the bantamweight champion. Harold Dade, who took the title from Ortiz.

People always ask me if I thought I should've fought for the title. Not really. I boxed pretty good and I was pretty smart but I didn't always train properly. Like I said, I was a journeyman fighter. I stopped after I failed an EEG in Denver, Colorado. I went there to box a guy named Corky Gonzalez, and when you get a license there, they make you take an EEG. So when I went to get paid after the fight, one of the commissioners said, "You failed the EEG, so we can't give you your money until you take the EEG again." I said, "If I failed the EEG, what did you let me fight for?" So they paid me. Then I took the thing again and they sent a letter to the California commission saying I had failed it again. Anyway, I laid off for three or four months, then I took it again in California and passed it.

When I quit, I had been boxing about ten years with time out for the Navy during the war. I was on a flat-bottom gasoline tanker in the Pacific. The good thing about it was, with all that gasoline they didn't go looking for trouble. When we hit an island, as soon as they got the beach, we'd come in close, hook up the hose, and start pumping gas. I was a third-class petty officer, a shipfitter. Which was like a plumber.

I never fought in Madison Square Garden, but after I was in

the invasion of the Philippines, I fought in Manila Square Garden. I was on shore patrol there so I looked around for a gym. I found one and told the guy I'd like to get a fight. Manila Square Garden was a little arena, one of the few places that survived the bombing. I got me two hundred pesos, which in those days was a hundred dollars, which was pretty good. After that I started training fighters while I was still in service, and when I stopped fighting, I just kept doing it.

I don't think I learned how to train fighters from watching other trainers. But maybe I took something from the manager I had, Harry Winkler. I boxed with him from the time I was sixteen until I quit at twenty-seven. In the beginning, I tried to use the things he taught me. He was really from the old school. Jab. Straight right hand. Not too much for body punching. When I first started training fighters, I was a little bit that way, but after that I don't think I trained fighters much at all like I did in the beginning.

I think the techniques change. Maybe not as much in boxing as in some other sports. But one thing Harry Winkler used to do, he had me block punches away from my body. Like when you block a left hook, he had you block it way out here, pick it off. The way he had you block, if the guy threw a hook to the body or a hook to the head, it was like two different moves. The way I teach guys now, it's the same move if it's close to you. Through the years you take a little from this guy, a little from that guy.

The jab is the only punch you don't put your weight in. You shouldn't shift your weight from one foot to another. If you're a little bit back on your right foot in good position to throw a straight right hand, when you throw your jab and the jab lands, you should still be in that position. There shouldn't be anything going out there except your arm. And you don't try to lean forward. If you're not close enough, you take a little short step to get yourself in close and remain in the same basic position.

When you throw a straight right hand, all your weight should be on your right foot. When the right lands, your weight should be shifted to your left foot. That's how you get your weight turned into it.

With an uppercut, a lot of guys will go way down and then come up. But the basics are, your shoulder should be going straight across while just your arm is making that swinging movement. Then you turn your shoulder. The left hook is exactly the same thing except you change the angle of your arm depending on the other guy. If the other guy is coming in a little bit low or if he's twisting away from your right hand with his head down, you throw the left hook on a little bit of an up-angle. If the other guy drops down just a little bit and you throw it on an up-angle, he'll duck right into it.

My two favorite punches are the jab and the left hook to the body or to the head. Carlos Palomino had a real good left hook. Don Jordan had a strong, hard jab. He was a converted southpaw.

But it's like Angelo Dundee once told me, "It really doesn't matter that much who's in the corner, it's who's on the stool." Unless you have the material, I don't care what kind of a trainer you are, you're not going to make it. I'm speaking as a manger too. With the exception of Gerrie Coetzee, I don't think I ever trained any fighters except my own. I trained Coetzee when he won the WBA heavyweight title from Michael Dokes with a tenth-round knock-out in 1983 at the Richfield Coliseum outside Cleveland.

Coetzee is just a super nice guy. That big clock on the wall over there and that ivory carving, he gave me those. He still calls me every so often.

Coetzee was a tough guy. Before his fight with Greg Page in Johannesburg in 1984, he broke his left hand in two places, but he kept training. The X-rays showed two clean breaks. I asked him, "Are you really going to fight with your left hand like that?" He said, "If I break the other hand, I'm still going to fight." I said, "That's the stupidest thing I ever heard. You've got the heavyweight title. If the other guy had the title and you were gambling to win it, I could see it. But the other guy has to wait for you."

He looked at me and said, "I never call fights off." But he lost the title. Page stopped him in the eighth round.

Coetzee always had trouble with his hands. He had so much trouble with his right hand he finally had to have it fused. Most people thought that right hand was like a hammer. But to me, it was more of a hindrance than a help. He hurt that hand all the time. In the gym he hardly used that right hand. When he did, it didn't look that devastating. I thought, this guy hits harder with his hook than he does with that bionic right hand. But his hands were brittle. He had two brothers. One had twelve broken hands. Nothing much you can do about it.

If you count Coetzee, who I just trained, I had six champions. The other five I managed and trained. Carlos Palomino, Mando Ramos, Raul Rojas, Don Jordan, and Rodolfo Gonzalez.

By the time I got Gonzalez, he was more or less considered to be washed up. He'd been around for quite a long time. But when he came to me, I said, "Give it a try, you got nothing to lose." He wound up winning the WBC lightweight title in 1972, then he made a couple of successful defenses. He was very strong for a lightweight, a tremendous body puncher. He had a good left hook to the liver. I don't know why, but a lot of Mexican fighters seem to develop that punch.

I don't know why Mexicans make good fighters. I'm not into that. But maybe it's due to their ancestry. You very seldom see a Mexican fighter who isn't aggressive, who doesn't have a lot of guts. Maybe the ones who become fighters grow up hard and develop that character. That confidence. That ego.

I never thought ego was a problem with a fighter. Deep down you've got to have ego. Carlos Palomino is a real quiet reserved guy who didn't have too much to say. But deep down there was never anybody he was worried about fighting. That's one thing most of the real good fighters have in common. In boxing, so much of what you do is mental. I think the worst thing is to have that confidence, that ego, when you can't fight anymore. I've told guys to quit but they go fight for somebody else.

Mando Ramos, the last fight I had him in, he fought a guy named Tootie Pineda and got stopped in five.

Tootie was just a tough club fighter, and afterwards I said, "Mando, I never thought I'd see the day you could lose to a guy like that. Don't ever go in the gym again. Don't ever fight again." He looked at me and said, "You don't need to tell me it's over. I know it's over." He laid off a little while, but the next thing I know he's fighting in Europe. He had nine more fights. He didn't want to leave the stage. It's like when somebody asked Sugar Ray Leonard a while back why he was still fighting when he was in great shape financially and he said, "It's simple. I like to fight." Most fighters always think they can fight. If they haven't fought for twenty-five years, they still think they can fight. And if they lost after twenty-five years, they'd blame the trainer.

Boxing is like everything else. If you lose, you never blame yourself. Always somebody else. The obvious guy to blame is the trainer. I think it was Ray Arcel who said, "The trainer is usually the guy to go, because there's no contract." But I only trained one guy that I didn't manage, so my fighters couldn't do much about it.

I've had fights where I trained a guy a certain way to take advantage of the other guy's mistakes. Most of those fights the other guy came out and did something unexpected and nothing worked out like we planned. But there were a couple of fights where everything worked out exactly. Raul Rojas fought a guy named Pavorito Moreno, one of the most devastating punchers ever to come out of Mexico. They fought at the Olympic Auditorium, a great fight with a controversial ending. The other guy got cut and they stopped it. They just about had a riot. The other guy's manager was about ready to jump on Rojas, so I stepped in front of Rojas like I'm going to protect him. Rojas should've been stepping in front of me.

Anyway, before the rematch, I was watching tapes of the first fight and saw where every time Moreno jabbed, he went way up on his left foot and his left hand went down. We just worked and worked on when Moreno would jab, I'd have Rojas come over the top with his right hand. We practiced that and Rojas stopped him in two. But usually it works out better on paper than it does in the ring.

That's the same fight I had a problem with Aileen Eaton, the lady promoter. Aileen Eaton was the greatest thing that ever happened to boxing in California. She developed every fighter I had in those years. And every fighter that anybody else had. If you had a fighter who looked like he could develop into a real attraction, she didn't hesitate for a second to bring a guy over from Europe even if she knew she'd lose money on this fight. She'd say, "Can your guy beat this other guy?" I'd say, "I think he can." She'd make the fight.

Anyway, when Ramos fought Moreno the second time after a sellout at the Olympic the first time, I don't remember the exact amounts Aileen offered us but I said something like, "Look, if the thing does fifty thousand dollars, we want twenty-five percent of the net gate. If it goes over fifty thousand, we want twenty-seven and a half. And if it goes over a hundred thousand, we want thirty percent." She said, "Oh, we can't do that."

We argued all day. We were there for hours, back and forth.

Aileen finally said, "Okay, okay, I'll take it in and have the secretary type it." When she brought it back, I looked at the percentages. Everything looked good. I signed it. I thought I had everything I wanted. Ramos took Moreno apart. The crowd went crazy. They drew over a hundred thousand dollars. Everything was great. But when I got paid that night, I said, "Wait a second, this can't be right." Aileen said, "I don't have all the figures in front of me." Anyway, I took the check and had a few drinks to celebrate, but I kept thinking that something was wrong.

When I got home, I did what I should've done in the beginning, I looked at the contract. What the contract said wasn't thirty percent of the net gate if it went over a hundred thousand, it was thirty percent of everything over a hundred thousand. It made a real big difference in the final amount.

I was just so mad, I called her house at three in the morning. Her maid answered and refused to disturb her. I had to talk to somebody, so I called Mickey Davies, her matchmaker. I reminded him that he was in the office when we were bargaining and I said, "This is the way I understood the contract, and I know she understood it that way, but that wasn't the way she wrote it up." He said, "The way you're saying it, that's the way you said it at the time, and I thought it was very clear." I said, "I'm going to cut off my nose to spite my face, but I'm never going to fight for Aileen Eaton again unless she makes this right."

That morning I went down to see her. I was in a rage I was so mad. But when I went in there, she had her son there, Gene LaBell, a professional wrestler, 235 pounds. My temper went away. I was able to control myself immediately.

I told her, "You know the contract isn't the same as what we agreed to." She said, "I believe that you thought that's what we agreed to, but why won't you give me the same consideration to think that what the contract says is what I thought we agreed to?" Then she said, "We'll split the difference." So she saved a little bit. But even with that, Aileen Eaton was great, she really was. I had a lot of respect for her then and I have a whole lot more respect for her now. Boxing isn't anywhere near what it used to be.

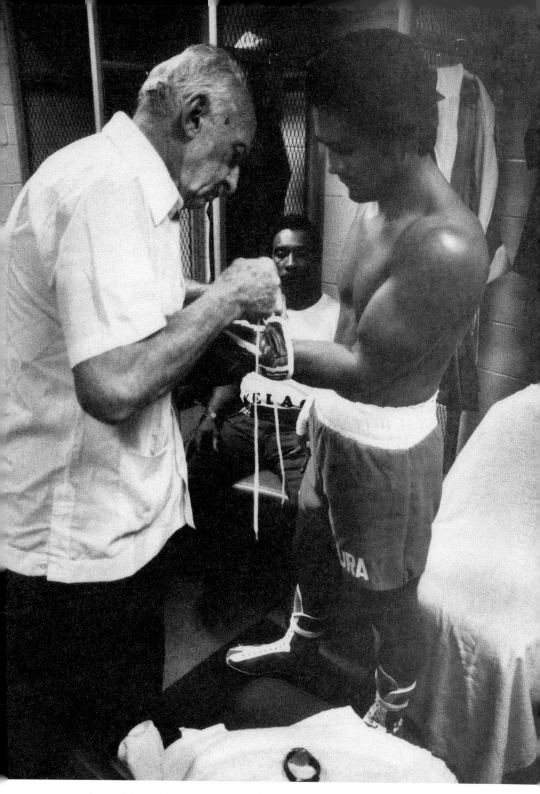

Nobody gloved boxers longer than Ray Arcel, here with Roberto Duran *(right)*.

Ray Arcel:

"Tough Times Make Monkeys Eat Red Peppers"

$$\equiv$$

In the living room of Ray Arcel's ninth-floor apartment on Lexington Avenue, he was surrounded by boxing. John Groth's painting of Stillman's Gym where the old trainer toiled for decades. Joe Brown's bronze sculpture of Mickey Walker about to throw a left hook while knocking down Georgie Ward's jab. Posters of Larry Holmes and Roberto Duran promotions that involved the last of his eighteen champions.

"Twenty champions," he said with a laugh. "If you count Duran and Barney Ross each as two."

Dapper as always, Ray Arcel was wearing a black sleeveless sweater over a shirt and tie, gray slacks, and brown suede shoes. But he wasn't wearing glasses. When he talked about a punch, he would get up from his chair and demonstrate it. Spry indeed for a boxing oracle who was born on August 30, 1899, in Terre Haute, Indiana.

"He brought class, dignity, and a high degree of professionalism to boxing," another longtime trainer, Eddie Futch, once said. "I admired him from afar. When I came to New York in 1942, I watched him. I listened to him."

Ray Arcel's other champions were Ezzard Charles, Jim Braddock, Bob Olin, Tony Zale, Billy Soose, Ceferino Garcia, Lou Brouillard, Teddy Yarosz, Freddie Steele, Jackie (Kid) Berg, Alfonso (Peppermint) Frazier, Abe Goldstein, Frankie Genaro, Sixto Escobar, and Charley Phil Rosenberg, a bantamweight who often had trouble making the weight. To supervise Charley Phil's intake before one title fight, Arcel prepared his meals and slept in an adjoining bed. One night Arcel awoke as Charley Phil went to the bathroom.

"What are you doing?" the trainer asked.

"I'm just going to the bathroom," the fighter said. "And then I'm going to just gargle some water."

"Go ahead," Arcel said," I'm watching your Adam's apple to make sure you don't swallow any."

In the years when Joe Louis ruled the heavyweight division, Ray Arcel often worked the corner of the champion's opponents. So often that he earned the nickname "the Meat Wagon" for carting the fallen challengers out of the ring after Louis had pummeled them.

"Louis once drove Paulino Uzcudun's teeth right through his mouthpiece," he said. "It was one of the hardest punches I've ever seen. Uzcudun went on his face."

As a New York City teenager growing up in Harlem, then primarily an Italian neighborhood, Arcel had what he calls "a few two-dollar fights" before deciding to devote himself to training boxers. His first job was hurrying up the steps to the corner between rounds and swinging a towel in front of the fighter sitting on the stool.

"Not to cool him off," he recalled. "To keep all the cigar smoke out of his face."

Slim and silver-haired now, he lives with his wife, Stephanie, known as Steve, who accompanies him whenever he attends a boxing card.

"Best thing I ever did in my life was marry her," he said. "She's a doll."

There's nobody else in boxing quite like him. Nobody who goes back as far. Nobody who remembers Jack Dempsey and Benny Leonard as vividly as he does. Nobody who has had so many champions who speak so glowingly of him. At a 1988 boxing dinner at the Downtown Athletic Club honoring him as its Boxing Man of the Century, several of his champions attended.

"He not only taught me boxing," Billy Soose said, "he taught me values."

"He's the greatest trainer in the world," Jackie (Kid) Berg said, dissolving into sobs of tears. "If it wasn't for him, I wouldn't be here."

But when Ray Arcel got up to speak, he momentarily groped for words.

"I don't know what I did to deserve all this," Ray Arcel finally said, "but I'm very proud of my friendships that are more important to me than all the money in the world."

Just as his friendship is more important to others.

=

Boxing is brain over brawn. I don't care how much ability you've got as a fighter. If you can't think, you're just another bum in the park.

And the trainer has to be able to think. Years ago the trainer didn't need three or four guys in the corner. He worked himself. All I needed was somebody to help me with the stool or the bucket. Not only me, that went for every one of the good trainers. Whitey Bimstein, Dan Florio, Charlie Goldman. We were in Stillman's Gym on Eighth Avenue near Madison Square Garden eight hours a day. Maybe more. Then you had fights every night. Sometimes two or three. I used to go from one club to another the same night. On a Tuesday night I'd work in the Broadway Arena early, then I'd get in my little jalopy and go up to White Plains for the main bout there. Sometimes I'd send Whitey someplace or he'd send me. We were partners for ten years.

If I say I worked with two thousand fighters, maybe I worked with more. Whitey and I, one thing we always took pride in, none of our fighters ever got hurt. When the fight was over, we never went home. We stayed with our fighter. If the fighter was in a hotel or he was living home, wherever he was, we saw to it that he took a hot bath and we gave him a rub before we went home. Today most trainers count their money first. It's not boxing anymore. It's exploitation.

The trainers of that day knew every boxer was different. No two were alike. What was food for one was poison for another. If you trained one fighter one way, you could not train another fighter the same way because he may not have the same ability. Or he may not have been able to think. Any trainer has to have a fighter who can fight. You might teach him, you might show him. But this man you're working with has to learn the characteristics that spell success. Mental energy. Self-control. Determination. The most important is mental energy. How to think. When you're in that ring by yourself, you've got to know what you're doing and what you're facing. You can't fall asleep.

The great fighters knew how to fight to start with, but we would discuss what mental energy was. When you're boxing, talk to yourself. This guy is trying to jab me, make him miss and then I'll counter with a hook. I learned that from Benny Leonard, because that's what he did. He was the fastest-thinking fighter I ever saw.

When it was whispered around that Leonard, the lightweight champion of the world from 1917 to 1924, was training at the old Stillman's up on 125th Street, the gym was mobbed. At first there was no admission charge and you couldn't move in the place. But then it got so crowded whenever Leonard was there, they started charging fifteen cents. Leonard even had a private dressing room. They built a wall around the one toilet seat in the gym. Anybody who had to go had to knock on the door and if Leonard was in there, he had to let the guy in.

The other fighters dressed in a little room. When they got through working out, they would sit and talk about their experiences. Leonard would come in there and tell the kids, "Think, think. Learn how to think." Some kids never knew what he was talking about, but I'd always bring kids over and I'd tell them, "Now listen to this."

Leonard would tell them, "You've got to talk to yourself. 'I'm going to jab this guy' or 'I'm going to hook this guy.'" How could you obtain knowledge in a better way than from the master himself? Kids would walk out of that gymnasium and say, "Benny Leonard told me . . ." This was the height of their existence. Not only the kids but the guys who worked with the fighters. We learned all those tricks by listening to what was Leonard's main stock in trade: to teach.

Most of the good fighters then, they had nothing else to do. There was no television, no radio, no place to go unless you went to the ballgame. So they sat around and picked up knowledge.

Whitey Bimstein and I were always very close. We were talking one day in 1925 and he said, "You know, Ray, there's a lot of work around here. We could handle a lot of fighters together." Stillman's Gym was starting to bloom. It's an apartment house now, but then it was only a couple of blocks away from what was then the new Madison Square Garden and there were a lot of fighters around. Whitey and I were partners from 1925 to 1934. Before the Depression, if you got fifty dollars from a fight, you got a lot of money. But you'd have nights where you might only get a couple of bucks from two or three kids. If the fighter got twenty bucks, he'd give you two. Maybe Whitey would get the guys ready in the dressing room and I'd be in the corner. Or vice versa. On a good night, maybe we'd go home with twenty dollars apiece, maybe twenty-five. But in 1934 we had to split up. It was the height of the Depression. Nobody was making anything. Whitey came to me one day and said, "Ray, I think we better go on our own. You're not making anything. I'm not making anything. If I make ten bucks, I got to give you five. If you make ten bucks, you got to give me five. That's no good."

One thing I would have to say about myself, the fighter was the most important part of my life. Which was wrong. But I didn't realize it at that time. It was wrong because I had a family, my first wife, Hazel, and our two children. I would go to training camp for months. They weren't just ordinary fights. They were important fights. Mostly championship fights. Tough times make monkeys eat red peppers.

Splitting up worked out for both Whitey and me. I got a lot of work around that time. It's all right to say that I worked with a lot of champions, a lot of good fighters. But they knew how to fight. If they didn't know how to fight, they wouldn't have been champions. I helped them, sure, but they knew how to fight and they knew how to think. But they had to have condition. That's where I came in. I was a cross-country runner in high school. I knew how to run. I used to show my fighters how to run. Walk, jog, sprint. Walk fast maybe half a mile. Break into a little jog for maybe a mile. Then sprint for half a mile. Really go, really go. By sprinting you're sharpening your wind. Then start walking again.

It was always up to the trainer to tell how much work the fighter needed from day to day. When shall he keep running. When shall he stop. When shall he take a day off.

You had to think for all your fighters. Not that they couldn't think. Nobody walked in that ring that couldn't think. He was a dead duck if he did. Barney Ross once won a fight just with his brain. In the Tournament of Champions in 1937 at the Polo Grounds, five titles were up for grabs. Ross was defending the world welterweight title against Ceferino Garcia from the Philippines, a helluva fighter. Real good. He could box. He could punch. He later won the middleweight title. Two days before the fight, Barney's last day of boxing, his last round, I called time and he went to pat his sparring partner on the back. But somehow he hit his right thumb on the guy's head. He fractured his thumb, a very slight fracture. But it's two days before the fight.

Barney's managers, Sam Pian and Art Winch, were talking about calling off the fight, but Barney says, "I'm fighting." I say, "How can you fight?" and Barney says, "I've been listening to you telling me, 'Use that left hand. Jab and hook, jab and hook. I'm sick and tired of listening to you, but now I'm going to do what you've been screaming at me to do." The night of the fight I bandaged his hand to take the pressure off the thumb after his own doctor gave him a shot of novocaine. That shot only lasted four or five rounds, but he put on an exhibition of boxing par excellence.

Barney defended his title for fifteen rounds against one of the best fighters in the world. He jabbed and he hooked and he feinted the guy into knots. He made him miss. He countered. He twisted him out of position. He just caught punches with his right hand. He never threw a right hand. He just made believe he was going to throw a right hand, then he'd throw a hook. He gave an exhibition of boxing that made an indelible impression on me. From the first round on that night, I had to go to the bathroom. I had to go but I didn't care, I didn't leave that corner. Nobody could have gotten me out of there. Here was a man giving a performance. That's what you call talent. After he got a unanimous decision he just patted me on the back and said, "You gonna bother me again?" He was a wonderful, wonderful man.

The next year Barney lost the title to Henry Armstrong, his last fight. In the corner, Sam Pian and Art Winch and I were thinking about stopping it. After the twelfth round, Arthur Donovan, the referee, came over to the corner and said, "I'm not going to stop this fight. It's up to you guys. You're going to be responsible for anything that happens, so use your own judgment." Barney looked up at Sam and Art and myself and said, "If you guys stop this fight, I'll never talk to you the rest of my life."

Armstrong was at the top of his game. He'd already won the featherweight title and later that year he won the lightweight title. He gave Barney a bad licking the last three rounds. Barney had lumps on his head. His eyes were swollen. His ears were swollen. When we got him back to the hotel, I put hot towels on him. That night I slept alongside him. I wouldn't leave him. He had just been married. But he was so busted up, we didn't let his wife in there to see him. She was screaming blue murder, but Sam went over to Barney and said, "Look at yourself in the mirror. You don't want her to see you like this. Let's wait a day or two." Barney was smart. He kept her out. I stayed with him for four days and four nights until he looked a little better.

By then I'd been around boxers for more than thirty years. The first time I saw Jack Dempsey was when he came to New York in 1916 for three fights. We used to hang out in a barber shop in Harlem, at 111th Street and Lenox Avenue. The shop was owned by John Reisler, who was a boxing promoter. John the Barber. He told us he had a fighter who could knock a building down, so the whole gang of us went up to the Harlem Sporting Club to see him. It cost you a quarter to get in.

Dempsey looked like nothing. John Lester Johnson actually outboxed him for ten rounds, but I don't think Dempsey even cared. It was a no-decision fight, so it didn't affect his record. Dempsey was just a rough and tough barroom fighter. Then he got mixed up with Jack [Doc] Kearns, and he won the title from Jess Willard in Toledo in 1919. That's the Dempsey I remember when people ask me who was the greatest heavyweight champion I ever saw. Some young people think Muhammad Ali was the greatest, but I would never say Ali. I've always said, "Who was better than Dempsey the day he knocked out Willard to win the title? Who would have beaten him?" You can go down the list. Joe Louis might've had a chance, maybe Ali would've had a chance. Ali was a good boxer. He was better as Cassius Clay than as Muhammad Ali, because of his three-and-a-half-year layoff. That layoff was unfair. I always thought that according to the American way, you had a chance to say no to the military. There were many guys that said no.

With Ali, with his Black Muslim religion, his way of thinking, the whole situation, he was a victim of his own people. And he still is. But I thought he got a rough deal. I hated to see it happen.

Getting back to Dempsey, he was a saloon boxer. With him every part of your body was a legal target. That was legitimate then. In those years Dempsey had a couple of people around him who were good friends of mine, so I stayed around him whenever I could. When he fought Georges Carpentier at Boyle's Thirty Acres in Jersey City, I think that was the first big promotion that Tex Rickard ever had. Rickard guaranteed Dempsey three hundred thousand dollars and Carpentier two hundred thousand, and to build the fight up, they talked about Carpentier the great French war hero against Dempsey, who the American Legion had gone to work on. During the war there was a picture of Dempsey supposedly working in a Philadelphia shipyard wearing patent-leather shoes.

Carpentier was an overstuffed light heavyweight. Good fighter. Good boxer. I think Dempsey planned to take him along for the ride, but Carpentier snuck a right hand in on Dempsey. Once you do that to Dempsey, he's a barroom fighter. He don't go for that nonsense. He flattened him in four rounds.

The first time I was actually very close to Dempsey was when I went out to Los Angeles with Charley Phil Rosenberg and stayed at Dempsey's hotel, the Barbara. The address was Sixth and Bonnie Brae, a nice big hotel. We lived there and hung out there for about six months. Dempsey was married to Estelle Taylor, the movie actress. She used to come into the hotel restaurant with him and sit around with us. Her pet name for him was Ginsberg.

In the morning Dempsey would go down to the gym and fool around with Jim Londos, who was the wrestling champion at the time. They would get on the mat and pull and tug. Jack needed some action. He wasn't boxing. Him and Kearns were on the outs because Kearns didn't want him to marry Estelle Taylor, but he was in love with the woman and she was his wife. You had to respect that.

When we'd be in the restaurant with them, Estelle wouldn't have much patience with the guys hanging around. One night I told him, "Jack, you need to get in action. You can knock all these bums out in one round." He said, "I'll get into action soon." He wanted a fight where instead of knocking a guy out in a round or two, he could go the limit. They put him in with Tom Gibbons in Shelby, Montana. It went fifteen rounds, but that was the fight where there was a big commotion about the banks closing in Shelby.

After that Jack got ready for the Luis Firpo fight, but even after going fifteen with Gibbons, when we watched Jack work, we could see the truth of the old saying "To rest is to rust."

The old Dempsey drive wasn't there. Against Firpo, he got hit on the button, but he got through it very lucky because he was strong and determined and the referee, Jack Gallagher, let him do whatever he wanted. He went to work on Firpo, and when he did, he really let loose with both hands. One thing about Dempsey, when he hit you, you stayed hit. But after that he started playing around too much, then he lost the two Tunney fights. The sad part about Dempsey, he should've been the only guy anybody ever thought of when they thought about the greatest heavyweight champion. I mean, he had everything. He could punch, he could box. He was mean and determined.

I went over to Philadelphia and saw Dempsey's first fight with Tunney in the pouring rain. I knew Dempsey lost it. Tunney outboxed him. Smart, cagey, good defensive boxer. Nobody ever realized how far Tunney could have gone, But he married forty million dollars when he married Polly Lauder, whose grandfather had been a first cousin of Andrew Carnegie and the first treasurer of the Carnegie Steel Company.

Tunney was a soft-spoken guy and I admired him as a boxer. But he was a loner. He was different than other boxers. When he traveled to Philadelphia for the Dempsey fight from his training camp at Speculator, New York, up in the Adirondack Mountains, he rode in a small plane. In those years most people were afraid to fly, especially in a small plane, but Tunney wasn't. He was different.

I was with Jim Braddock in 1935 when he won the heavyweight title from Max Baer. Wonderful man. But with the Depression, Jim was still dead broke. He was struggling, working on the docks for what were pennies. Somebody decided to give him a dinner. He hardly had anything to eat and I think it was Jimmy Johnston who said to him, "Well, Jim, they finally gave you a dinner." You had to live through those years in order to know the types of people who were around boxing. Some I liked very much. But most of them, no.

When Jim signed to defend the title against Joe Louis, I honestly didn't think Jim had a chance. Jim had been laying off, he was broke. Louis was already a great fighter. I didn't tell Jim much, just don't get hurt. Jim knew how good Louis was. Jim told his manager, Joe Gould, "I'm going to take a chance. I'm going to let everything go in the first round." Joe Gould told him, "If you can, do it." Jim nailed him in the first round. But he was in with a great fighter and Louis stopped him in the fourth.

Some people always thought that Joe Gould made a deal with Mike Jacobs that was supposed to give Gould ten percent of Louis's purses for the rest of Louis's career. But it was ten percent out of Jacobs's profits from Louis's fights, not ten percent out of Louis's money. The people with Louis weren't that type of persons.

That wasn't the first time I was across from Joe Louis's corner. Three years before, I worked with Charley Massera in Joe's eleventh pro fight. Jack Blackburn was Joe's trainer, and when Jack was around New York and Philadelphia, I got very friendly with him. Jack had been a helluva fighter, a lightweight who could lick heavyweights. But he had been in jail for killing a guy. So after he got out, I saw him in Chicago before the Massera fight and I asked him about Louis.

I've never forgotten Jack's answer. He said, "Ray, I always told you I was gonna have a champion. I got the man now."

He sure did. Joe flattened Massera in three rounds. After that I worked against Joe with Jack Sharkey and George Brescia, then with Jim Braddock, Nathan Mann, John Henry Lewis, Johnny Paycheck, Paulino Uzcudun, Al McCoy, Buddy Baer twice, Lou Nova, Ezzard Charles, and Cesar Brion. That's fourteen fights. I don't know if it was the Al McCoy fight or one of the Buddy Baer fights, when the fighters and their cornermen got to the center of the ring for the referee's instructions, Joe looked at me and said, "You heah again?" Everybody busted out laughing. There was always something so nice about Joe. He knew I was only there to pick the guy up.

I loved Joe Louis. One of the greatest human beings I ever knew. When he got older and lived in Las Vegas, my heart would drop when I saw him sitting in a wheelchair at ringside. I'd go over to him and lean down and say, "Joe, I'm heah again." He'd always laugh.

The night Joe fought Nathan Mann, they had Everlast make up form-fitting gloves for Joe, but they just had a pair of ordinary gloves for Nathan. I had trained Nathan ever since he was a kid, but when I squawked about the specially made gloves Joe had, Mike Jacobs interfered. I knew Mike, I knew all about him. It was none of my business what he did, but when he said, "You don't like this, do you?" I said, "No, I don't, because I build and you destroy."

Mike didn't talk to me after that, but I wasn't surprised. Mike was never concerned with fighters, only with money.

When Ancil Hoffman, the California avocado grower who was Max Baer's manager, insisted on a cash guarantee of two hundred thousand dollars before Baer fought Joe Louis in 1935, Mike took Ancil into the bank vault where his safe-deposit box was.

"You should have seen it," Ancil said later. "Stacks and stacks of big bills."

Money was all Mike cared about, just like money is all Don King and Bob Arum and the Duvas care about now. Money is the sickness of the boxing business. Maybe the sickness of the world. That's what I mean when I say the trainer of that day was not only a trainer, he was a fighter's friend. For the trainer of that day, there wasn't any money around, so your whole concern was the fighter. And sometimes the fighter's whole concern was trying to support his whole family with whatever money he could make. Not just his wife and kids, but his parents and his brothers and sisters.

During the Depression it wasn't that the other members of the fighter's family didn't want to work, it was that there wasn't any work.

I remember fighters telling me, "I can't box today, Ray." When I asked why not, they'd say, "Because I haven't had anything to eat." So as the trainer, you would try to take care of the fighter as best you could. The trainer was the one guy in boxing the fighter could always depend on. It's a different world now. It's different money.

But there's one thing that's never different. Most fighters know some fear. I don't mean they're afraid to fight, but they're a little nervous about it.

If you get into a fight on the street, you don't have time to get nervous. But when you're booked for a fight a month in advance, you don't go to bed alone. Any guy who was booked to fight Joe Louis went to bed with Joe Louis on his mind every night. Unless

you're that rare human being who can develop a feeling of supe-
riority in your own mind and know you'll take care of the job,
you're going to be nervous. When some guys went into the ring,
they were petrified. Nervous tension. But because they were so
nervous, some of them fought their bravest fights.

Bob Olin was like that. Four nights before he was to defend the
light heavyweight title in 1935 against John Henry Lewis in St.
Louis, he woke me up in the middle of the night. He had his
pants and an overcoat on over his pajamas and he was as white as
a sheet.

I can still hear him saying, "I'm going to die. I'm going to die."
I put him back to bed. I stroked his forehead and held his hand.
I talked to him like a baby. I told him, "Just forget about the fight.
Just go to sleep." In the morning I called a friend of mine and
told him that I was sick, that I needed to see a doctor. When we
got to the doctor's office, I introduced myself as Marty Sampson,
the name of our sparring partner, and I introduced Olin as me.
I said, "Doctor, my friend Ray Arcel doesn't feel well. I wish you'd
examine him." Olin stripped down and the doctor checked him
for an hour. Finally he looked at Olin and said, "Mr. Arcel, if I
had your physical condition and your build, I'd be a prizefighter."

After Olin went outside, the doctor turned to me and said, "Mr.
Sampson, what happened to frighten that man?" I said, "What do
you mean?" The doctor said, "That man is afraid of something.
He's suffering from extreme nervousness and nervous indiges-
tion. That's all that's the matter with him."

I knew Olin was dying a thousand deaths, but he kept training.
He ran in the morning. He worked out in the afternoon. In the
dressing room the night of the fight, the perspiration actually ran
from under his arms. But when the bell rang, he fought one of
the greatest fights you ever saw in your life. He lost the title to
John Henry Lewis on a fifteen-round decision, but you should
have seen the crowd outside Olin's dressing room. There was an
old black lady there and I can still hear her saying, "Let me look
at that man. Let me look at a man with guts like that."

One of the trials and tribulations of the trainer who was in full
charge, the one thing that always depressed me and made me feel
miserable, was the fact that in those years long before the civil-
rights movement you couldn't always get decent living quarters
when you traveled with a black fighter.

One time I took Jimmy Bivins to a fight down to Washington,

the capital of our country. We went to a hotel where I thought the manager was a friend of mine. He had a room for Jimmy, but I wouldn't have put an animal in that room. We left and we went over to another hotel where I knew the manager.

When Jimmy and I got there, I told the manager, "I had to bring my valet with me." He looked at me and said, "I've heard a lot of things, but you always come up with a lulu." He said, "Who's the guy?" I said, "Jimmy Bivins." He said, "Is he here alone or is he with a whole gang?" I said, "Alone. Let him stay in my room. You don't have to sign him in." He said, "What are you going to do about his food?" I said, "You tell me." He said, "When you order dinner and the guy comes up with the food, put him in the bathroom." I said, "How about me?" He said, "You eat in the coffee shop."

We were there four or five days. Jimmy was the kind of guy you could talk to. I told him, "Jimmy, we're in trouble. You're black and I'm a Jew, we're both in the same boat." He laughed but others didn't.

Traveling with Ezzard Charles was a problem. In 1951 he was the heavyweight champion of the world. The year before he had outpointed Joe Louis for the vacated title and now he's going to box Joey Maxim in Chicago. Jim Norris was the promoter and he told me, "I own the Western Hotel. Go over there and make the arrangements for your entire group." We had sparring partners, hero-worshippers, hangers-on. I don't know if Ezzard got that from Ray Robinson or who, but he always traveled with about ten guys.

The whole gang of us walked into the Western Hotel, and when I went over to talk to the manager, he said, "We don't allow any niggers in this hotel."

I said, "Do you own the hotel?" He said, "I run the hotel." I said, "I thought Jim Norris was the boss of the hotel. Let's call Jim on the phone." He gets Jim on the phone and I said, "Jim, I'm over at the Western Hotel, but your manager says he doesn't allow any niggers in the hotel." Jim said, "Put him on." When the manager got on, I could hear Jim tell him, "You give them anything they want." That's all I had to hear. After the manager got off the phone, I told him, "I don't want anybody allowed down the corridor where our rooms are. I want to be able to order from the kitchen whatever any of us want to eat." We never had a problem and Charles won the fight.

The next year, after Charles lost the title to Jersey Joe Walcott, his manager, Tom Tannas, booked him in Ogden, Utah, against Rex Layne, a Utah heavyweight he had stopped in eleven rounds in Pittsburgh the year before. Tom told me he had called out there and made all the arrangements. When I got to Ogden a few days before Ezzard and everybody else, I had a list of people to contact.

I went to the hotel on the list and asked for the manager. I told him my name and said, "I understand that arrangements have been made for Ezzard Charles and his group to live here and eat here." He looked at me and said, "Who made the arrangements?" I said, "Your mayor is supposed to have talked to Ezzard Charles's manager." He said, "We don't allow any niggers in this hotel." I knew I was in trouble. But then he said, "How many are there?" I said, "Twelve." He said, "All niggers?" I said, "No. I stay with them all the time." He said, "I'm sorry, I can't do anything." I said, "If you can't accommodate me, maybe you can tell me where I could get some rooms, but I want a decent place. No slipshod joints."

"About a mile and a half up the road," he said. "The fellow just built a group of cottages. From what I hear, it's pretty nice. Go up there, but don't tell him what you told me."

I drove up there, walked in, and said, "I'd like to rent a few rooms, but I'd like to see them first." They were nice. Big double beds. Not top-notch but clean, new. I said, "What's the cost of the room?" He said, "Two to a room, thirty-five dollars a night." I said, "I'll pay you in advance for six rooms for ten days." Tom Tannas had given me cash. I had a bundle. About five thousand dollars. I pulled out that roll and started to count. Six times thirty-five times ten. His eyes were popping out of his head. I put the money on his desk. I said, "I need a receipt and I want a key for each room." I wasn't going to wait until Charles arrived and then ask him for the keys and take a chance on him giving me my money back.

I've got rooms and now I go to see the promoter to find out where we're going to train. He told me, "It's all set. You drive over to Salt Lake City and train in the ballpark."

Salt Lake City was about thirty miles away. I just looked at the promoter and said, "I've been in this business a long time, and excuse me if I say something wrong, but Ezzard Charles is the former heavyweight champion of the world. We don't train in ballparks. We don't travel thirty miles there and thirty miles back.

We have to have a gymnasium." He said, "The little gym I got isn't big enough?" I said, "Is there a dance hall?" He said, "There's a roller-skating rink." We went up there and the owner said, "You can train here, but I don't have any gymnasium equipment." The promoter had a portable ring, but then the roller-rink owner said, "You'll have to take the ring down by four o'clock every afternoon. That's when the people start to come in to roller skate."

I took it, but I was fit to be tied. I told the promoter, "I don't know why you brought us out here. You didn't even have a place for us to train." He said, "I thought you'd train at the ballpark." I said, "Where? Between first base and home? Or between third base and home? Or on the pitcher's mound?"

But at the roller rink, I was thinking, where are we going to eat? Twelve people, not just one. In those days I had more guts than brains. I went back to the hotel that we couldn't stay in. I thanked the manager for sending me up the road, then I said, "I still need a place to eat. Do you have an area in your hotel where we could eat? I'll give you a menu ahead of time. Steak, chicken. Whatever Charles eats, everybody eats." He said, "I never met a guy like you." I felt I had him now, so I said, "If you need extra waiters, I'll pay for them." He said, "No, if I take care of you, I'll take care of you the whole way." Then he said, "What time do you want to eat?" I said, "Twice a day. Breakfast at nine-thirty. Dinner at five-thirty." He said, "No hanging out in the lobby." I said, "I give you my word. After we eat, we're out."

Now I'm set. We've got a place to sleep and a place to eat. We've got a place to train even though I'm still hoping to find a better place than the roller rink. The next day I go down to the train station to meet Charles, who didn't like to fly. We put everybody in my car and in a couple of cabs and drive out to our rooms.

The owner and his wife are there to meet us. When they saw everybody getting out of the cabs, they realized I was the only white guy. The owner called me aside and said, "You don't tell me Negro." I said, "This is Ezzard Charles, the former heavyweight champion of the world. What are you worried about?" He said, "No music. No dancing. No girls." I said, "Ezzard Charles is a boxer. He goes to bed at nine o'clock. He gets up early to run. During the day we go to the gymnasium to train. When he comes back, he stays in his room and reads. Don't worry. When we leave here, you will thank me." At least I eased the owner and his wife.

When we went to train in the roller rink the next day, I told

Ezzard, "This is the best place we could find. You've got to be patient. Some of your pals have to help put up the ring and take it down every day. But you don't have to worry about that. When you're through working, go back to where we're staying. I'll meet you back there."

After a couple days of putting up the ring and taking it down, I was walking along the street in Ogden, talking to myself, when I bump into a guy I knew in New York who was stationed at a nearby Air Force base. We talked for a couple of minutes about why I was out there, then I mentioned, "Do you know if there's a good gymnasium around here?" He said, "We've got a brand-new boxing gym at the base." I said, "I bet you guys don't have much entertainment up there." He said, "Very little." I said, "I'd like to bring Ezzard Charles out there to work out." He said, "C'mon up right now."

Everything in the gym was brand-new. I went in to talk to the colonel, and when I told him how I'd love to have Ezzard Charles work out there, I thought he was going to kiss me.

I went back to tell Charles, and I said, "Snooks," that was his nickname but I don't know why or how, I said, "Snooks, when you get through sparring, I want you to invite one of the soldiers to come up and spar with you. But Snooks, if you lay a glove so much as this on the guy, the bottle is going to fly across the ring at you." We went there every day, and it was great. He just played around with the soldiers who came up to spar with him. All the soldiers loved him. Even the generals came in and thanked him.

The night of the fight in Ogden, it was in a rodeo arena. The promoter had to put chairs on the dirt at ringside. He didn't have enough chairs, so the Air Force generals had a truck loaded with extra chairs from the base. The generals sat with their wives in the first row. Jack Dempsey was the referee, the only voting official. I made sure to introduce Jack to all the generals.

Just before the fight started, I told Jack, "I was the one who wanted you to referee this fight. I figured you would do a good job. Don't do anything to hurt me." It went ten rounds. All the newspapermen thought Charles won decisively but Jack scored the fight seven rounds even, two for Layne, one for Charles. When Jack walked out of the ring, I told him, "I'm terribly disappointed." Jack just kept walking. Many of his early fights were in Salt Lake City. He even had a couple in Ogden. And the guy

Charles fought, Rex Layne, was from Utah, so maybe Jack had to do somebody out there a favor. Charles never complained. He was very close-mouthed. He knew I was his friend. I never even told him the trouble I had getting the rooms, getting a place to eat. Those were the incidents, aside from training a fighter, that most people don't realize went on.

Most people also don't realize what a great boxer Ezzard Charles was. The word "great" is misused. When a man is great in his field, this is a God-given gift. Nobody can make another man great. Charles was naturally great. The only difference between him and Ray Robinson was, Robinson was a great puncher. But when Charles was a middleweight, I don't know if Robinson could've beaten him.

The first time I realized Charles was a great boxer was in 1942 when he fought Charley Burley in Pittsburgh twice in five weeks. You must understand that Charley Burley was the best fighter I ever saw who not only never won a title but never got any glory. In those days, if you were a good black fighter, nobody wanted to fight you. To get fights, Burley fought anybody who'd fight him. He didn't care if the other guy weighed 180 pounds. He'd say, "What the weighing-in about?" One time I was kidding around with Ray Robinson and I said, "Charley's one of the best fighters in the world, Ray—why don't you give him a shot?" Ray looked at me and said, "I thought you was my friend." He knew how good Burley was.

But when Charles fought Burley the first time, Burley was a three-to-one favorite. I think Charles won eight of the ten rounds. Nobody could believe it. In the rematch Burley was still a three-to-one favorite but Charles got the decision again. That's how great a fighter Charles was.

Charles was never given due credit for his ability. Nobody even talks about him anymore. Don't forget that as the heavyweight champion, Charles lived in the shadow of Joe Louis just like Larry Holmes later lived in the shadow of Muhammad Ali. Around the time that Charles was champion, Rocky Marciano was coming along and Ray Robinson was still fighting. When Charles was younger, he did a lot of his boxing in Cincinnati, where he grew up, and in Pittsburgh. He didn't show in New York until later. He had to overcome a lot within himself. He had a strong inferiority complex. If he met a black beggar on the street, he'd give him some money and stop to talk to him. But if he met a white beggar, he'd give him some money but that would be it. This inferiority complex was ingrained in his soul since he was a kid. After his mother left Lawrenceville, Georgia, to get a better job, he was raised by his grandmother and his great-grandmother, who once had been slaves. That lives with you.

Knowing him, I never asked him many questions. As his trainer, my conversations were always just a few words. I'd say, "I think you ought to take a day off." He'd look at me and say, "How am I going to get in shape?" I'd say, "I think you ought to take a day off so that you'll be able to get in shape."

Looking back now, it's easy to see that Ezzard was in the early stages of the illness that eventually killed him. Multiple sclerosis. But at the time I just thought he was getting older. He wasn't able to do the things he had always done. He'd get tired. His coordination wasn't there. But he had tremendous courage. He proved that in his two fights with Marciano, who was a helluva fighter, a helluva puncher. But the first time I saw Marciano he looked like just an out-and-out catcher. I used to get up to Boston a lot. The promoter there, Sam Silverman, asked me to go to Providence with him one night.

"You're going to see a fight like you never saw in your life," Sam said. "There's a kid I want you to see. His name is Marciano."

That night I saw two kids murdering one another, and Sam said, "Whattya think?" I said, "Well, you put two bums in there, you're always going to have a fight. They're both looking to knock each other's brains out." But Sam said, "There's something about this guy, he can punch." I said, "He hit the other guy twenty times on the chin and never even budged him." Sam said, "Yeah, but do you know how many times he got hit on the chin?" I said, "Then it was a perfect fight. If I were you, I'd put that match in every week. You'd sell out."

The first time I knew Marciano had something was when I went to Providence in 1949 and saw him box Ted Lowry ten rounds. I knew Lowry could box. I watched Marciano get the decision on aggressiveness, but I knew right then and there that this guy had something. I saw a marked improvement from the first time. The improvement was the left jab. When I saw that, I thought, well, this guy is learning. Charlie Goldman, a great trainer who always wore a black derby even in the gym, had been working with him and teaching him that jab.

Marciano had more than twenty-five fights in Providence, and when I went back there the next year to see him box Lowry again, he gave Lowry a licking and I said to Sam Silverman, "You have developed a helluva fighter."

When I was promoting *The Saturday Night Fights* for ABC television, Sam and I developed a lot of fighters in the New England area. I couldn't operate in New York. Jim Norris and his entourage, the International Boxing Club, was operating in New York, so I had to go to all the other places. One Saturday afternoon in 1953 I was talking to another trainer, Willie Ketchum, outside the Boston Garden when I got hit on the head from behind.

I don't know who hit me or what I got hit with. Some of the cops there were friends of mine. They knew me. I used to give 'em tickets to the fights. One of 'em told me, "You tell us who did it, there'll be a funeral. Just tell us who." I said, "If I knew, I would tell you."

But I learned a long time ago, what would I gain? Supposing I knew who did it and supposing I would want to see him go to jail. Could I get up in the morning and go out on the road with my fighter? Could I do all the things I wanted to do? I had enough experience in my early years when I had to fight to exist. My father was a great teacher, a very smart guy. He was in the candy-nuts-and-fruit business in Terre Haute, Indiana, and he tried to do the same thing in New York and he couldn't make it. I mean, we were poor. But he always told me, "Watch your step and never try to get even. Because you never get even." So what I learned early in life held me in good stead when I got hit in the head.

I was persona non grata with Jim Norris just like I'd been with Mike Jacobs. I never had anything to do with either of them. If I trained a fighter and they were interested in a fighter, it was none of my business. The manager was the one I did business with.

They couldn't control me. They learned that right away. I was never in their company. I might bump into them now and then, but I never went to places they went. Jacobs did exactly what Norris did later. Jacobs controlled boxing. He controlled the New York State Athletic Commission, but I never hung around Jacobs Beach much. That's what they called the sidewalk on the corner of Broadway and Forty-ninth Street where the Brill Building was, where Jacobs's office was. If he had a fight and I wanted a ticket, I'd ask for a ticket and the young lady who handed 'em out would give it to me. That's all. I had no business dealings with them in no shape or form. I dealt with managers. I wouldn't deal with a fighter unless I knew who his manager was.

After I got hit on the head, I stayed in boxing for another year. I tried to promote on my own in the same areas where I promoted on television, but I couldn't make it financially. I had just been married to Steve, and I was saying to myself, I'm getting sick and tired of this, I think I'll move into another field. One night I was having dinner in Toots Shor's with Harry Kessler and he offered me a job with his company, Meonite casting materials. We made all the castings for Mack trucks.

Steve and I would go to the Garden to see the fights, but I never thought about getting back into boxing until Carlos Eleta called me. We had been friends from the forties. He sent me fighters. I looked after them and booked them in four-round bouts, six-round bouts. I never took any money from them. Whatever they earned was just enough for them to live on. But when Carlos called me in 1972, he wanted me to come down to Panama to work with Alfonso [Peppermint] Frazier, who was challenging an Argentine, Nicolino Loche, for the junior welterweight title.

On the phone Carlos told me, "I'm promoting the show here in Panama City and I have to guarantee Loche a hundred thousand dollars. That's a lot of money. But if I feel Frazier can win the title, it'll be worth it. You're the only man who can help me." I thought, one fight, why not?

When I got there, I knew that in order for me to tell Frazier what to do I had to know what Loche could do. Loche was training in secret at night. But the guy who drove Loche, his name was Chiclet, he was driving me during the day. I asked him how I could get in to see Loche, and he said, "Dress like a Panamanian." You should've seen me. I put dark glasses on and wore a Panama hat. At the door they weren't letting anybody in, but Chiclet told them, "He's my friend" and they let me in. Loche had a style that reminded me of Johnny Dundee, the featherweight champion in the twenties who had over three hundred fights. Loche would feint you and keep backing up until he got near the ropes. Then he had an uncanny ability to twist you into the ropes. He'd take you by surprise. By the time you realized where you were, he'd bang the hell out of you.

I'm watching Loche do this, and as I'm watching, there's a guy walking up and down staring at me. I know he's staring but I'm watching the fighter.

After Loche finishes, the guy came over to me and said, "You Panamanian?" I said, "No." He said, "Where you from?" I said, "New York." He said, "What are you doing in Panama?" I said, "I'm here on vacation." He said, "You come to Panama on vacation!" as if I must be crazy. Finally the guy said, "I know you. Stillman's Gym." He was a newspaperman from the Argentine who had seen me in Stillman's. Then he said, "You going to work with Frazer?" I said, "I don't know." He said, "Why don't you know?" I said, "Because nobody asked me."

That night I talked to Frazer, who spoke English well. He had lived in Brooklyn for a couple of years. He was a good boxer but not a trickster. I showed him what Loche was going to do, then I said, "The minute he starts backing up like that, don't follow him. Just stand there and look at him. Just stand there. Don't do anything. Just watch him go back."

The night of the fight, the place is mobbed. There must've been twenty thousand people there. Carlos Eleta is in the dressing room with us and he's listening to me tell Frazer, "Remember now, when he starts to back up, just stand there and look at him and wave at him." When the fight began, sure enough, Loche started to back up but Frazer just stood there and waved his glove. When he did that, those twenty thousand lunatics let loose. You never heard screaming and hollering like that in all your life. Frazer won the fight right then and there. The other guy couldn't fight anymore.

When I was down there, Carlos kept saying he wanted me to work with this kid named Roberto Duran, but I told him, "I'm interested in Frazer now, I can't be interested in Duran." But later I went back to work with Duran, who was getting ready to challenge Ken Buchanan for the lightweight title.

I had seen Duran the year before. I was walking on Central Park West and I bumped into Joey Leonard, Benny Leonard's brother. Joey said, "There's a guy fighting in the Garden who's one of the best boxers I ever looked at. His name's Ken Buchanan and he's another Benny Valgar." Benny Valgar was the first boxer who made me realize it's brain over brawn, the first boxer I ever saw who could feint another man out of position. I said, "Nobody's another Benny Valgar." But if Joey liked Buchanan that much, I figured I'd go see him. Buchanan had won the world lightweight title from Ismael Laguna of Panama the year before, and now he was defending the title against Laguna. When I saw Buchanan I saw a good boxer, a British boxer from Scotland, but I didn't see any Benny Valgar. I didn't see any mental energy. I didn't see a lot of things that the average guy wouldn't be looking for, but Buchanan was very good. On the same card was this kid from Panama, Roberto Duran, fighting Benny Huertas, a good club fighter.

Duran knocked Huertas out in the first round. But the strange thing was, when he came out of the ring, he came over to where Steve and I were sitting and shook hands with us. I'd never seen him before in my life. I figured Carlos Eleta had put him up to it, but Carlos didn't even know Steve and I were there.

So when I went to Panama to work with Duran, I knew Duran was good, but I wanted to find out how good. I took Freddie Brown, a trainer I'd worked with for a long time. I told Freddie, "Don't try to tell this guy how much you know. Let's leave him alone and find out how much he knows." Immediately we could see that this kid had a tremendous amount of natural ability. The next time he fought in the Garden, he won the lightweight title from Buchanan. Freddie and I never had to tell Duran how to fight or what to do. He knew how to fight. He knew what to do. If he looked at the corner, the only thing I had to do was pretend to jab. I knew once he was using his jab, he would have no trouble.

Even more important, Duran knew how to think. When you talk about great fighters, always remember there was a guy by the name of Roberto Duran. He never was given the opportunity to really display his wares because at his peak, he was overshadowed by Muhammad Ali.

I used to tell everybody around Duran, "Don't you dare tell him what to do. Leave him alone. He knows what to do." Freddie Brown tried to shadowbox with him, but I told Freddie, "Just condition him. See that he's in shape." Duran had an ass on him and you had to get his legs in shape. Walking and roadwork. He was not a good eater. You had to put a leash on him. Food, women. Wherever he went, women threw themselves at him.

When Duran took the world welterweight title from Sugar Ray Leonard in a fifteen-round decision in Montreal in 1980, he probably would've knocked Leonard out if it hadn't been for all the confusion leading up to that fight. The Monday before, we had to go to the hospital for his physical exam. When he got back to the gym, Duran was working when I get a phone call. I got on and a voice said, "We are sorry to tell you that Duran cannot fight Friday night." I said, "What?" He said, "Duran has a heart condition." I said, "You mean to tell me Duran has a heart condition? He doesn't even have a heart."

I was trying to be funny, but this was no laughing matter. Somehow a heart problem had showed up in Duran's physical. Duran had to be examined again the next morning. I called Carlos Eleta at our hotel and told him what happened, then Carlos called General Omar Torrijos.

Torrijos put Panama's finest heart specialist on an Army plane that got him to Montreal late that night. The next morning Duran was cleared to fight, but he had been in the hospital for three hours. I didn't know if he would be able to fight an ordinary guy, much less Sugar Ray Leonard. When the exam was over, I told Freddie Brown to take Duran back to the hotel.

"Put him right to bed," I told Freddie. "Right to bed. No place else. Give him some toast and tea and let him sleep all he wants."

Duran didn't work out that Tuesday, then Wednesday he did a little roadwork and we brought him into the gym to fool around. Thursday he did some roadwork. Friday night, the night of the fight, we kept telling him to take his time. He was ready to go, but we tried to hold him back. If we had let him go and he hadn't knocked the guy out, he would've gone to pieces. This way, if we kept him on a steady pace and didn't waste his energy, we knew he could last. I kept telling him, "Good, good. Box, box." That's all he had to hear. You didn't have to tell Duran to use his left hand. All he wanted to know was that he was all right. He went ahead and won the fight.

In the *no más* fight in New Orleans five months later, Duran's excuse for turning away from Leonard in the eighth round was that he had overeaten after the weigh-in. That was nonsense.

I just think Duran couldn't accept Leonard's clowning, that Leonard got his goat and he couldn't handle it. That was the worst experience of my life. Back in the hotel that night my phone kept ringing. I had a call from a guy I knew in New York who said, "I've known you for many, many years. I never thought you'd get mixed up in a fix." Between rounds I kept telling Duran, "If you crowd him, you can keep him from going through all these motions." That's what Duran had done in Montreal, and I kept reminding him, "Remember Montreal. Shove him. Push him." Duran was in good shape. He had trained well. If anybody told me that Duran would quit, if I had a gun I would've shot the guy who told me that. Duran would fight a cageful of lions. If you told him another fighter would make him quit, he'd get a gun and kill you.

I've never talked to Duran about why he quit. Never asked him for an explanation. I know him well enough to let bygones be bygones. I learned a long time ago that speech is silver, that silence is golden. The secret of being a trainer is to know and understand the individual you're working with. Know when to say something. Know when to be quiet.

I never worked with Duran again. When he finally fought Leonard for the third time in 1989, I thought he would be more aggressive, but he tried to outbox Leonard, who was in there just to shadowbox and grab whatever he could financially. But the blame doesn't go to Leonard, it goes to Duran for trying to outbox him. The blame also goes to Duran's corner. Those people in his corner were strangers. They didn't know what they were doing. They were just there for a payday.

Outdoors in Las Vegas on a cold December night, Duran's corner let him come out first and stand around in the ring for ten minutes waiting for Leonard to come out. They should've told Leonard, "When you go out, we'll go out." Leonard used all the tricks and got away with them. Leonard's corner even had a blanket over his shoulders.

Duran wanted me to work with him when he fought Wilfredo Benitez early in 1982 for the junior middleweight title. But I was helping Larry Holmes get ready to defend the heavyweight title against Gerry Cooney, the most racially promoted fight I ever remember. I always had great respect for Mills Lane as a referee, but the night of that fight Mills became an Irishman. Larry got hit low about eight times, and when he came back to the corner after the twelfth round I had some words for him.

"You're backing away from this guy," I told him. "You're letting this guy take the lead from you. Are you going to let this bum take the title from you? Go out there and be the boss."

Larry knocked him out in the next round. I never had to tell Larry how to fight. From the time I started working with him in 1979 when he got up from a knockdown to knock out Earnie

Shavers I just told him, "Be the boss. Be the boss." People still don't realize how good Larry Holmes was, because he lived in the shadow of Muhammad Ali, but let me tell you something. He taught Ali how to jab. Ali was one of the best fighters I ever saw. I'm not underrating him. But I don't care how good you are, you can always learn something, and Larry Holmes taught him how to jab.

Don King kept Larry around as one of Ali's sparring partners instead of booking him for fights. Larry was a suppressed fighter for several years. I would have liked to have seen Larry in there with Ali when Ali was at his best. But when I tell that to people, they say, "I thought you knew something about boxing." And I say, "I may not know something about boxing, but I may know something about boxers."

Larry Holmes was never given the sense of pride and confidence and a feeling of belonging that a fighter needs. I kept telling him, "You're one of the best heavyweight boxers I ever saw. Jack Sharkey was the best heavyweight boxer I ever saw, and I compare you with him. You've got what most of these bums don't have. You have a left hand." I don't care where you go, you'll never see a better fight than Larry had with Ken Norton in 1978 for the WBC heavyweight title. Larry won it with his jab and his heart.

But coming after Ali like he did, Larry always felt nobody respected him. In the short time I was around him, I always told him, "When you're finished boxing, people are going to realize what a great fighter you really are."

I think most people were just starting to realize what a great fighter Larry was when he made the mistake of insulting Rocky Marciano's memory. After he lost the title to Michael Spinks in their first fight in 1985, he took the microphone in the interview area and talked about how "I'm thirty-five fighting young men and he was twenty-five fighting old men. To be technical, Rocky Marciano couldn't carry my jockstrap." I'll never understand why Larry said that. I always found him to be one of the nicest men I ever met. But you have to remember that here's a guy that felt he had enough ability to beat anybody and was never given a chance for a long time. In those years the best he could say was that he was a sparring partner. Why? Because he was being used and he had no other way to overcome it.

After all my years in boxing, nothing has changed. If you're a trainer, you're only as good as the fighter you work with. It's the same now as it was then. Yes, I worked with this fighter and that fighter. I helped him. I rubbed him. I reprimanded him. But he knew how to fight. When he gets in the ring, I can't fight for him. And if he can't fight, God help him.

Yes, the trainer of yesterday knew boxing, he knew when his fighter made a mistake. But when I started in boxing, I learned one thing from Dai Dollings, who told me, "If you want to be a good trainer, you must know what your fighter can do. But you also must know the faults and the assets of your fighter's opponent." You can't just go out there and tell your fighter to fight. But if you can tell him, "This guy drops his left hand after he jabs," then you're telling him what to do. Those are the things you had to know. You had to make a study of it. Years ago there were no videotapes, no television. You were lucky if you were able to make a telephone call. Sometimes you had to find out in the first round. If we had time, there wasn't a four-round bout to the main event that we didn't stand in the back and watch every fighter perform.

As a teenager, I lived in Manhattan, 106th Street between Second and Third Avenues, right next to St. Cecilia's grammar school, the only Jewish family in strictly an Italian neighborhood. The street guys had a peculiar way of expressing themselves. Me and my brother Solomon were always a Jew this or a Jew that.

One of those wise guys would say, "You Jews ain't got any guts. You won't fight." Now I had to. If I got killed, I had to. One thing you had to do was make the other guys respect you. Then I went to the Union Settlement House and boxed there, and finally I hung around Grupp's Gym asking Dai Dollings a million questions. Dai was a Welshman from Cardiff who lived down on Fifteenth Street, but the gym was on 116th Street, five miles away, a hundred blocks. Dai was so cheap, he would walk both ways. Rain, hail, snow, it made no difference. I, like a fool, I was so interested in asking him questions, I'd walk down to his house with him. And since I didn't have the nickel to come back uptown, I'd walk all the way back to my house.

Dai Dollings had trained marathon runners in Wales, then he got tied up with Ted [Kid] Lewis, the English boxer who came over here and won the world welterweight title in 1915 from Jack Britton. Ted [Kid] Lewis—his real name was Gershon Mendeloff—introduced the mouthpiece. He had crooked teeth, and when he got hit, his upper lip always got cut. Somebody in a London dental clinic made a rubber gum shield to put in his mouth.

Ted had four or five gum shields, so Dai Dollings, he made me the keeper of the gum shields. I'd guard them as if they were all the assets I had in the world. In the dressing room before his workout he would fit one in his mouth, look in the mirror, feel it to make sure it was just right, then he'd ask me, "Do you have the others?" After a while I was putting his bathrobe on, cutting his bandages off.

Over their careers, Ted [Kid] Lewis and Jack Britton fought twenty times, from New York to New Orleans, from Boston to Toronto. Between them they ruled the welterweight division for seven years. Finally, when Britton was the champ, they're matched in Madison Square Garden in 1921—the last time they fought, as it turned out.

Ted's manager was Jimmy Johnston. Jack Britton's manager was Dumb Dan Morgan. But if Dumb Dan was dumb, if you had managers like that around today, you would see boxing. Now they're in the center of the ring. In the corner Dai Dollings told me to go out there and listen to what they say. Just as the referee is giving the instructions, Dan Morgan points to the mouthpiece and says, "That man has a foreign substance in his mouth and he must take it out." Jimmy Johnston started to scream. Jimmy said, "After nineteen fights, you dirty rotten s.o.b." Dan must've seen it before in those nineteen previous fights, but Britton was defending the title and Dan wanted every advantage. I thought Jimmy and Dan were going to have a fight right there. But they went over to the chief inspector, Walter Hooke, who ruled that a mouthpiece was a foreign substance. Ted had to take it out. Britton won a unanimous fifteen-round decision.

These were the experiences that I inherited. You could see how it was done, why it was done, and how to do it. But sometimes I outsmarted myself.

Doc Bagley was another of my teachers. I watched him work the corners and swing the towel and handle a cut. He chewed tobacco. If his fighter got cut, he'd take a wad of tobacco out of his mouth and put it on the cut. I thought, if only I could do that. One night he sent me over to Jersey City to work with a fighter. My first time in charge of a corner. So on the way over I bought a plug of chewing tobacco. I was praying for the guy to get cut so I could put a wad of tobacco on it. But I'd never chewed tobacco before. I had to crawl under the ring to throw up. When they finally found me, I was so sick they called an ambulance. I never did see the end of that fight.

Chewing tobacco was something I learned not to do, but mostly I was learning what to do. Like knowing and understanding your fighter so that you were able to detect if he had enough work. Many times he'd ask, "How many rounds am I going today?" I'd say," Four." But after he boxed two, I'd take him out. I knew he was ready. What am I going to do? Put a show on? Have him go stale on me?

Some fighters were ready no matter what, because they had mental discipline. When Tony Zale was in the Coast Guard in Puerto Rico during World War II, if he had a night off, he wouldn't go out, he'd stay on the base and work out. Tony was a devout Catholic, nothing tempted him. He had the middleweight title before he went in service, and he wanted to keep it when he got out. His mental discipline paid off. Before he fought Rocky Graziano at Yankee Stadium in 1946, he had a bad left elbow. I had to stay up nights massaging it. This was one of the most vicious fights I've ever seen. The fifth round was just a murderous round. Graziano was winning hands down. But when Tony got back to the corner, I said, "This is the last round. Hit the guy with your best punch." Tony knocked him out with a left hook.

Their second fight, in July the next year, I'll never understand why they had it indoors in the Chicago Stadium instead of outdoors in a ballpark. With the ring lights, the temperature had to be 110 degrees. Tony was winning until the heat got him.

The third fight, in Newark's Ruppert Stadium the following year, Tony decided he would take it to him right from the start. Graziano fought back, but you could see that Tony was going to win. Tony was a clean-living guy, and it paid off.

If your fighter didn't look ready, you had to find out why. You'd ask him if he went to bed early, if he slept well. Jackie [Kid] Berg thought he was God's gift to the ladies. You had to put a ball and chain on him. When he came over here from England in 1928, his manager, Sol Gold, wanted him to box in Chicago, because Goldie had a lot of boxing friends there. Jackie fought a draw with Billy Petrolle, then they fought again and Petrolle knocked him out. Out there Goldie didn't watch him and Jackie was running loose. But once I had him, he never escaped.

Jackie won the world junior welterweight title in 1930, and later that year he was getting ready to defend it against Billy Petrolle at the Garden. Before that fight I took him home every night to St. Alban's, where I lived. He had dinner with me, we'd sit and talk, then I'd tuck him in.

Jackie was a rough, tough guy who made the other guy fight every minute of the round. Now he's in there with Billy Petrolle, the Fargo Express, a good puncher and a good fighter. They're going at it hook, line, and sinker with about a minute left in the round when Petrolle hit him with a left hook in the belly. I didn't think Jackie would be able to last the round, but he did. When the bell rang, I jumped in the ring. His nickname was Yiddle, and I said, 'Yiddle, how do you feel?" He looked at me and said, "Lovely, thank you. And you?"

Jackie won the decision. He was a sensational performer. He had almost two hundred fights. But some kids should never have one fight. And for some kids, their worst enemy is their own family. His father. His uncles. His brothers.

Any fighter that has his father or any of his relatives around him can never make it. I once had a kid, I've forgotten his name, that I was trying to teach. He was a lovely young man. I put him in there to box in the gym, and I told him, "Keep your right hand up and jab with your left. If this guy tries to jab you, catch his jab in your right hand." He went out there and instead of trying to do what I asked him to do, he was trying for a knockout.

In the dressing room later, I told him, "I'm your friend, I like you very much, but I don't want you to box anymore. If you want to do it for fun, okay, but I don't want you to come here and get your brains kicked out." He started to cry, then he went home and told his family.

Next thing I hear, his father and his brother are coming to the gym to beat me up. That didn't bother me. If anybody took a punch at me, I knew how to make him miss and counter. But now they arrive and they're screaming at me, "You're taking advantage of him. You're taking his money." I said, "What money? He hasn't earned any money." Then I told them, "You're his father and you're his brother. But I'm his friend and he should never box again. He can't make it. He's going to get hurt." They walked out calling me a Jew bastard, all that stuff. The kid went to somebody else's gym and had one fight. He got knocked out.

His father and his brother wanted him to be a fighter for them, not for himself. The worst enemy a fighter has is his family.

I've always been very proud of one thing, and I say it without any fear of contradiction. There wasn't one fighter I ever worked with that ever got hurt. At least not with me in his corner. The minute I knew that he couldn't fight anymore, he didn't fight. The night Ezzard Charles got knocked out by Marciano, I didn't work with him, because I was promoting *The Saturday Night Fights* then. But his manager, Tom Tannas, asked me to talk to him about retiring.

I got him alone and I said, "Snooks, you're going to be angry at what I tell you. I don't want you to fight anymore." He shook his head and didn't say anything. He just walked away. He fought two more years, took a year off, then fought another two years.

Ray Robinson had tremendous talent. He won the welterweight title, then he held the middleweight title a total of five times. But he was his own worst enemy. After he collapsed from the heat in the Joey Maxim fight, he retired to be a hoofer. I said to him, "You and I are friends, so let me ask you a serious question: Is this just a temporary thing or are you giving up boxing forever?" He said, "I'm going to make the theater my career." Two years later, he was back.

Robinson won the middleweight title three times in his comeback, but that's when he started to take lickings. Those fights destroyed him. Just like all those fights after the Manila fight destroyed Muhammad Ali.

Robinson was a teenager the first time I saw him. George Gainford called me one day in 1939 and said, "I want you to look at the next champion." I said, "George, you're always giving me this crap about 'the next champion' and now you're giving it to me again." He said, "Come up and look for yourself." I couldn't resist. I went up to the Salem-Crescent Gym in Harlem and all I had to do was see this kid put his hands up. Class. Class. He was still an amateur then, but if you knew boxing, you knew this kid was somebody special.

Having been around Benny Leonard, if anybody was ever close to Leonard, it was Robinson. When people ask me who's the greatest boxer, pound for pound, I ever saw, I hesitate to say either one, but Leonard's mental energy surpassed anybody else's.

Benny Leonard was a picture. He was the one fighter who I felt could name the round with anybody. He could make you do the things you didn't want to do. If you were a counterpuncher, he made you lead. If you were aggressive, he made you back up. He knew where to hit you. The solar plexus. The liver. He knew all the spots. He'd aim for those spots. If you look up his record, you will see that he always fought good fighters. If you didn't know how to fight, nobody would match you with Benny Leonard.

But you live through those years and you see what happens to some fighters and you say to yourself, who is the beneficiary of boxing? Bob Arum, Don King, the Duvas. They move in quick. They tie up every fighter they can lay their hands on. That's the business.

Years ago we had men who knew what boxing was all about. Some of them were evil. Tough times make monkeys eat red peppers. And those were tough times. Everybody was trying to grab a buck because they had families that had to eat. You had managers like Joe Woodman and George Lawrence who were con men. They were always talking about a big promotion in South America, about how they needed cable money and all that. But it was fun. Nobody got hurt. Maybe a guy got taken for a hundred bucks. But nobody really got hurt and it was fun. It's not fun now. I don't see anybody laughing in boxing anymore.

I naturally don't think boxing should be abolished, but the way boxing is today, it wouldn't make any difference. It won't be long before the television networks tire of handing out all this money. Sooner or later, the lack of talent will be even worse than it is now.

Boxing is not really boxing today. It's theater. Some kids might look good. But they don't learn their trade. They're not polished. If you take a piece of gold out of the ground, you know it's gold. But you have to clean it. You have to polish it. You have to give it a form. But there aren't many guys capable of polishing a fighter. I went to a weigh-in in Atlantic City not long ago and I couldn't believe what went on. Twenty guys are running around giving orders and none of them knew what the hell it's all about. It can't get better. Not as long as some of these fighters are being paid a million dollars or more even though they really don't know how to fight. With all due respect to the heavyweight champion, imagine him in there with Dempsey or Louis or Muhammad Ali.

I don't know whether you heard all these stories before, but the story of boxing is the story of the trainer. Because the trainer is the boss, the trainer is the pillar of hope for every fighter. It's like watching a child grow day to day. There's just something about it. I just wish I had a better power of expression.

Bill Slayton lifts Ken Norton to the WBC heavyweight title.

Bill Slayton:

"You Know I'm an Only Child"

———

Tall and muscular, Bill Slayton is a big man with a cheerful manner that hides his sadness. In 1970 his son Raymond, who worked for the Board of Education in Los Angeles, was arrested for making a disturbance while sitting on a neighbor's roof at dawn.

"Raymond came home the night before acting peculiar, back when PCP started getting popular in the drug community," he recalled. "He asked if he could borrow my flute and he was downstairs playing the flute when I went to bed. At six o'clock the next morning I hear this noise. The police are outside and they've got my son in handcuffs. He wasn't himself. He was saying things he never said. They took him down to the main jail, and when I went to see him the next day, they told me he refused the visit. When I got home I told my wife, Jackie, what the police had said, but we couldn't understand it. That afternoon a sheriff came by and told us, 'Your son hung himself in jail.' My wife was no good after that. My wife was a fun person, but she went into depression. Nine years later she died. I don't know what happened, but I know Raymond didn't hang himself."

They had five other children: Howard, Norma, Penny, Randall, and Arlia. Their grandson, Raymond, Jr., also lived with them. But until Bill Slayton began working with Ken Norton in 1974, he was a little-known Los Angeles trainer who just enjoyed being around boxing.

"When I was a kid," he was saying now, "I'd go to the gym that Mr. Bill Brown ran. Old Bill Brown, but he demanded that you call him Mr. Brown, and everybody did. Mr. Brown didn't drink, didn't smoke. Some of the guys hanging around the gym didn't like Mr. Brown because he didn't play pinochle. Mr. Brown was a straight, quiet person, so they didn't associate too much with him, but they'd always say, 'Mr. Brown is a good man, a good man.' Duke Holloway was another guy around the gym. I loved Duke's humor. Duke wore a derby. Duke smoked a cigar. Duke could've played Kingfish on *Amos 'n' Andy*. Duke would have a towel on his shoulder, another towel in his back pocket, a cigar in his mouth, and half a pint of Christian Brothers brandy in his other back pocket. One day a boy came in and said, 'Duke, what's the first thing you're going to teach me?' Duke looked at him and said, 'I think the first thing I'm gonna teach you is how to fall, because I think you're gonna do a lot of that. When you fall, I want you to have some class.' "

Bill Slayton, born on April 4, 1922, has carried on their boxing legacy. He's known for his honesty and his humor.

"Mr. Brown showed me that it paid to be a straight, quiet person," he said. "But after a workout you don't want to be talking about boxing, boxing. That's why I'm always cracking jokes. I'm telling stories. I'm keeping my fighter laughing. Duke Holloway showed me that was important too."

Once a semipro football player, Slayton grew up in Los Angeles, the son of a city maintenance worker. He later boxed in the Army while in the Pacific during World War II.

"I had a good mother with a good outlook on life," he said. "My mother always told me, 'Search yourself before you condemn somebody else and you'll never have any problems. Instead of getting mad at somebody else, maybe you were wrong. Check yourself first. And always talk nice about somebody.' What she told me has always been my golden rule. I don't go to church every Sunday, but I live within my own feelings about what's

right and what's wrong. I can sleep at night."
Not everybody in boxing has that clear a conscience.

$\mathbf{I}$'d been working with fighters off
and on in the Main Street Gym in L.A., but I wasn't making any
money. I hadn't even thought about making money. I was working in trucking as a driver and a yard foreman. I had an income.
I didn't think about boxing as an income. I just loved boxing. I
loved to teach. I had guys like Adolph Pruitt, he fought for the
title four times. But whatever money I made, I gave it right back.
I'd buy equipment for the gym, things like that. My wife, Jackie,
used to get mad at me because I'd cosign loans for guys and not
even tell her about it. Then when the guy wouldn't pay, the letters
would come to the house. Just little loans, nothing big. But one
guy never did pay and I had to come up with eight-hundred
dollars.

Back in 1970 I had worked with Chuck Leslie against Ken Norton, who got a ten-round decision. I didn't speak to Kenny, he
didn't speak to me. I thought he was an arrogant, cocky guy who
acted like he's better than you. But I learned he's a beautiful
guy.

In 1974 they were looking for a trainer for Kenny, because Eddie Futch had left him to go with Joe Frazier after Yank Durham
died. Kenny's manager, Bob Biron, told Eddie that it would be a
conflict of interest for him to train both fighters.

But when Kenny talked to me about the job, he was very sar-
castic. He said, "What do you think about lifting weights?" I said,
"Light weights are cool, but I don't believe too much in weights."
Then he started to say, "What do you think about . . ."

I said, "Hold it, Ken, we can go on with this cat-and-mouse
game forever. Just let me work with you for three weeks. If you
don't like what's happening, we'll shake hands and I'll be on my
way. You won't owe me nothin'." He said, "Fair enough."

By the time I got hired, I had only six weeks to get Kenny ready
for a heavyweight title shot against George Foreman in Caracas,

Venezuela, in March 1974. But when Kenny started training with me he didn't like the Main Street Gym because there were mostly Mexican fighters who didn't know who Ken Norton was. We had to go over to the Hoover Street Gym, which had mostly black fighters. At first no matter what I said, he doubted it. But I had patience and I learned how to reverse things on him. Make him feel it was his idea.

I'd tell him, "Man, the way you were throwing your hook today, that was beautiful." Then he'd do it more because he figured it was his idea. He didn't want to do anything you suggested, but if he thought it was his idea, he'd do it forever.

Even with only six weeks before his title shot, Kenny got into good shape. Kenny trained harder than any fighter I ever had. But when we got to Caracas, a guy named Jack Cohen who was around Ken, he had been around the bad boys in New York and he knew how a fighter could be doped. Jack didn't want Ken to eat in this place or that place. Then he took us outside Caracas to a little town where they had an aerobics gym but no ring. We had to spend a week and a half sparring on this mat. Kenny was very upset with that. Then we come into town and we had this hassle about Foreman threatening to call the fight off because of a bad leg. Everybody knew he was faking the injury.

The night of the fight, it got worse. Bob Biron told me, "They're trying to shove this referee on us." We didn't want that particular referee because George had this thing of pushing you, then hitting you. We wanted to make sure we had a referee who wouldn't let George get away with that. We ended up getting a referee that Bob agreed to. Jimmy Rondeau.

When all this was going on, Bob told me, "Don't say anything to Ken, but don't leave the hotel until I call you." Now we're waiting for Bob to call. Ken's family is waiting with us. We're still waiting there in the hotel when the undercard comes on television. We haven't even left for the arena and the early fights on the undercard are already on television. We're supposed to be in the ring at ten minutes after ten, and now it's after nine, but we're still in the hotel waiting for Bob to call. Hedgemon Lewis, who was working with me, kept telling me, "Ken is going out of his mind." I knew we couldn't wait any longer. We took off.

We had a van for Ken's family and a limo for Kenny, Hedgemon, me, and three city policemen. We told the driver we were in a hurry, so around corners he's going up on the sidewalk. We're not even there and Ken is upset.

When we finally get to the arena, we don't know where the dressing room is, but we saw Bob and he said, "I've been trying to get you guys but the phone was tied up." By now Kenny is walking stiffly. I can see disgust on his face. He's down, completely down. Joe Louis came into the dressing room and told him, "You got your chance now. Good luck to you." Kenny just sat there. Blah. He didn't look ready to me, but I'd only been with him six weeks so I didn't know how he was before other fights. Then he got in the ring and he still had that hangdog look.

As soon as Kenny got hit in the second round, I threw the towel in and I thought, well, there goes my chance to be this guy's trainer.

But when we got back to L.A., Kenny told Bob Biron, "I didn't follow Bill's battle plan. Bill told me things and I just didn't do 'em." That took me off the hook. We went up to Seattle to fight Boone Kirkman, who was Jesus Christ up there. The place was sold out, but Kenny dusts him in eight rounds. In the dressing room all the people were telling Kenny, "You're gonna be the champ. You beat the best."

I'm taking Kenny's shoes off and when I hear Kenny say, "What do you mean, the best? He wasn't shit." I hit him on the leg. "What's the matter with you?" I said. "Always praise the other guy high. If you beat him, that puts you even higher."

That's what I always liked about Joe Louis. He was low-key. Joe was my hero as a kid. He always praised the other guy, he always had a lucky night. I hate braggarts. I hate guys who are always going around talking what they're going to do. Just do it, then give the other guy praise behind it. That makes you look better.

After the Kirkman fight, Kenny had a long layoff so I told Bob Biron, "We've got to get Kenny a fight where he can really get his confidence back even if it's against a bum. You don't set nothing up but you get him somebody you know he can destroy."

I found the ideal guy, Rico Brooks. He had upset Ron Stander. I was there when he did it. He was a tough fighter but he was thirty-four, thirty-five, and he was thinking about retiring. I told him, "Rico, how would you like to make yourself thirty-five hundred dollars?" He said, "Fighting who?" I said, "Fighting Norton." He said, "Oh, man, no. I'm going to retire." I said, "Look, Rico, you do what you want to do, man, but you got a chance to make thirty-five hundred dollars."

I didn't tell Rico what to do. All I said was, "You got a chance to make some easy money before you retire, Rico, you got nothing to lose, man." He finally agreed.

We put it on in Oklahoma City in March 1975. All we wanted to do was get Kenny back on track. The night of the fight, I happened to see Rico and he told me, "I'm not going to let this big sonofabitch kick hell out of me. I ain't gonna let him do that." I said, "Rico, I'm not telling you how to fight, I just want to make sure you're here, that's all." Sure enough, Rico went out there in the first round and Ken hit him with a pretty good jab and hit him with that right hand and Rico went down. I thought, God, so quick.

Everybody jumped in the ring. Kenny was ecstatic. Nobody seemed mad about it. I was concerned about Rico, but when I went over to see him, he said, "How'd I do?" I said, "Aw, man, I thought you might be hurt." He said, "He hit me pretty good, but I could've got up." That was his last fight. He took his thirty-five hundred and went back home. He had come there all by himself. Whatever he made was clear money.

In boxing, it's known as getting an opponent. You can't say anything to fix it. But a guy can go in there on his own and he'll go so long and then he'll say to himself, aw, man, why should I take a beating? You don't tell a guy to lay down. You don't tell a guy nothing. But you get a guy as an opponent who you're expecting will lose so that your fighter will get that confidence he needs. At that time Ken Norton needed that confidence. For a fighter, a lot of it is having that confidence in yourself.

Some fighters are very cocky openly but in the back of their mind they feel insecure. To me, guys that holler are hollering out of fear.

Ali always hollered. Maybe it wasn't exactly fear, but he needed to talk himself up. Having all those other guys around him, telling him he was the Greatest all the time, and him saying, "I am, I am." First thing you know, you believe it. Some guys need that. Other guys don't need it. Kenny was the kind of guy who needed praise more than anything else. He used to get his butt kicked sparring. The only guy he beat up sparring was Eddie Jones, who once fought for the light heavyweight title. Eddie sparred with

Ali, he sparred with all of 'em, but Kenny always looked good against him. So the last guy I always put in there to spar with Kenny was Eddie Jones. That way Kenny would always come out of his workout feeling good.

Kenny always trained hard, but sometimes he wouldn't listen to what I was telling him. Sometimes he couldn't get nothing going right. So he'd turn his back on me and stand over in a neutral corner and stare out at the people at the Massacre Canyon resort where we went before big fights. When he did that, I'd tell the other sparring partners to do things I knew he had problems with. Afterwards we'd put Eddie Jones in there and then Kenny would feel pretty good after he kicked Eddie's butt but he'd still be mad at me.

When we got back to the room, I wouldn't say nothing to him. We had adjoining rooms. He'd go to his room and I'd go to mine. Pretty soon he'd come over to my room and say, "Sorry I blew up today." I'd say, "You got to watch your temper, man. Whenever you lose your composure, you forget everything you know." He'd say, "Yeah, but my jab was working good." I'd say, "Yeah, but you were getting hit with right hands." Then he'd say, "I didn't say nothing about the right hands, I said my jab was working good." I'd say, "Yeah, your jab was all right."

That's how I learned that you had to give Kenny the positive points before you bring in the negatives. I'd always praise him first. After that I could tell him all the bad things he did and he would accept them.

These are the things you have to learn about guys in order to get the most out of them. The cocky guy, you have to knock him down in front of people, you have to embarrass him in front of people. But if you did that to Kenny, he'd sulk for months.

When Kenny and I really got tight was when he fought Jerry Quarry in Madison Square Garden later that March. I had Quarry in the amateurs when he was sixteen years old. His fifth pro fight, Jerry's father and a trainer named Johnny Flores were trying to ace me out. I told them, "If you guys don't need me, I don't need you." I had never made any money with Jerry anyway. If he made five-hundred dollars in a preliminary, I made fifty, that's all. I bowed out.

Jerry had a few more fights, but then he told his dad that he didn't feel he was learning anything, that he wanted me back. His father asked me if I'd come back. I started training him for his first big fight, with Eddie Machen.

Jerry was already good enough to have Rocky Marciano thinking about buying his contract for fifty-thousand dollars, which was big money then. But when Jerry was training, I told his dad, "This kid isn't ready." In workouts he'd be winded in three rounds. His dad said, "We can't pull out." I said, "We can say his hand's hurt." They went through with it anyway. Jerry was ready to quit in the seventh round, but I told him, "Irishmen don't quit." His family came from Oklahoma. They were poor. They didn't have nothing. He'd come to the gym from that tire company he worked for. "Now you got nice clothes, Jerry," I told him. "Now you got a chance for more nice clothes. Irishmen don't quit." He made it through ten rounds but lost the decision.

One problem I had with Jerry was that he lived down in Orange County. I told his dad, "I can't go pick him up in the morning to run. I got to go to my trucking job in the morning." The guy who did pick him up, they'd almost get in a fight to get him on the trail. I told his dad, "I think a guy has to contribute something himself. If he wants to be a fighter, he's got to show some interest himself."

So they took me away from Jerry, but today he tells me, "If I'd stayed with you, I could've done this, I could've done that." He really respects me and he's really a nice guy. But I tell him, "Jerry, that's the fate of everything. Hindsight is always good. At that time you didn't have control of your life." Then when Norton was up in the Catskills training for the Quarry fight, I saw the Quarry family when we went over to Grossinger's for a press conference.

I went over and shook hands with Jerry. I gave him and his mother a big hug like I always did, because when Jerry won the Nationals she was the only one who gave me any consideration.

Kenny saw me hug them. Kenny never did like Jerry. Afterwards Kenny said to me, "What are you doing talking to him?" I said, "Hey, man, I know the guy for years. We're friends. I wasn't telling him any secrets. This is what boxing is all about. Fight tonight. Friends tomorrow."

I used to tell Kenny all the time, "You're spoiled, man." And he'd say, "You know I'm an only child." His aunts and his mother, they all spoiled him.

So after we hashed out me talking to the Quarry family, Kenny said, "I'm going to kick his ass." I said, "I want you to knock him out. That's what we're here for." He stopped Jerry in five, the best fight Kenny ever fought. Afterwards I went over to Jerry's room. The doctors had him on the table because he was busted up. He asked me, "Did I disgrace myself?" I said, "You fought like a true Irishman."

But with Kenny, you couldn't brag on nobody. If you told Kenny that somebody has a helluva left hook, he'd say, "Yeah, but you can hit him with right hands all day long." I'd say, "Ken, I didn't say that. There's a lot of mistakes a person makes, but my mother always told me, 'Always tell the good things about people. Everybody knows the bad things.' " Then he'd say, "Why don't you do that with me then?"

I knew how to get his goat. I always knew how to praise him first, then I could give him a little something negative. But you couldn't give him too much negative because if you told him anything he did wrong, to him that was a negative thought.

I'd say, "You know what you were doing there with your right hand. You ought to do that more just like you said you were going to do." Then he'd say, "Yeah, that's good." I made him think it was his idea. That type of person, you have to make them feel that they're the one who's creating this. Kenny is a Leo—his birthday is August 5. I get along with Leos very well. I'm Kenny's daughter's godfather. That's how close we are. I consider myself one of his friends. Kenny's very hard to get close to. He don't trust many people. But if you get close to him, he's a wonderful man.

After the Quarry fight, Kenny kept knocking guys out, then he fought Ali in Yankee Stadium, September 28, 1976.

People always say Kenny gave Ali three tough fights, but I thought he won all three of 'em. Not just the first one in San Diego when he broke Ali's jaw but the second one in L.A. just before I started training him and the third one in Yankee Stadium. With Kenny, fighting Ali was an ego thing. It started when Kenny fought on the Ali card in Lake Tahoe in 1972. Ali was between titles. He stopped Bob Foster in eight after Kenny stopped Henry Clark in nine. That was the night Clark got his check and went into the casino and lost every penny he just made. About three grand. But when they were training, Kenny would woof at Ali and Ali would yell, "I want you next." Ali was playing, but

Kenny was serious. And when Ali fought him in San Diego in March 1973, Kenny broke his jaw and got the decision.

Then they fought a rematch in L.A. that September. The way I got the story, Kenny was riding on cloud nine but he had Eddie Jones working with him as a sparring partner. Eddie had just become a Black Muslim, and Eddie supposedly was telling Ali everything that was going on.

Ken heard rumors that Eddie was passing things on. That Kenny was fooling with girls, that Kenny wasn't training like he should. That was before I started to train him, so I had no control over it. But no matter what fighter I'm working with, I always tell our sparring partners about loyalty. When they go to work for somebody in training camp, they've got to be loyal to him. They've got to keep his secrets. If they see he's got a hurt hand, don't tell the other camp.

With all the rumors, Ken didn't believe 'em until after the fight. Kenny once told me that when they announced Ali as the winner of a twelve-round split decision, Eddie Jones jumped higher than anybody. The next thing you know, Eddie was working in Ali's camp. Kenny eventually hired Eddie back as a sparring partner, because he always liked Eddie. But when Kenny sparred with him, he'd be punching hell out of Eddie and saying, "You told Ali all those things about me."

Before the third fight in Yankee Stadium, we trained at Grossinger's in the Catskills and Ali was over at the Concord, a few miles away.

As soon as we got there, Kenny told me, "I don't want Ali or any of his guys coming over here to bug me." Sure enough, one night all these guys came over to harass us. Ali wasn't with them, but Angelo Dundee was there, with Gene Kilroy, Lloyd Wells, and a few others. They never got in. Grossinger's had a gate at the bottom of the hill with a security guard. The guard turned 'em around. Another time, they knew Kenny was superstitious about black cats. If he was out running and he saw a black cat ahead of him, if he had to go ten miles around, he'd go around. So they sent Kenny a box with a black cat in it.

Ali also hired Dick Sadler, who had been George Foreman's trainer, to harass Kenny about losing to Foreman two years before. At a press conference Ali told Kenny, "I got Dick Sadler here and I'm going to whip your butt like George Foreman did."

I looked at Sadler and said, "You're working with Ali now—no wonder George said you put something in his coffee before he lost to Ali in Zaire." Ali turned to me and said, "Nigger, you crazy." That's exactly what he said. I knew I had hit a nerve. I later told one of Ali's people, Wali Youngblood, to tell Sadler that I was kidding. Sadler just disappeared.

As for the fight, I thought we won it. That was the best shape Kenny was ever in in his life. Between rounds he never sat on the stool and he never took a swallow of water. All I did was wash his mouthpiece out and put it in his mouth. I never even gave him a rinse.

It was cool that night. Between the early rounds Ali stood up too, but he sat down around the eighth. During training Kenny had a sore rib. Nothing serious, and we knew Ali wasn't a body puncher. Kenny never got hit hard on that rib one time. My battle plan for Ali was different than Eddie Futch's. My plan was for Kenny to use his herky-jerky style and jab off it. That confused Ali, broke his rhythm up.

I told Kenny, "Cut him off, keep going to his right. Step over on him and keep him going to his right, because he can't jab unless he's going to his left. When he's going to his right, he can't do nothing." We nullified Ali's jab.

Everybody that fought Ali's style, Larry Holmes, all of 'em, they're always jabbing. But if they have to go to their right, they're dead. Anytime I see that type of fighter, I tell my fighter to cut him off and make him go to his right. During the fight I kept telling Kenny, "Keep sticking that jab. Keep cutting him off. You're the baddest man out here." Before the fifteenth round I told him, "You got it made, man, just keep the pressure on him." Kenny kept the pressure on him. All the way. I just was so sure that we had won that fight. I think Ali was sure we'd won too. Ali was dejected in the corner. He thought he'd lost.

When the decision was announced, Kenny almost cried. In the dressing room, he was talking about being through with boxing. He wanted to beat Ali so bad.

When there's a big fight like that, Ali is always going to draw the most money. The referee and the judges knew that if Norton had the title, Norton would bring in a few million dollars. But they also knew that if Ali had the title, Ali would bring in a lot more million dollars. Ali's name was more important. I told everybody that it wasn't a fixed fight, but sometimes people realize who the "house fighter" is. Nobody told 'em, "That's my fighter over there in the red corner," but always notice the color of the padding in the corner. It's usually red or blue.

The house fighters are usually all in one corner or the other. Top Rank has 'em. Don King has 'em. Most promoters have their corners.

In L.A., the promoters don't decide the corners. You flip a disk. But most other places, if you're betting, try to figure out which is the house corner. Nine out of ten times you're going to make more money than the next guy because the blue corner or the red corner, whichever it is that night, is the house corner. But with Kenny, we were never in the house corner, because Bob Biron was always a lone wolf. Bob never stayed with one promoter. He went from here to there to wherever was the most lucrative. Bob always said, "Whoever comes up with the most money."

After the Ali fight, the next year Kenny signed to fight Duane Bobick at Madison Square Garden, because by then Eddie Futch was working with Bobick.

Kenny had a vendetta going with Eddie because Eddie had left him to work with Joe Frazier, who had retired by now. Kenny kept saying, "Eddie thinks he's smart. Eddie thinks Bobick can beat me. I'm going to show Eddie, I'm going to show him." Kenny showed him all right. First-round knockout. Then we fought Jimmy Young, knowing that the WBC was threatening to strip Ali of their title. If that happened, the winner of Norton-Young would be sanctioned as the WBC champion. Kenny won a fifteen-round decision and a few months later he was the WBC champion.

Kenny's title defense against Larry Holmes was one of the great heavyweight fights. Going into the fifteenth round, I told him, "It's close. You got to go out there and give me three good minutes." He went out there and he went as long as he could. He trained for fifteen rounds and he gave his all. It wasn't that he saved something.

I thought Kenny was winning that round for two minutes and thirty seconds, but he punched himself out. In the last thirty seconds, Larry really scored, but if it went another thirty seconds, Larry might have dropped. Every time I see a tape of that round, Kenny threw more punches and landed more punches. But the last thirty seconds Larry came on at the end to steal the judges' eye.

The next year Kenny got knocked out by Earnie Shavers in the first round, but his heart wasn't in it. He had a real bad rib and he didn't like heavy punchers. He didn't even like to train with heavy punchers. He was leery of 'em.

Before the Shavers fight, Kenny said, "This is going to be it for me." But afterwards he decided to buy a new home that cost about eight-hundred-thousand dollars. I told him, "You got the money. You got all your marbles. You don't need two more fights." He said, "Two fights, I'll make me a million dollars." Then he said, "Ain't you gonna work with me?" I said, "Kenny, you know I'll be with you, man, whatever you decide to do, because if it's not right, I'll protect you. I'll throw the goddam towel in." He fought Tex Cobb in San Antonio, he got two hundred and fifty thousand. Then he fought Gerry Cooney in the Garden for seven hundred and fifty thousand.

Kenny got caught in the first round. Cooney came out and jumped right on him, and that's something we didn't plan on. Cooney caught him cold. If he had beat Cooney, he probably would've had another fight because it's hard to turn down a couple of million bucks.

I've had other fighters. Me and Duke Durden who works for Don King were good friends for a long time. Duke always told me, "I'm going to get you a fighter, either Greg Page or Michael Dokes." I'd been around Page, who was a loudmouth kid who didn't know what was happening. I didn't know much about Dokes, who was rumored to be on drugs when he lost the WBA heavyweight title to Gerrie Coetzee, and when I started working with him, he was hard to get along with. Sarcastic, arrogant. But then he got into trouble, and his manager, Marty Cohen, told me about Mike's drug problems. But the last few years he's been clean.

It's a tough world out there. I tell all these young guys every day how easy it is to get in a bind with guys who are supposed to be your friends, but they're around you only because you got money. These guys want to keep you in that same low class they're in. They don't want you to get ahead of 'em. They want to drag you down to that same hole they're in.

Boxing has some of the most rotten people you'll ever meet. Not all of 'em, but ninety percent of the people in boxing are rotten. One day a big guy as tall as that door, a gangster-looking guy, a white guy, drove up in a Rolls-Royce and came into the gym with two Doberman pinschers. I loaned one of my young fighters six-thousand dollars to stay away from this guy, and he did. But when another of my young fighters told me he was going to go with the big guy, I said, "Then you have to get somebody else to train you." He said, "Why?" I said, "I got a good name. I'd rather have my name than money."

My intuition usually works out right. Sure enough, the big guy got in trouble and had to leave the country. I heard he went to Brazil but they brought him back. He's in jail now.

That was the great thing about Bob Biron. If it hadn't been for him and Ken Norton, I wouldn't have my gym now. My first fight with Kenny, the Foreman fight, I was on salary for six weeks, twelve-thousand dollars, then I got a three-thousand-dollar bonus. After that I got ten percent down the line. The Ali fight I got almost two hundred and fifty thousand dollars. I own three houses and my gym now. Kenny had that auto accident where he woke up in the hospital and he's getting around okay now. But if he ever went broke, I'd sell one of my houses and give him the money if he needed it. I owe everything to what Ken Norton did for me.

Between rounds, Lou Duva shapes Pernell Whitaker's strategy.

Lou Duva:

"I'm Always Fighting for My Fighters"

═══

His office was cluttered with boxing gloves, robes, a leather headgear, framed photos of Rocky Marciano, laminated plaques of newspaper articles. But when Lou Duva is on the road with his fighters, the Main Events, Inc., offices in West Paterson, New Jersey, are in good hands. His family's hands.

"My son Danny is the promoter, and his wife, Kathy, does the publicity," he was saying now. "My daughter Donna is the office manager and also handles the travel and hotels. My son Dino is the comptroller, he's a CPA. My daughter Deanne is the book-keeper, and my other daughter, Denise, used to work here."

Once a trainer and now primarily a manager, Lou Duva reigns as the patriarch of one of boxing's closest families.

"My kids spoke Italian, American, and boxing," he said. "My kids grew up reading *Ring* magazine, not comic books."

His wife, Enes, died in 1987 of multiple sclerosis after he spent six years searching for a cure at various medical centers.

"She was the backbone," he said. "We'd have parties on Thanksgiving and Christmas and she'd invite my fighters and their girlfriends. They always got gifts. They always ate. Some-times we didn't eat, but they always ate. She just loved what I was doing. She loved me, I guess, that's what it amounted to."

He met Enes in Paterson, New Jersey, where he had been born on May 28, 1922, the son of parents from Foggia, Italy, near Naples.

"I was in a minstrel show when I met Enes," he said. "I was an end man, a clown. Her sister was a singer. The first time I seen Enes, I said, 'Don't go away, I'm going to marry you.' She said, 'Are you crazy?' Sure enough, I started taking her out and I married her. She was just a skinny little girl, but every time I got out of line, she'd knock me on my ass."

In those years Lou Duva owned a trucking business. He later was a bail bondsman and a Teamsters boss.

"When people say Teamsters, right away they think the trucking business and shakedown artists," he said. "I represented hospital workers, nursing-home workers, civil-service employees. I didn't represent any private manufacturers. I mean, who the hell could I shake down? The governor of New Jersey? The mayor of a town?"

Now his only business is boxing. Over the years he has worked with thirteen champions: Evander Holyfield, Mark Breland, Pernell Whitaker, Meldrick Taylor, Joey Giardello, Johnny Bumphus, Rocky Lothridge, Livingstone Bramble, Bobby Czyz, John-John Molina, and Mike McCallum.

But as a trainer or a manager or a promoter, Lou Duva has remained what he once was and still is, a fighter. As a kid in Paterson he followed his older brother Carl to the American Gym behind a bar on West Broadway, not far from the dye house where their father worked.

"I had twenty-two pro fights. I think I lost four," he said. "I learned all the mistakes because I did everything wrong. I knew all the shortcuts. Taking a shower and telling 'em I'd worked out. Unscrewing the weights on the scale so I could knock off five pounds. So whenever a fighter tries to give me the bullshit, I know."

While stationed at Camp Hood during World War II, he was offered twenty dollars to box in a weekend smoker in Killeen, Texas.

"The guy running the smoker told me he needed somebody for a pretty good Texas fighter who was coming in that weekend," he recalled. "He gave me the bullshit about not being able to remember the guy's name, all that there stuff. I said, 'For

twenty dollars, I don't care who he is.' Then I find out it's Lew
Jenkins, who had won the world lightweight title two years earlier. As luck would have it, he got drunk and never showed up.
I boxed somebody else for ten dollars. If he had showed up, I
probably would have got knocked on my ass. But to this day I
could always say I fought Lew Jenkins."

One way or another, Lou Duva has fought just about everybody else.

$$\equiv$$

D id you know Rocky Marciano
wanted to make a comeback? Right after Ingemar Johansson
knocked out Floyd Patterson to win the heavyweight title in 1959,
Rocky had a deal where he was going to fight the Swede for a
million and a quarter. Tax-free. A lot of money in those days. I
know. I was going to train him.

That's when Cus D'Amato came up with Patterson's hidden
contract for the return bout. That ended Rocky's comeback before it even started. He was only thirty-six, he was all set to do it.
He didn't quit in 1956 because of his back. I still think to this day
that he quit because he didn't want to do business with his manager, Al Weill, any longer. Al Weill was a lousy human being. He
really used to rough up Rocky, he wouldn't do nothing for Rocky,
and when Rocky found Weill was robbing him, that turned Rocky
off. Weill was Frankie Carbo's front man, Weill and Billy Brown.

What a great guy Rocky was. We used to have more fun, Rocky
and me. Eating contests. Anyplace we could find food. Veal,
chicken, pasta, anything. He'd eat the whole menu.

We used to hang down my club in Jersey, the Italian Circle
Club in Paterson. I'd say, "Rocky, I need some help on this here
fight show. I want to bring you in as referee." He'd say, "No problem." He'd do anything for you. I'll never forget one time he was
driving back home to Brockton, Massachusetts, when we were
having a big birthday dinner in Jersey for one of our local politicians. We got tipped off that this politician's scheme to shake some
people down for money had just been uncovered. Rocky had a

phone in his car, maybe the first guy I ever knew with a phone in his car. We got him on his car phone and turned him around. That night Rocky was this politician's birthday present. Rocky had never met the guy. But we told Rocky all about him and Rocky got up and told everybody that this guy was his lifelong friend. All the people there loved it.

I still got so many of Rocky's clothes in my house. He used to keep some clothes there so he didn't have to carry a lot of luggage back and forth. He was my partner in Gladiator Arena in Totowa before the name was changed to Ice World.

They talk about Rocky being cheap and all that there stuff. He was cheap. But I seen him show up for nothing at so many church father-and-son affairs. I seen him when he was offered twenty-five hundred dollars for a guest appearance as a referee. He'd make the deal, then he'd get on the phone and call Jersey Joe Walcott or Willie Pep and tell them, "Can you take my spot?" Just to give them a payday.

The day his plane went down in Iowa in 1969, he'd just called me. He told me he'd just made three deals. One was with Andy Granatelli for STP to search for young heavyweight fighters. Another was with Lou Perini, who had owned the Milwaukee Braves and the Boston Braves before that, to start Rocky Marciano Frozen Foods; he was giving me the Jersey franchises. The third was with National Car Rental.

Rocky was so thrilled with the deal with Granatelli, who was going to subsidize us to go out and look for a white hope. We were going to get Joe Louis and Jersey Joe Walcott for show. I was going to be the actual trainer and maneuverer. And where would you go for heavyweights? To football camps.

On the phone that day, Rocky was calling me from Chicago, and he told me, "Look, I've got to go over to Iowa, then I'm going to Florida to see Barbara and then I'll fly up to Jersey and we'll get together." Maybe three hours later I was driving along in my car when it came over the radio that his plane crashed. He was a good guy. He was my friend. He was everybody's friend. You should've seen his wake. I went up there with Vic Marsillo, who would've managed him if his comeback had gone through, and Lou Monte, the singer. Mob guys from all over the country were there with their broads. We partied all night at the motel. Lou Monte sang. Guys got up and told stories. They'd laugh, then they'd cry. Then they'd laugh again, then they'd cry again. In the morning the pallbearers were all crying like babies. It's something I'll never forget.

What a fighter. The night Ezzard Charles split Rocky's nose, how he fought and won with all that blood all over him I'll never know. Rocky was so tough, so strong, so fearless. But he was smart enough to know that when he went in that ring he had to have some fear. Because if he didn't have some fear, knowing his style and all, he'd get killed in the ring.

Everybody wonders how Rocky would've done with Muhammad Ali, and we'll never know. But when they had their computer fight, Rocky was forty-four, forty-five, then, but he gave Ali a message. We were having dinner one night with Ali in New York when Rocky nudged me and said, "Ask Ali if I can still punch." I said, "Hey, champ, Rocky can't punch anymore, can he?" Ali said, "Man, you crazy?" He lifted up his shirt and showed us where his ribs were all red.

Rocky told me the story later on. Whenever people were around at the filming, Ali was always onstage trying to show Rocky up, trying to knock Rocky's toupee off. But whenever Ali did that, Rocky would dig a few punches into Ali's ribs. Ali walked out of there holding his ribs and Rocky was what, forty-four, forty-five years old?

Jersey Joe Walcott once told me that when Rocky nailed you, all of a sudden you just became numb all over. Rocky had so much heart. He told me that when he got up after being knocked down by Archie Moore in what turned out to be his last fight, he looked around and said to himself, what the hell am I doing down here? After he got up, he thought Moore was turning white, that Moore didn't believe Rocky could get up from his right hand. Rocky knocked him out in the ninth round, then retired early the next year undefeated: 49–0 with forty-three knockouts.

Like I say, Rocky was my partner. And when Evander Holyfield knocked out Buster Douglas to win the heavyweight title, did you see me jump up on the ropes in three of the four corners and point to the sky? I was pointing to Rocky. He was my partner when he was alive and he's still my partner.

I've had a lot of other champions, but Evander was different. Evander was my first heavyweight champion. You know when I fell in love with him? At the 1984 Olympics in Los Angeles after he got disqualified by the New Zealand referee and had to settle for a bronze medal. He never hollered. He never blamed the referee. What mental strength. I knew right then that he knew how to handle a crisis.

Before the Douglas fight, Steve Wynn, the owner of the Mirage, rubbed Evander the wrong way when he called him "the other guy." Evander showed who the other guy was.

In the ring before the bell for the first round, I told Evander, "You waited a long time for this. Just remember one thing: I want you to start setting the tempo right away. Don't catch his jab. Slip it, then throw your jab." After the first round, I told him, "You're boxing beautiful, but don't get lazy with your jab. Move it up to two, three jabs. Make him run." After the second round, I told him, "You're still boxing beautiful. Just slip and turn, when you get the chance, drop down and go to the belly." But then Douglas missed that uppercut and Evander hit him with as perfect a right hand as you can throw. That punch was like one of Rocky Marciano's right hands.

I knew Rocky from when he first started training at Long Pond Inn on Greenwood Lake up on the New Jersey–New York border. Vic Marsillo was my goomba. I got to know Vic at Stillman's gym back when I was driving a truck in the garment area over in New York. For me, going to Stillman's was like being an apprentice plumber or an apprentice electrician. I was learning my trade.

I used to go upstairs and watch the great trainers like Ray Arcel, Whitey Bimstein, Mannie Seamon, Chickie Ferrara, Freddie Brown, the Florio brothers, watch them handle their fighters in the three rings. Then watch the managers maneuvering on the pay phones in the back. There must've been a dozen phone booths, but no doors on the booths. That was their office. Phony calls and all that there stuff. They'd be on the phone pretending to work on a match, but it was all bullshit. Stealing phone calls. If a promoter wanted to talk to a certain manager about getting a fighter to fill in a show at the last minute, the manager who answered the phone would tell him the other manager wasn't around but he had a fighter who would fill in. The managers were always maneuvering.

Afterwards they'd all go over to the Garden cafeteria for coffee, and I'd go with them. I used to hang with these guys until I had to get back to my truck. That's how I learned. Like the job Vic

Marsillo did with Ray Robinson to get his middleweight title back. Vic conned Sid Flaherty into guaranteeing Robinson a shot at Bobo Olson's title if Robinson beat Rocky Castellani. Flaherty thought Castellani would win, but Robinson got a ten-round decision over Castellani and then knocked out Olson in two.

When you hang with guys like Vic Marsillo, Bill Daly, and Jack Kearns you learn a lot of things. Kearns was a wily old guy. He could set up things like you couldn't believe. There were a lot of things going on. Like the Joey Maxim–Irish Bob Murphy thing. He had both fighters. Murphy was a three-to-one favorite, but they're getting him loaded every night. Maxim punched the shit out of him to keep the light heavyweight title. I grew up in that atmosphere. I seen all that maneuvering. It was like poetry in motion. They ain't got managers now. Anybody that owns a restaurant or got an insurance agency and wants to be on television, he puts a tie on, buys a fighter, and he's a manager. Forget it. The television networks, the promoters, they run boxing now.

Don King, Bob Arum, they're supposed to be promoters, but those old guys would put them in their pocket. Those old guys knew what it was all about. They set up deals. They set up scores. They set up stings.

Don King, Bob Arum, they're amateurs. If you go back thirty, forty years, I would rather trust those people and their word than Don King or Bob Arum. As bad as those people were back then, their word was their bond. As bad as they were, once you made a deal, you had a deal. Would you bet on King on a deal? Would you bet on Arum on a deal? Contract or no contract, first thing you know they're throwing twelve lawyers at you. And you can't afford to fight that.

Good, bad, or indifferent, when Rocky Marciano had his restaurant on Madison Avenue in New York, he fronted it for Frankie Carbo, who owned it. Good, bad, or indifferent. In that time, sure Carbo and his people were doing things, understand, but you had some sense of honor, some sense of loyalty.

Fighters couldn't operate then like they do today. You bring 'em up, you teach 'em everything. Then they leave you. They got three lawyers, they got six accountants. Stuff like that there. In those days you had one promoter. You had some recourse. If you were the right fighter and you were with the right manager, understand, if you had the connections, you had no problem. You were more or less using them connections as a blocking back. Sure, you'd give up a piece, but so what? You'd get fights. Look at Joey Giardello. He may be a perfect example. Joey couldn't get a fight until the people behind him said, "Okay." Then he started getting anything he wanted.

Take the other side of it, take George Benton. He didn't have the connections. He was the uncrowned middleweight champion. His people down in Philadelphia didn't have the connections. He didn't want to hook up with the promoter there, Herman Taylor, so George never got a title fight.

George and I kid about it now. I screwed him out of a middleweight title fight with Dick Tiger. George was the number-one contender, but I maneuvered Joey into the title fight because I had the connections. I sat down with the right people and worked out the right deal. I never sat down with Carbo, but there were other people I sat down with. It wasn't so much giving up a piece. It was more or less a friendship thing. Whenever they wanted a fighter trained, whenever they wanted anything done, when I say done I'm talking about promoting a show or doing this or that, I always obliged. I used to go in my pockets for all the money, but I was always involved in some way with helping out, understand. I was never involved to the point where I was part of a plot.

When you promoted a show, they would say, "This is what you're getting." It was that kind of thing. No negotiations. They'd tell you what you were getting. But if I had a kid who was a good prospect, if he was my fighter then he was my fighter.

The way it is today, I've got an advantage that some fighters, some managers, and some promotional groups haven't got. The advantage I got is that my son Danny is a lawyer who knows boxing. He knows contracts. He was a labor lawyer. He knows how to negotiate. When I get sued now, he handles it. When I got sued for a million dollars by Jose Sulaiman, I thought, sonofabitch, look at that, I got twelve dollars in my pocket but I'm being sued for a million. I must be a success.

One of the great stories in boxing is when Danny promoted Michael Spinks and Dwight Qawi for the light heavyweight title in 1983 in Atlantic City. We walk in there to talk about the seating arrangement and the guy there says, "Let's take out the charts from the last big fight here." The charts were from the fight I put together when Joey Giardello took the middleweight title from

Dick Tiger in 1963. Twenty years between big fights. Twenty years between father and son. That's a helluva story.

The Giardello-Tiger fight, we did a hundred and eighty-three thousand dollars and we could've done four hundred and eighty-three thousand, but every cop, every usher, was my partner. During the undercard I looked around at all the people in the Convention Hall and I thought, this place is really loading up. I went over to the ticket windows and asked how much they had taken in and I was told, "Nobody's buying nothing." That's when one of my security guards, an Italian guy, took me aside and told me, "Lou, go downstairs and take a look." Everybody down there was parking their car, walking through the tunnels, giving the cop five dollars, and boom, they're upstairs without having to buy a ticket, then they give the usher another five dollars and they got a seat. But what the hell, we had a lot of fun that night. Especially when Joey won the title. Everybody had dumped him. He was down and out until I talked him into letting me promote his shot at the title.

Now that Joey was champ, he wanted me to get him a big-money fight right away, but I said, "Joey, the best way to do this is let me get you a bum a month. We'll go on tour. We'll pick up fifteen thousand dollars, maybe twenty thousand. We'll get guys you can knock out in two, three rounds. Just take off your clothes. Pick yourself up some easy money." He said, "Okay, that's what we'll do."

While I was lining up a couple of fights, Joey went back to his old haunts. As soon as he had some money, guys were coming out from under rocks. We were starting to argue back and forth. Finally I said, "I'm going to take one more shot at making you some money. But if you don't want to cooperate, let's call everything off." In the meantime, he gets talked into fighting Rocky Rivero, a tough sonofabitch. Not once but twice. Then he held onto the title against Rubin [Hurricane] Carter, but he turned down the best deal. I got him a hundred and twenty-five thousand dollars guaranteed, a lot of money in those days, to go to Italy to fight Nino Benvenuti, who was then the European middleweight champion. The deal was, if Benvenuti wins, we get another hundred and twenty-five thousand guaranteed for the rematch wherever we want it.

Joey stood to make a quarter of a million dollars, a lot of money in those days. And he needed the money. I also had Rocky Marciano in the middle. I worked it out so he'd be the referee in Italy, and if they robbed us, we'd have him as the referee in Jersey, where they had a one-man rule at the time. The referee in Jersey had the only scorecard. No judges. After all that, Joey turned it down. He told me, "We're going to get robbed over there," and I said, "But when they come over here, we're going to rob them." I couldn't make him understand that. Then he fought Dick Tiger back and lost the title.

Joey's still my friend. But as soon as a fighter starts to make good money, he becomes a different animal. All of a sudden, they got fourteen new guys hanging around them, fourteen advisers. They listen to those fourteen new guys instead of to the guys who's been around them from the beginning, the guys who really know what's right and wrong. My toughest job with my fighters is when I tell 'em the truth. That's when I fight with my fighters. Livingstone Bramble, when he won the WBA lightweight championship from Ray Mancini, he thought he knew everything. Nobody but nobody, I don't care who it is, nobody knows completely what boxing's all about. There's always something you should learn, always something you should do. There's always some direction you should take to improve yourself. Because if you don't, you don't improve.

Bramble thought he was a superstar, but like I kid everybody, there's only one superstar in the whole stable. Me. I'm the loudmouth. I'm the front. If a kid is an amateur, a four-round fighter, or a champion of the world, I don't give a damn. I always give the preference to the guy that has the next fight coming up.

Like when Bramble was the champion, we were starting to work with the 1984 Olympic kids like Evander Holyfield, Pernell Whitaker, Meldrick Taylor, Mark Breland, and Tyrell Biggs. Me and George Benton would set up a schedule. But if Bramble was supposed to be in the gym at one o'clock, now he's not there. Quarter after, he's still not there. So you tell another fighter to get in the ring. But all of a sudden Bramble walks in and says, "Get that guy out of the ring." I'd tell him, "No, you wait for him now." Because if you show that a champion is more important than a kid, now you've got a problem both ways. With the kid and with the champion. That's how I get my fighters to do the job. Because they know I'll break their balls. They knew I'll ride herd on them.

I've always maintained that I don't own these fighters, I work for these fighters. Just let me do my job. If I do it wrong, get rid of me. Every fighter I have, I don't just sign him to a contract. I have to make sure I can live with him. And that he can live with me. If we can't live together, how can I get the best out of him? And how can he get the best out of me?

If I think he's a rat bastard, if I think he's cheating on his training, if I think he's got a bad personal life, if I think he's on drugs, how can I really move him? At the same time, if he feels that I'm not doing right by him, if I'm not getting him the right fights, then he's got a right to ask me about it. I work twenty-four hours a day, seven days a week. I've got an organization, but everything works off what I'm doing. Don't forget I had three fighters that I really did a job on. Scott Frank, white. Bobby Czyz, white. Vinny Pazienza, white. I know how to maneuver these guys. How to market these guys. We created something, but after a while they started reading their own press clippings and thought they could fight.

I don't know of anybody else who fights for his fighters like I do. I don't mean pretending to fight, that's bullshit. I mean ready to fight. I'm always fighting for my fighters. The time I went after Roger Mayweather in Vegas in 1988 was the biggest, but only because of where it was and because it was on television. But I was fighting for my fighters when there was no big television shows.

The thing with Mayweather was, he was hitting Vinny Pazienza after the bell. He done it four times. I know Vinny's temperament. He's coming back to the corner muttering, "I'll kill this sonofabitch." I got to say in all deference to Mayweather, who I don't like, he fought the best fight of his life. Vinny was made to order for him, but he fought the best fight of his life. But he's a dirty fighter and he hit Vinny four times after the bell. Now the last round ends and the referee goes over and breaks 'em up. While he does that, I'm thinking, Vinny's going to go after him. While I'm hurrying up the stairs and through the ropes, you can look at the tape, you see Vinny swerve off and Mayweather swerve off. Just as I get there, Mayweather looks at me and says, "What are you going to do about it? I beat your man." I said, "You got to be a jerkoff. You hit him after the bell four times. The referee never done nothing about it."

As we're arguing and cursing, a 330-pound security guard grabs me. As he does that, he trips. As he trips, I go down with him. And when I go down with him, boom, he pops me in the eye. When I get up, I'm so mad I'm going after Mayweather, and now everybody grabs me. But that's the whole story.

Some people thought I threw punches at the referee Mills Lane, but Mills said, "Lou never threw a punch at me." I never even threw a punch at Mayweather, never. Cursed at him, went after him, yes, I did do that. Now the Nevada commission wants to follow it up because the television people played it up big, the newspapers played it up big. The windup is, they're going to suspend me, they're going to take my license away. But in the hearing, we slowed down the tape. They said, "Look, just apologize and we'll fine you seven hundred and fifty dollars. You're bailed out, we're bailed out." That's what we did.

Earlier that same year, Pernell Whitaker got robbed in Paris when he challenged Jose Luis Ramirez for the WBC lightweight title. I laid everything out before the fight. I told the WBC president, Jose Sulaiman, "I know I'm going to get robbed, because I won't sign for options with Don King." The guy that's the WBC supervisor for Sulaiman, he gave us a piece of paper at the weigh-in. The guy said, "You must sign this piece of paper." I said, "I'm not signing this paper." He said, "You must sign for an option." I said, "I'm not signing an option." He said, "You must sign it or there's no fight." I said, "Then there's no fight."

I knew I was going to get the business. The only judge I got a fair shake from was Harry Gibbs, who voted for Whitaker. Before they announced the decision, I got the word that we had lost. The judges from France and Brazil screwed us. I'm not just saying this. All the French newspapers had it as the biggest robbery in boxing.

To make a long story short, I accused Sulaiman of being a thief. I accused King of being a thief. Sulaiman sued me for a million dollars. That's when I knew I was a success. The windup is, my son Danny went to work on those guys. We subpoenaed all of Sulaiman's records, all of King's records. Naturally when you start doing that, they get smart and sit down and make a deal. Sulaiman dropped the suit and I put out a statement that I didn't have any "direct evidence" that he had fixed the fight.

Danny and all my kids have always been around boxing. One night I had Christy Elliott fighting Ned Allese in Elizabeth on St.

Patrick's Day. We needed about twelve thousand dollars to break even. I had about eleven thousand in. I said, "We're going to make a score on this one." When the kids asked if they could have the concessions, I said, "Sure." In those days you got a twenty-five-dollar license, you give ten percent to a charity, and you can sell beer. But the windup is, that afternoon it starts snowing like hell. Like a jerk I gave refunds. I blow about two thousand dollars. But every Irishman and Italian who showed up wound up getting drunk on beer. Because of the snow, nobody left until two in the morning. The kids made about six thousand on the concessions. The next day they took off for Florida with their six thousand and I'm two thousand in the hole. I said, "Next time, Danny, you run the fight and I'll take the concessions."

Danny really got into boxing around the time I was working for Bob Arum as a matchmaker. I didn't last too long. I didn't like the way Arum operated.

I was running a show for Arum in St. Louis in 1977, Leon Spinks against Pedro Agosto, Leon's fourth pro fight. Danny was just out of Seton Hall Law School, so I brought him out there with me. Mitt Barnes had Leon then. Mitt was the head of the Teamsters in St. Louis, and he fell in love with Danny's knowledge of boxing. Mitt said to me, "I'd like your kid to work for me." I said, "He just took the bar exam. He's got to see what happens." Mitt said, "Lawyer or no lawyer, I'd like him to work for me." Danny represented Mitt when Butch Lewis was trying to buy Leon from him. At the time the price was like a hundred and twenty-five thousand, but Butch backed off. Next thing you know, Leon beats Ali and the windup is, Butch has to pay over a million. Danny's first payday was like two hundred thousand dollars. But that's how Danny got involved. He started from scratch. Now he's one of the biggest promoters in boxing.

You always hear how big King and Arum are, but I got an advantage. Me and Danny will fight them and their lawyers. I think Danny's got an eight-one record against Arum. I think Danny's got King shut out, three-zip.

I'll never forget the time I had it out with Sugar Ray Leonard's lawyer, Mike Trainer. He was trying to downplay the role I play in boxing with my son Danny when we put on the first Hearns-Leonard fight. Trainer's telling me, "What's the big deal about this?" I said, "Let me tell you something, Mike. You never had a fighter. You don't know which is the right hand or the left hand. You're lucky you came up with one of the greatest fighters in the era. But I'd like to see you manage Livingstone Bramble, then let me see how smart you are." Trainer likes to deal with Arum now, but I ignore Arum.

I know what Arum's all about. He professes to be the overlord of boxing. He professes to be the savior of boxing. That's strictly bullshit. As far as he's concerned, you're just another face. Just another number. He hugs people and all that, but he wouldn't know whether some up-and-coming kid has personal problems, whether he's got an injury, whether he's got a bad heart, whether he shouldn't fight. He doesn't know and he doesn't care.

King's no better. King tried to steal Livingstone Bramble from me, but I let him steal Bramble for two hundred and fifty thousand dollars. Bramble had his snakes, he was a nut. We capitalized on it. We made him nuttier. But as a fighter, he was just an ordinary strong fighter. But if there was one style he could beat, it was Mancini's style, and we wound up beating him. Then he accused me of stealing fifty thousand dollars from him. He went through a couple of lawyers, he went through a couple of accountants. They all told him he was wrong, that we were giving him the right count. Everything was done with the lawyers and Danny, all that. I don't know where Bramble is. I don't know and I could care less. I'm glad King stole him. I wanted King to steal him.

Me and King just don't get along. Me and him got into it hot and heavy after Tyson knocked Tyrell Biggs out in Atlantic City. Biggs is on the stool, we're trying to revive him, when King comes over near the corner. King is cursing me and yelling, "What do you think of your fighter now?"

I yell, "You talking to me?" I'm jumping through the ropes to get at him when a state trooper grabs me, then some other troopers and the security guards hustled King out of there. I was still hot. I told the security guards, "I don't want to see Don King anywhere around the post-fight press conference." King didn't show up. He knew if he did, I'd rip his head off. It's not that I willfully look to fight for my fighters. It's just a natural thing for me. I love my fighters. If I don't love a fighter, I don't care how good he was, I don't care if he was going to be champion of the world. If I don't love him, I don't want him around. But I really love my fighters. Every punch they catch, I catch. If I could take the punches for them, I would take the punches.

What I'm trying to say is, I've gone through every facet. I don't think there's anybody in boxing that's got the situation I've got. I've got two families. My fistic family and my blood family.

That's why Tony Ayala, Jr., was absolutely my biggest disappointment. This guy was a fighter but I thought he was like my son. I found him down in San Antonio, Texas, when he was an amateur. He could knock you dead with either hand. He was a cinch to be a champion of the world. I thought we were going to make a million dollars with this kid. Hell, I thought we were going to make twenty-five million dollars. I knew his father, his mother. Mexicans are more or less related to me as an Italian. And when he got into trouble, he was living with me up there in Jersey.

I'll never forget the night. He was going out New Year's Eve with my nephew and a young state trooper. That's when he screwed up. He got sentenced to thirty-five years in Jersey for raping a thirty-year-old schoolteacher in her house. He's not even eligible for parole until 1998. That night he was drunk and all that there stuff. He'd had that trouble before in San Antonio, I found out later. I always took everybody on their word. Whatever they told me, I believed. Had I known he had a couple of problems before—but I didn't know.

The windup is, when we checked everything out, we had to pay this off, we had to pay that off. Every time Tony got in trouble in Texas, his father would send him up here. His father would give me the bullshit, the kid's not acting right and stuff like that there. But his father knew he was messing around, that he was drinking and busting up bars. His father would tell me, "He's only a kid growing up." Then after a fight he would disappear. We'd be having a party and he'd never show up. I'd ask where he was and somebody would tell me, "You know Tony, he's got a broad." I'd says, "There's broads here." The windup is, he was going out and drinking and stuff like that there.

But what a fighter. His meanness. You couldn't believe how mean he was. As mean as he was, that's how meek he was. He'd be sitting there in the house for two, three hours, wouldn't say a word. But broads turned him on. Ugly broads. He was married to a beautiful Mexican girl, but ugly broads turned him on.

Mean. In one fight, after he knocked the guy down, he spit on him. The first time he ever got knocked down, by Mario Maldonado in Syracuse, just as he got up, the bell ended the round. He came back to the corner and said, "I'm going to kill this guy. I'm going to kill him." I'm trying to calm him down. I put the mouth-piece in, he goes out. Whoom, the guy's mouthpiece went flying, I thought the other guy's head went into the third row. The guy went down in a heap. That was all. I don't think the referee counted.

Another time he's in San Antonio to fight Robbie Epps, but in the press conference Epps said something contrary to Tony's father. Tony didn't say nothing, but I knew he was mad as hell. I told him, "Tony, forget about what the guy said, just go out and fight your planned fight." But he went right after the guy. As the guy is sagging down, he pushes the referee off and keeps hitting the guy. I had to jump into the ring and wrestle him down, nail him down.

Another time, the guy he was fighting had said something about his mother. After he knocks the guy down, he started kicking him. You couldn't believe how mean this kid was in the ring. But as soon as the fight's over, you don't hear one word. You're talking about Jekyll and Hyde, you couldn't believe this kid. But what a fighter. When he got into trouble, he was 22–0 with nineteen knockouts. Not even twenty years old. He'd just signed for one point one million dollars to fight Davey Moore for the WBA junior middleweight title. Then he was going to fight Roberto Duran. What a fight that would've been. What a fight it almost was. Right there on Broadway in New York City after we came out of Gallagher's restaurant one summer night in 1982, only a few months before he got into that trouble.

When we left Gallagher's on West Fifty-second Street, I said, "Let's take a walk down Broadway." After we make the turn down Broadway, I see four or five Spanish guys in a doorway. They got a bottle. They're singing and whooping it up.

I turned to Tony and said, "That's the way to live. Those guys don't care about nothing." Then he said, "That looks like Duran over there." I said, "What would Duran be doing here?" He said, "No, no, that's Duran." I looked over and sure enough, it's Duran. He's wearing an open shirt with a belly on him. He's between fights. I said, "Hey, Roberto." He said, "Hey, Lou." But now Duran recognizes Tony and they're staring at each other. You can feel the ice cubes coming out all over the place. Duran said, "*Torito*"— that's Spanish for "little bull." They talked a little in Spanish, then Duran turned to me and said, "We fight one day. We fight one day." By now their faces were about a foot apart. Tony just said, real slow, "Yeah, we fight one day. I can't wait. I can't wait." They just stared at each other for a few seconds, then we kept walking.

You talk about *High Noon*. This was one of the greatest scenes in boxing. Right there on Broadway on a summer night. You talk about all the great fights in boxing history. Ayala-Duran would've been the greatest brawl of all times. No referee. Put 'em in a cage and let 'em fight.

Emanuel Steward, the headmaster of the Kronk Gym in Detroit.

Emanuel Steward:

"Certain Things You Can't Rush"

≡

When the door opened, the aroma of sizzling chicken sweetened the eighth-floor room in the Trump Regency Hotel overlooking the surf and the boardwalk in Atlantic City, New Jersey.

"I'm cooking Michael's dinner," Emanuel Steward explained.

Through the open door leading to the connecting room, Michael Moorer could be seen sprawled on the bed watching television. But the manager and trainer of the Kronk Center boxers in Detroit, Michigan, was hurrying in and out of his bathroom, where he had plugged in his electric pans.

"Chicken, pasta, peas and carrots," Steward was saying now. "Then a cup of grapes for dessert and bottled water."

On his arrival the day before, Steward and his assistant, Prentiss Byrd, had purchased the food at a supermarket.

"I've got a red-and-gold Rolls-Royce, big beautiful wheels and all that," he said, "But as pretty as that car is, if I go on a trip and don't have enough gas to get me where I want to go, it don't function. There's some type of fuel source that makes everybody go."

On the windowsill were several huge oranges, not far from a steamer trunk full of other fresh and canned foods.

"Unless you go to a gourmet restaurant, you can't get this kind of meal and then it's a two-hour dinner," he said. "Michael wants to eat quick and go to bed. It's no trouble. I boil the chicken. I take the broth and pour it over his pasta. It won't put on any weight but it's a good source of energy. I've learned that you've got to keep a fighter's energy level high. He can't starve himself. He just must eat the proper food with the proper portions plus certain vitamin combinations that help prevent colds."

The day of the fight, Steward prepares oatmeal for his boxer's breakfast. He also has plenty of bananas and grapes available.

"You need the bananas to maintain your potassium level under those hot lights, and grapes are the best sugar for energy," he said. "But the meal you really fight on is the one the night before the fight. And there's nothing like pure bottled water. It converts into red blood cells quickly, which carries oxygen quicker than anything else. So there's a lot more to training a fighter than just teaching a guy how to box."

Born on July 7, 1944, in Welch, West Virginia, Steward was eight years old when he received a pair of Jack Dempsey boxing gloves for Christmas.

"I loved the art of boxing," he said. "I just was so fascinated with being able to hit somebody, then make them miss."

In time, Steward moved to Detroit, developed into a national Golden Gloves champion, but spurned the 1964 Olympic Trials in order to be an electrician. He married his childhood sweetheart; he and Marie have two grown daughters, Sylvia and Sylvette.

As the Kronk Center boxing coach, Steward has produced such champions as Thomas Hearns, Mike McCallum, Dennis Andries, Milt McCrory, Hilmer Kenty, Jimmy Paul, Duane Thomas, John David Jackson, and Michael Moorer.

"At first the Kronk colors were blue and gold," Steward said with a laugh. "But then one of my boxers came home from the Marines with a red-and-gold Marine boxing robe. It had 'Marine Boxing Team' on the back, so I covered it with a big blue patch with 'Kronk Boxing Team' in gold letters. That's how we got our colors of red, blue, and gold. I didn't have no robes then. But now we do."

Now the Kronk boxers even have their own traveling chef.

===

Control of the camp. You can lose fights by not having control of the camp, complete control of everything that's going on with the fighter. Looking back, I think me not having control of the camp was a big factor in Tommy Hearns losing to Sugar Ray Leonard in 1981 and losing to Marvin Hagler in 1985.

Before the Leonard fight, we were training up in Traverse City, Michigan, at Sugar Loaf, a beautiful resort. One of my friends was recovering from a heart attack, so I invited him to stay with us. But what happened was, Tommy likes to play softball. They had a softball game one day with the sportswriters and Tommy played first base. One game, that's all right. But the next day, I'm on the phone taking care of some business deals when I see everybody jump in the van and take off. Then I see Prentiss Byrd walking to his car.

I said, "Prentiss, what's going on?" He said, "They got another softball game today." I said, "Hold it. I don't want Tommy playing softball anymore. One game was enough. We're too close to a multimillion-dollar fight. When you get there, tell Tommy he can't play."

At the softball field, Prentiss went up to Tommy and said, "Emanuel doesn't want you to play today." Tommy went, "Aw, man, I want to play." But he was ready to go along with what Prentiss told him until this friend of mine who I'd invited to camp said, "Why don't you quit messing with him? Let the boy play. He needs to be able to do something. He's got to have some say-so in his own training camp. Muhammad Ali ran his camp. Everybody else runs their camp."

That's all Tommy needed to hear. Tommy said, "Yeah, man, I'm going to play." Now all the other people are around and Prentiss said, "Let me tell you what my boss told me, that you're not playing."

Tommy said, "Well, the hell with you and your boss." Tommy had never said anything like that before. Never. And right away this friend of mine said, "That's right, Tommy, you stand up for yourself. You got to have some say-so in your camp. You got to have some fun." Before I heard about what had been said there, I'm still on the phone in my room when I hear a door slam. Boom. I go look and Tommy's back. I said, "What are you doing here?" He said, "I'm tired of this damn stuff. I can't do nothing. You and Prentiss won't let me do nothing." I said, "Look, do you realize what could happen? You've got all of your life to play softball. Forget the money involved in this fight. Just think of all the people counting on you to be ready for this fight."

Just then Prentiss was at the door. Prentiss told him, "Tommy, if you don't want us to say anything to you when you're wrong, the hell with it, I'm gone." Tommy looked up and said, "I'm sorry, man, I don't want you to go." But that set a tone.

When we got to Vegas for the fight, it was like Tommy was still thinking that he had to have some say-so in the camp. Three days before the fight, Tommy got to sparring real good. During the last round I went over to Shelly Saltman, our public-address announcer, and had him tell the crowd that this was Tommy's last day of sparring. But the next day, two days before the fight, Tommy looked at me and said, "I'm going to spar today." I said, "You're not sparring. You're ready now. If you spar today, you're going to overtrain." He said, "I'm going to spar." I said, "You're not sparring." He walked over to Shelly and said, "Tell the crowd I'm sparring today." Shelly announced, "Although the champ's manager said yesterday that was the last day of sparring, the champ is going to box six rounds today."

The day before the fight, Tommy didn't go to the gym. But about three o'clock in the afternoon I said, "Tommy, let's work out here in the room, then we'll check your weight so we know where we stand." What we wanted to do was have him put on his stuff and turn up the heat in the room, let him move around and sweat for six rounds, then we check his weight.

The weigh-in was at eight the next morning. If he was overweight after his little workout in the room, he didn't have much time to try to lose weight, because I wanted him to eat at five o'clock. I like a fighter to eat early the night before the weigh-in. If you eat late, like eight o'clock, that food is still going to be in your system. But if you eat at five o'clock, that gives you time to have a bowel movement, because the food gets a chance to work through your body.

As soon as I told Tommy that I wanted him to eat at five o'clock, he said, "I'm not going to work out now. I'm going to work out at five thirty." I said, "That's too late." But he said, "I'm going to work out at five-thirty." That's the way his attitude had gotten to be.

What happened was, I was scheduled to do an interview at five-thirty with some sportswriters. I wasn't even with Tommy when he did whatever he did. When he got through, I guess he felt he was 147 and decided not to eat anything instead of having some pasta and going for a walk to help digest it. Then that night he had his entourage of people in his suite at Caesars Palace at one end of the hall and I had a party for some of my friends in my suite at the other end of the hall.

Anyway, the next morning I'm expecting to see a big welterweight but Tommy looks like a skinny welterweight with a sunken-in face. When he got on the scale, he was 145.

For our previous few fights, the script was for Tommy to just make the 147-pound welterweight limit. He'd been 146½ for Pipino Cuevas, who he won the title from, 146½ for Louis Primera, 146 for Randy Shields, and 147 for Pablo Baez, but now he's only 145 at the weigh-in for what was the biggest fight of his career at that time. That's when I learned about the importance of nutrients. That's what happened in that fight. He didn't have enough energy. When he got hit in the sixth round, he was hurt. Tommy Hearns, who's got a good chin and never been hurt. But when he got hit this time, he didn't have nothing in his body to have resistance to the punch. In the last rounds, he was just fighting on all his moves, boxing with what little energy he had left. When he came back to the corner at the end of the twelfth round, everything was gone. The next round, the referee stopped it.

People said, "Look what Ray Leonard did—ain't that great?" But we lost that fight in our own damn camp. I fought with myself later for not fighting with him over what happened in the camp, but I learned once you you lose control of the camp, it don't work. That's why Tommy's the easiest fighter in the world to train now. He'll say, "Whatever Emanuel says." He learned his lesson. I'll ask him, "Who do you want to spar with today?" He'll say, "It's up to you. You're the boss."

The Hagler fight was not quite the same, but almost the same. Control of the camp. Control of what's going on. We got Tommy in excellent condition down in Miami, then we go out to Vegas and everything seems fine. But the day of the fight, all his buddies were flocking in from Detroit, from all over. They're all saying, "What can we do for you, champ, what can we do?" It's about four o'clock, the fight is about seven-thirty that night Vegas time. We're all sitting around when I get a call to come downstairs. Some people were asking about tickets. I'm gone for fifteen minutes. When I come back, Tommy's stretched out watching TV and one of his buddies is rubbing Tommy's legs. I yelled, "What the hell are you doing?" He said, "Tommy said his legs were tight. I was just loosening 'em up." I yelled, "All you get the hell out of here."

Prentiss had come in with me. Prentiss looked at me, I looked at Prentiss. We knew it was over. All the months of training and some guy is rubbing down Tommy's legs about three hours before the fight. Because a rubdown is what you get when you're through with a workout so your muscles will be stretched.

We weren't going to say anything to Tommy about it. Why get him all upset? But when he gets up to go get his trunks and all his stuff, when he stands up, he says, "Why are my legs so damn tired?" By the time he came in the ring, his legs were all messed up. Then he broke his hand in the very first round. But he's got so much balls, if he had his regular legs, he'd have knocked Hagler on out. When he had Hagler cut in the third round, all he had to do was dance and box and tick off the clock. But he didn't have his legs and Hagler knocked him out. That's why I say teaching a guy how you want him to box and getting him into condition, that's one thing. But you got to have control of the camp. That's why when you see me at a fight now, I'll have a nice suite in my contract but I give it away. I don't stay in it myself. I stay with the fighter.

As long as you stay with the fighter, you'd be surprised what a difference it makes. Psychologically, he feels strong. It's like having his mother around. He feels secure. If the fighter sneezes, I say, "Hold it." I go right in, get a cold tablet, mix up some honey, give it to him right now. You got control of all that. When you got too many people in your camp, that's when you got a problem. They don't know what the hell they're doing but they got to do something to justify themselves feeling important.

Tommy's second fight with Leonard, the draw in 1989, I had total control of the camp all the way through. But the day before the fight something happened that we never expected. I was downstairs walking through the casino when one of Tommy's buddies stopped me and said, "I've been trying to find you. Tommy's brother Henry killed his girlfriend back home in Tommy's house." I said, "Does Tommy know?" He said, "Not yet." I came upstairs and Tommy was in his bedroom all by himself. Sitting in his pajamas, playing solitaire. I said, "I want to talk to you." I closed the door to his room. I explained it to him, then I called his momma in and told her. She started screaming, she couldn't believe it.

I was fortunate that I told Tommy, that he didn't find out from someone else. If he had, he might've hired a private jet and gone home. You never know what people will do when something like that happens. But after I told him about what happened, I said, "There's nothing you can do that's going to change anything. I don't want to put your brother down, but it's not just your brother that's involved in all this. You've got too many people out here depending on you in this fight. You've worked too hard to get to this point. You're just going to have to put this out of your mind and do something for all these other people who came out here. Tomorrow night you've got to fight the fight of your life."

As soon as Tommy found out his mother was going home, he wanted to go with her, but I told him, "You ain't going nowhere. You're not making no calls. I'll handle it." I got his mother, his sister, and a couple of other people plane tickets out that night at eleven o'clock under fictitious names so nobody would know who was on the plane. I had the tickets delivered to me at the hotel, then I got a van to take everybody to the airport.

Those are things you got to deal with if you've got fighters. And that was hard. That was hard. Not just the idea of your brother shooting his girlfriend, but knowing that somebody in your own house got their brains blown out. I don't know if anybody else could have handled that as well as Tommy did. But after all these years together, you get a relationship going for you. Like when he was having trouble with Leonard in the fifth round and the sixth round, I just hugged him. That's all it took. He came out fighting all over again. When he was getting ready to go into the ring to spar in training camp before the first Leonard fight, he'd get all his music blasting. But before this second fight, I told him, "No music while you're sparring. I want you concentrating on what

I want you to do." He said, "Fine." Nobody played no music. That was a difference right there. It helped him put his whole career back together.

For a fighter, putting his career back together is harder than dealing with his first career. Especially going into a fight like that second Leonard fight where everyone thought Tommy was going to get knocked out. Based on his two fights in 1988, people had a right to think that.

Tommy got stopped by Iran Barkley, then he got knocked down by James Kinchen and just barely survived. He did enough boxing to win the decision fair and square, but he had no legs. He'd only been training thirty days. The first day he ran five miles, trying to cram it all in. After two weeks, he couldn't run. His legs were all sore. Then he couldn't train at all. If a young fighter is fighting every six weeks or so, that's different. Anybody who fights that often is never really out of shape. But as a fighter gets older, if he only fights two or three times a year, or once a year like Tommy did in 1989, he can't get in shape in thirty days. Before we broke up, I still ran maybe twice a week even when Tommy didn't have a fight coming up. We live in the same neighborhood, and when I got through running in the morning, sometimes I stopped by his house just to wake him up. Just to let him know that I'm running.

One morning Tommy asked me, "Why are you running again?" I said, "Because when we get to training camp, I've got to put those mitts on and get in the ring with you." I've got to be in some kind of shape. At least not too far out of shape."

That's when I said to Tommy, "Why don't you start running with me? I'll pick you up tomorrow." That's how it started. He'd run one day, take two days off. The first day we ran, his legs were sore. But then he had two days off before he ran again, then another two days off. So in a week's time he ran twice. The next week, he runs a little bit more. Finally he gets to where he's running every other day. Then every day. Doing it that way, he never has any stiffness, because it's gradual, gradual. But it takes about ten weeks to get to that stage. It's the same with your face. If you haven't been boxing, as soon as you get hit with the first few punches, your face starts swelling. But then it toughens up. Same thing with your nose. The first day or two, your nose might bleed. Then it toughens up. But it takes time. You can't come in and do it in thirty days.

One of my favorite hobbies is my vegetable garden, but I can't rush it. I know that it's going to take so many days for those seeds to grow into maturation. Ninety days, seventy-five days, whatever it says on the package. I clean my soil, put fertilizer in it, take all the weeds out, set up my sprinkler system, make sure it's in the best spot for the sun, then I put my corn out there. But if that package of seeds says it's going to take seventy-five days, it'll take seventy-five days. Once in a while maybe seventy days if you're lucky. But you know damn well it's not going to be ready in thirty days. I don't care what you do. Certain things you can't rush.

It's the same with getting a fighter in shape. And with getting a trainer in shape. Not just physically, but mentally. If a trainer works a fight every two years, he's not going to be as sharp as the guy who's in somebody's corner every few weeks or sometimes two or three times a week. It's nothing for me to work a corner in California on Monday night, be in New Orleans on Thursday night, be back in Detroit on Saturday night, then go to Atlantic City for a show the following Saturday. You worry all the time about a fighter being rusty, but a trainer can be rusty too. Maybe the rules have changed in whatever state he's working. If he doesn't know the new rules, the stuff he makes up to take care of a cut might get his fighter disqualified.

Sometimes it's just knowing how much gauze and tape you can or can't use in wrapping a fighter's hands. Different states have different rules. One time in Atlantic City, the guy the other corner sent to watch me wrap Michael Moorer's hands said, "Hold it, you can't use but one roll of gauze." I said, "No, it's a roll and a half." I've got an advantage over guys who don't know those things because I'm working all the time.

I'm also thinking all the time about what I can use to motivate my fighters, something that they're sensitive to. Like with Dennis Andries, he's really crazy about his two little sons. I once told him, "If you don't want to work hard for your two little boys, if you don't want to take them on a nice vacation . . ." That got him going.

Rodney Trausel's daddy idolized his older brother Benny. If you walked into their house, his daddy would say, "Look at Benny's trophies, look at what Benny did." Rodney was just as good a little fighter as Benny, but the father didn't pay Rodney no attention. Everything was Benny, Benny, Benny. So what happens. Here we are in the 1977 National AAU Junior Olympic championships, the welterweight final. Here's little Rodney, who weighed 144 pounds, fighting Bobby Czyz, who had three straight knockouts. Bobby Czyz was guaranteed to win it. The first round, Rodney almost got stopped, but he got through it. In the corner I told him, "Look, your brother Benny has never won a national championship, but if you win this fight, you'll be the national champion. When you get home your daddy is going to have to be bragging about you instead of Benny because your picture is going to be in all the papers as the national champion." He leaped up. The very next round, down went Bobby Czyz twice and Rodney went on to win the National Junior Olympic championship.

I could've told Rodney to double up on the jab, turn the left hook, the right hand's got to go over. All that wouldn't have meant nothing. But when you start dealing with psychological things, they wake up.

In boxing everybody talks about styles, but when you start studying styles, you learn that it's not just styles. You learn that some fighters win not only on talent but on dedication. One night at a dinner in Massachusetts for Rocky Marciano, I spoke about how I always admired Marciano. For a little guy who wasn't much bigger than I am, I'm five-nine, his arms stopped here. He was slow and flat-footed, uncoordinated. His skin cut easily. He didn't start fighting regularly until he was nearly twenty-five. But he went on to be the world heavyweight champion. And never lost. Just on dedication. Give me a Marciano instead of all the pretty boys.

Look at Johnny Bratton. So much talent it was unreal. But he wasted it. Lost too many fights he should've won. Never won a world title. I had a kid like that. Bernard Mays. He was a brilliant child star. His nickname was Superbad. He's still a year or so younger than Tommy Hearns, but he eventually fell by the wayside.

The last time Bernard was going to a fight, they stopped him at the airport. Wouldn't let him get on the plane. He was too drunk. He's a diabetic now. He can't drink. He just sits at home in his mother's house. He's a real likable kid. Perfectly polite. What talent he had. But when you train a kid at twelve or thirteen or fourteen, no matter how much talent he has, you can't tell if he's going to be a star because there are so many tests out there that he's got to pass. It's like mines in a minefield. How many guys are going to get by all the mines? One guy goes to a party, gets the taste of alcohol, he can't get away. Another guy, a drug pusher gets him. Some guys, as soon as they're successful, if somebody says, "C'mon, man, we got a big party to go to tonight," they can't turn it down, they got to go to every party. Other guys, they can't say no to girls. They're going to press conferences and everybody's looking at them and offering them things. That's another of those mines that can explode.

Another thing is having resistance to advice. The fighter hears advice from every damn person. The garbage man. The mailman. They're telling him, "Your trainer's not doing right by you." He's got to listen to everybody giving him advice. That just confuses him.

Even if a fighter's got a straight head, a fast-talker will try to go through his parents. Especially the momma. Back when Don King came to town to try to get Tommy away from me, he had his lawyers go directly to Tommy's momma, Lois. They told her, "You're not going to make no money with this man," meaning me. Then he gave her a laugh and a smile and told her, "When you came to Tommy's fights, you're supposed to have a nice suite. Did you have a nice suite? No? Well you should have the best suite in the hotel. You should have a mink coat. And when Tommy goes on a publicity tour, you should be flown on that tour with him because you're the one who made him. Without you, he wouldn't be nothing. And when you go out shopping, you should have a limousine. This man's making all this money off of you and he doesn't give you a limousine?" You listen to that long enough, you believe it.

Long before the Mirage opened in Las Vegas late in 1989, its owner, Steve Wynn, and his boxing man, Bob Halloran, were calling Tommy at Tommy's home and trying to make deals directly with him. Steve Wynn is pissed with me. He was trying to offer ten million dollars to let Tommy fight Michael Nunn, but Tommy told him, "Look, call Emanuel." When he did, I told him, "If you had called me, you could've made the fight, but the way you went around behind my back, I don't want to have nothing to do with it. I don't feel comfortable being around you. I mean, you're messing with my fighter."

If you're a trainer or a manager, you can't let anybody mess with your fighter.

Emile Griffith never entered a ring without Gil Clancy *(right)* in his corner.

Gil Clancy:

"I Wish I'd Had Cooney When He Was a Kid"

===

High above New York City's honking traffic, in a small office on the thirtieth floor of the CBS Building, Gil Clancy sat at a metal desk alongside a pair of red leather boxing gloves. Not miniature boxing gloves. Real boxing gloves.

Never far from boxing gloves, Gil Clancy is now a CBS boxing analyst. But as a trainer and manager he guided Emile Griffith to the world welterweight and middleweight titles, and Rodrigo Valdez to the middleweight title. He worked with George Foreman after that heavyweight champion had been dethroned. He worked with Ken Buchanan when he was the lightweight champion. He trained them and dozens of others his way.

"There's an order to a fighter's workout," he was saying now. "The first thing he should do is loosening-up exercises. Some stretches. I had fighters doing that long before stretching became popular. Then I'd have them shadowbox. Then box. Then shadowbox a round. Then hit the heavy bag two rounds. Then shadowbox another round. Then skip rope two or three rounds. Then hit the speed bag. Then do their calisthenics. And that's it."

Why that order?

"Lots of reasons," he said. "The stretching and the shadow-boxing in the beginning loosened them up. Then they'd box and have guys punch back at them before they got tired. If you do things in reverse order, they're no longer fresh. Then they'd hit the heavy bag to get more work in. Then the rope-skipping for the stamina and the muscle tone. Finally the calisthenics to build up whatever part of the body you want to build up."

Spoken like a teacher. And that's what Clancy, born on May 30, 1922, was before he decided to make a living in boxing.

"I was working with fighters at the Lynch Center, a Police Athletic League gym in the Bronx, a full-time job, three in the afternoon to eleven at night, three-thousand dollars a year. I was married with kids, so it was really difficult, but I would teach school from nine until three and then go to the Lynch Center from three to eleven."

How could he be both places at three o'clock?

"I used to get my principal to let me out a few minutes early, then the guys at the Lynch Center knew I came a few minutes late. Lynch Center was really where I started to develop terrific fighters. Every year I had one or more Golden Gloves champions. I had guys on my team like Floyd Patterson, Tony Anthony, Frankie Ryff, Randy Sandy, Tiger Jones."

Before that Clancy had first begun to work with boxers at a PAL gym in South Jamaica, Queens. At a dance there one night, he was assigned to make sure that everybody there signed his or her name and address on a yellow legal pad.

"All of a sudden, one of my fighters, the kid's name was Weenie Johnson, I'll never forget his name, a strong little kid, he could fight, he came running down the stairs. I said, 'You've got to sign,' He said, 'No, no.' I said, 'You've got to sign.' He's trying to run past me. Just then, ten feet away, a guy shot a gun at both of us. Ten feet away and he missed the both of us. But later on that night, if I got the story straight, Weenie shot the other guy."

He and his wife, Nancy, whom he met at a basketball dance in Rockaway, Queens, have six children: Patricia, Gil Jr., Joan, John, Kathy, and Nancy.

"We still live in the first house we bought in Malverne, Long Island," he said. "We've improved it a few times, but it's still the same house."

Sitting in his CBS office, he was still the same Gil Clancy who never let a boyhood accident deter him. When he was about three years old, a sliver of steel flew from a pneumatic drill's pounding and lodged in his left eye.

"I can see out of the side of the eye, no problem," he said. "It's never stopped me from doing anything I ever wanted to do."

=

Several months after George Foreman got licked by Muhammad Ali, I got a phone call. "This is Mr. Moore." The fat guy, Fat Moore I called him, the nasty guy who was George's hatchet man. I said, "Yes." He said, "We're interested in having you train George Foreman, and we wonder if you'd be interested." I said, "Certainly I'd be interested." So they flew me to San Francisco and I made a deal to train him. I worked with him in Marshall, Texas, and Livermore, California, but I soon found out that George had strange ways about him.

The first time I went to see George, he told me, "I'm going to chop wood, I'm going to hit the heavy bag, I'm going to be stronger than ever." I said, "George, I don't want you to chop wood, I don't want you to hit the heavy bag. Your muscles are big enough. You're strong enough. What you need is just a little more hand speed." We worked on that, but he never liked me yelling at him, which didn't bother me a bit. If I saw him doing something wrong, he was told. But he was the kind of guy who never wanted to accept any kind of challenge. Unless he was sure he was going to win, he didn't want to do it.

Even before George took a real fight with me as his trainer, I had to get him two so-called exhibitions. But they were regular fights with eight-ounce gloves. One was with Jody Ballard at the Concord up in the Catskills, the other was with Eddie Brooks in San Francisco. They didn't fool around. They were exchanging shots. He knocked Ballard out in the second round.

So now George takes a real fight in Vegas with Ron Lyle, who hit him so hard he went down on his face. Most of the time when guys go down on their face, they don't come back. I dragged him to the corner. I looked him right in the eye and I said, "Who wants this more? Do you want it or does he want it?" He said, "I want it." I said, "Then, goddamm it, go out and get it." He knocked Lyle out in the fourth round. Just a great fight. Then I had him for Joe Frazier in the Nassau Coliseum. He knocked him out in the fifth round. I had him for Scott Ledoux in Utica. He knocked him out in the third round. I had him for Dino Dennis in Hollywood, Florida. He knocked him out in the fourth round. I had him for Pedro Agosto in Pensacola. He knocked him out in the fourth round. We were getting good results, but after each fight, I could see that my influence over him was eroding.

Then we came to the fight with Jimmy Young in San Juan, March 17, 1977, St. Patrick's Day. As soon as the fight was made, I told George, "Puerto Rico is a different climate. I want you down there at least three weeks before the fight." To get used to that heat.

Don King had set up a great training camp in the El San Juan Hotel. But when George told us he didn't want to train in that hotel, his brother Roy and me had to find another place. Each day George is supposed to arrive, but each day we get a message he'll be here tomorrow. The next day the same thing. He finally gets there only eight days before the fight. By then I'd had a big fight with King, who accused me of trying to sabotage his show because I won't let George train in the hotel. I told him, "You big dumb bastard, don't you think it's better for me to have George train in the hotel? You think I want to come out here wherever the hell we are?" King naturally blamed me for whatever went wrong, not George. I was the bad guy. But after George finally got there, if I saw him doing something wrong, I told him. Just like before.

So now one of the guys in George's camp, Big John, a nice guy, comes to me and says, "George don't want you to be correcting him in workouts anymore. He don't want you giving instructions in the corner the night of the fight. Charlie Shipes will tell him what to do." In the workout that day, no matter what George did, all Charlie's saying is, "You're doing good, champ. You're doing good." The next day Duane Bonds kicked the shit out of George and all Charlie's saying is, "You're doing good, champ. You're doing good."

The day after that, I came back to the hotel and told my wife,

"This is ridiculous. Shipes is trying to teach him tricks." Charlie was a pretty good welterweight who once fought for the title, but Charlie needed tricks. George Foreman needed tricks like he needed seven holes in his head. All that George ever had to do was punch. But I told my wife, "I've put in nearly two years with this guy, I'm going to stay and get paid." I was very aware of getting paid because of what happened before the Frazier fight in the Nassau Coliseum.

Around midnight the night before that fight, Fat Moore called me at home and said, "Gil, you know your contract with George, well, George says he's not going to pay you because this fight is right by your house here on Long Island and you didn't have to come out to California." I said, "What?" He said, "George says you can take it or leave it." I said, "You tell George good luck in the fight tomorrow night because I'm not going to be there." Bang, I hung up the phone. My wife said, "What was that all about?" I said, "Damn expensive phone call." I think I was supposed to get thirty thousand dollars for that fight. But at eight o'clock the next morning Moore called again. He said, "I guess there must have been some kind of misunderstanding. George would like you to be at the weigh-in." I said, "If I go to the weigh-in and if I'm in the corner tonight, I expect George to pay me." He said, "George will pay you. George wants you there."

But whoever it was, Fat Moore or George himself, one of them had tested me about getting paid. So when I was told not to correct George in his workouts and not to give him instructions in the corner in the Jimmy Young fight, I decided I'd just stick around to make sure I got paid.

Now we all go to the Roberto Clemente Coliseum the night of the fight. Hot like you can't believe. But the first thing George does in his dressing room is have Charlie Shipes tape up all the vents and all the doors. George thought somebody was going to pump in poison gas. Now there's no oxygen in that room. None. I was dying. Every once in a while I'd open the door, look around the hall like somebody was out there, and yell, "What was it you wanted?" Anything to bring a little air into that dressing room. Over in the other dressing room, as hot as it was, Jimmy Young had been down there three weeks. He was much more used to that heat than George was.

When they ring the bell, George goes out, grabs Jimmy Young, and pushes him down. Everybody boos. George does it again, everybody boos again, but Charlie Shipes turned to me and said, "You see those tricks?" I said, "Yeah, I see those tricks." Everybody's still booing. George was trying to show me, in my opinion, that Charlie taught him how to box.

I'm watching this shit go on round after round. Finally, after the sixth round, I elbowed Charlie out of the way and told George, "Listen, you big dumb bastard, just push this guy against the ropes and hit him in the body with your right hand. You can't miss him there. Then hit him with a left hook and let's get out of here." That's what he did, and he damn near knocked Jimmy Young out. But by the end of the round George was so exhausted from expending the energy in that heat with no air, that was it. For the rest of the fight, he was lucky to get through the twelve rounds. Then the decision went against him.

Back in the dressing room, we're standing around. Me, Shipes, his brother Roy, Fat Moore, a couple of other people. George goes in to take a shower in a little cubicle, almost like going to the john. Now he comes out of the shower and he's ranting and raving. He's yelling, "There's water all around me. There's water all around me. I see God. I see God." He's nude, but he's trying to run out the door into the hall. I hit him with my shoulder in the belly, then the other guys and I grab him and we stretched him out flat on the rubbing table. We're holding him down. But now I knew what happened, because he's vomiting brown stuff.

Only three weeks before, I had a fighter named Robbie Givens who had vomited brown stuff. Heat prostration. So when I saw George vomit brown stuff, I told everybody, "He's got heat prostration. Let's cool him down and get him to the hospital."

To this day, George thinks he saw God that night and that God told him not to fight anymore. He didn't fight again until his comeback in 1987, ten years later. But during all his ranting and raving in the dressing room that night in San Juan, he kept looking at me and saying, "Gil, you're specially blessed, you're specially blessed." He'd told me that before. Whenever my daughter Kathy came to training camp, George would tell me, "You're specially blessed to have a daughter like that." The next day, when my wife and I went to see him in the hospital, he had a silly grin on his face but he wouldn't concede that he was out of his head with heat prostration. He still talked about seeing God and that God told him not to fight anymore.

After that, I didn't talk to George until just before his comeback. He called me and said, "I'm thinking of boxing again." I said, "I'll tell you what, George, I'll be willing to come down to Texas and look at you. But if I tell you that you shouldn't fight anymore, you're going to have to pay attention." He said, "I'll call you." But by the time he called me, he'd already had a couple of fights. I told him, "Bob Arum has a deal with ESPN, he can put you on whenever you want to be put on. It's a solid promotion. Why don't you talk to Arum?" So he made a deal with Arum and fought in Vegas a few times.

When he stopped Dwight Muhammad Qawi in Vegas, I interviewed him in the ring. I said, "George, you're going to have to fight a guy in the Top Ten to get the people to believe in you." He said, "If I do that, you're going to have to come back and train me." I said, "George, all I can tell you is, you're going to have to fight somebody in the Top Ten."

The next day Arum calls me and tells me he's meeting with George to discuss his next opponent and would I stop by the Top Rank office. I said, "Bob, I'm a TV announcer, I don't belong in that office at all." He said, "Well, I'd just like you to come." I said, "Well, it's on my way to the airport." As soon as I got there, I told them, "I'm just a friend of the court. Bob, I'm not interested in what you do, and George, I'm not interested in what you do. I'll just sit here and listen."

Right away Arum got on George's case and said, "George, you're going to have to get somebody to train you. Maybe Gil would want to train you." I said, "Listen, I'm not interested in training fighters anymore, but what I'll do, George, when I come to the gym to see you before a fight I'm working on television, if you ask me what I think, I'll tell you what I think. I'd do the same thing for your opponent if he asked me. That's all I can do to help you. I'm not interested in training you."

Arum put on a couple of videotapes of guys who had been knocked out by Michael Dokes and asked George if he'd fight either one of them next. George told him, "I'll let you know." I found out later that George told Arum that both of those guys were too tough. So Arum, in his inimitable fashion, told George where to go.

That was the end of my relationship with George in his comeback. But he's smart. He's a schemer. I kept telling him, hell, everybody kept telling him, that he had to fight somebody in the

Top Ten to get people to believe in him. Little did I think then that I'd wind up training Gerry Cooney against him in Atlantic City early in 1990. When I told George I wasn't interested in training fighters anymore, I meant it. But then Tom Mara, a Long Island construction guy, asked me if I would train Gerry in a comeback fight with Foreman. When I told Tom I wasn't sure if I wanted to do it, Gerry asked me himself.

We went to Caesars Brookdale in the Poconos and worked hard. I honestly thought Gerry would win. He got into excellent condition. He listened. He was moving, boxing. Just like I wanted him to. I thought he'd be too fast for George and then when he got George into the late rounds, he'd stop him.

The first round, Gerry dominated it just like we planned. He was boxing, moving. When he came back to the corner, I told him, "You had a good round. Just relax. Keep boxing. Keep moving." But when the bell rang, instead of boxing and moving, he stood still. He suddenly had reverted to what he always tried to do in the past. Knock the other guy out. As soon as he stood still, George nailed him. And once George got him in trouble, George didn't miss a punch. Second-round knockout.

George has proved that he's smarter than all of us. Just fighting Cooney, he made a million dollars. He stood to make a few more million.

I just wish I had been able to train Gerry Cooney when he was a kid coming up. I definitely think he would've been the heavyweight champion. I also think he would not have had a lot of his other problems. Booze and all the other things. I think he was driven to all that. He could punch and he was so big. Ken Norton was the body beautiful, but when he got knocked out by Cooney, he looked like a midget. Cooney's problem was, everybody around him was too scary. His trainer, Victor Vallee, was scary. His comanagers, Mike Jones and Dennis Rappaport, were scary. If they were talking about future opponents for Cooney, if Victor Vallee told Jones and Rappaport, "Four fights ago, I saw this guy hit somebody with a good right hand," that was the end of that guy. They just wanted guys who weren't supposed to be able to fight at all.

When I was the Madison Square Garden matchmaker, I wanted to put Cooney in with Marvin Stinson, a Philadelphia heavyweight who wasn't much better than a sparring partner. Vallee killed that.

Vallee, Jones, and Rappaport absolutely ruined Cooney by turning down so many opponents. They convinced him that he couldn't fight. That he had to fight bums.

Believe me, there's a grapevine in the gym. One of Cooney's sparring partners had to tell him, "Hey, did you hear that Marvin Stinson thought he was going to fight you, but your managers wouldn't take him?" After you listen to that about ten times, you say to yourself, "If they think Marvin Stinson is too tough for me, maybe I can't fight."

I just know I could've done something with Cooney if I'd had him from the beginning, the way I had Emile Griffith from the day Howie Albert brought him over to me at the Parks Department gym on West Twenty-eighth Street. Emile was up from the Virgin Islands, working at Howie's hat factory, pushing carts through the traffic on the streets of New York's garment district. Howard entered Emile in the 1957 Golden Gloves without telling him. When the notice came in the mail for Emile to report for his Golden Gloves physical, he brought it to Howie and yelled, "What's all this about? I'm not a fighter." But he had such a good body, Howie convinced him to come over to the gym and let me look at him.

The day they showed up, I told Howie, "I usually work with a kid for a full year before I enter him in the Golden Gloves, but let me start him and see." We started him the same way we started everybody else. Left foot forward. Right foot back. Elbows in. But the most important thing was balance. Once you get their feet under them, once you get a foundation under them, then you teach them how to throw punches. Emile progressed so quickly that when the Golden Gloves were about to start, he knew how to hold his hands up, move around, and throw a good stiff jab. When he got to the finals and lost a close decision, I knew I had a fighter.

The next year Emile won the New York Golden Gloves, the Eastern Golden Gloves, and the National Golden Gloves. He was very industrious and studious. He didn't make the same mistake twice. When he turned pro, he won nineteen of his first twenty-one fights, losing only to Randy Sandy and Denny Moyer. That's when Teddy Brenner, the Garden matchmaker, called me and said, "I want to make Griffith with Florentino Fernandez."

Now if Florentino Fernandez hit a bull or a horse or an ox, he'd knock him out. I think he had twenty-five straight knockouts. I said, "Teddy, who needs Florentino Fernandez, the way he can punch? Remember how Billy Arnold got ruined by Rocky Graziano? With a puncher you always take a chance. But let me look at the films." I looked at the films, then I sat down with Emile and said, "This fight is mind over matter. This guy can punch, but every punch he throws is a little bit wide. Now, your natural tendency is to pull back, dance away, and dance around. But no, you can't do that. Every time this guy makes a move, you've got to step inside. Then move in behind your jab with combinations."

I went to see Teddy and told him, "We're thinking about the fight." He said, "I'll tell you what. If you beat Fernandez, you don't have to fight Luis Rodriguez next. If you win, you can fight Benny [Kid] Paret for the welterweight title." I said, "We'll take it."

I think Fernandez really hit Emile only once in the whole fight. Emile just did a job on him. Busted him all up. Back in the dressing room, Teddy Brenner comes running in and says, "Now you got to fight Luis Rodriguez," just the opposite of what he'd promised. At the time Luis was 35–0 with ten knockouts. Toughest guy in the world to fight. Durable, always moving. He would throw those fast little flurries that would catch the judges' eye. Tough to outpoint him. But Emile did. Then he fought Benny Paret in Miami Beach for the title. During the twelfth round Emile was going through the motions, so when he came back to the corner I said, "You can't miss this guy with a left hook. Now, goddamm it, go out and throw that left hook." Just as I said it, I slapped him in the face. Hard. He went out and hit Paret with a left hook and knocked him out with one punch in the thirteenth round. One left hook. Emile was the welterweight champion of the world.

The rematch in the Garden, that was a tough one. Emile had Paret on the deck. I thought Emile won it and most of the newspapermen thought he won it. But they gave it to Paret, a split decision.

Now we had to get the title back. So before the third fight I was really on Emile's case. I kept telling him, "You can't let Paret win a round this time. You're a better fighter than he is. Anytime you're inside with this guy, you've got to punch until he either falls or grabs you or the referee stops you. You can't stand there to admire your work no matter what. You've got to keep punching." Then at the weigh-in Paret insulted him. Paret used the word *maricón,* Spanish for "fag." Before the weigh-in Emile told me, "If he calls me anything, I'm going to hit him right there." I said, "Dummy, you don't throw a punch unless you get paid for it. You don't hit anybody." So when Paret called him *maricón,* Emile didn't throw a punch, but he didn't like it. Even so I've always thought that what happened at the weigh-in had absolutely nothing to do with what happened in the Garden that night.

Near the end of the sixth round Paret got off a perfect punch that damn near flattened Emile, but in the corner I could see that he was clear-eyed. I said, "He's going to be looking to knock you out, so he's going to be wide open. Just throw nice short straight punches." From then on Emile took him apart. Knocked him out in the twelfth round. If you remember, Paret unfortunately collapsed and died a few days later.

Everybody blamed the referee, Ruby Goldstein, for not stopping Emile from throwing punches. The fact is, Emile hit him with seventeen punches in five seconds. We counted them on the replay. Seventeen punches in five seconds. You can blame me for that just as much as you can blame the referee. I'm the guy that told Emile to keep punching no matter what. Another thing, Ruby Goldstein didn't have a chance to step in. All these Latin fighters, Benny used to do it, they'd go on the ropes, they'd cover up and let you throw some punches, then they'd flurry out. If Ruby had stepped in and stopped the fight, the Latin fans would've torn the Garden apart. They would've said Benny was only playing possum. So it was an unfortunate set of circumstances. And unfortunately Benny died.

Handling the death was very very difficult. Emile and I both got a lot of threats, a lot of bad mail calling Emile an ape, that kind of stuff. We had bodyguards for a couple of weeks. But we also got a lot of great positive letters.

We got a letter from a truck driver who had killed somebody in an accident, but he told us he still had to continue to be a truck driver. We got a letter from a surgeon who said he'd lost patients on the operating table, but he was gifted as a surgeon and Emile was gifted as a boxer so Emile certainly should continue his profession. We got a letter from a priest. But all the time Emile was seriously thinking about not fighting anymore. After he decided to keep fighting, I knew I couldn't put him in an over-the-weight fight. He wouldn't have done anything. But he loved his title. He loved being the champion. So I made him put his title on the line against Ralph Dupas in Vegas. I knew he'd train hard. Whenever he trained in Vegas, I'd tell him not to go out in the sun, to stay in the shade. I could be out on the deck of the pool but if he wanted to talk to me, he wouldn't even put his foot in the sun. That's how disciplined he was. So with his title on the line, I knew he'd train hard. I knew he'd perform. And he did. He won a unanimous fifteen-round decision. But even in that fight, you could see a little change in him. Unless the other guy hit him, Emile would just control the other guy. If the other guy got fresh, then he would put the other guy back in his place.

From then on, Emile was always like that. Sometimes the bell would ring and the other guy would come across the ring and hit Emile with a real good punch. In the corner I'd say to Howie, "Good." If the other guy hit him with a real good punch, you could actually almost see Emile's hair stand on end. Then he would be the Emile Griffith of old for a little while until the other guy behaved himself.

The next year, 1962, Emile lost the title to Luis Rodriguez in Dodger Stadium, a unanimous fifteen-round decision. But after he got the title back from Rodriguez in the Garden, we went to Pittsburgh for a nontitle fight with Rubin [Hurricane] Carter, a middleweight who could really punch. I told Emile, "This guy is very dangerous for three or four rounds, then he tightens up. He's a little muscle-bound. Just box him for the first three or four rounds. Then you'll be able to do what you want with him." But he'd met Rocky Graziano, who told him, "You can knock this guy out." In the first round Carter hit him high on the head and down he went. He got up and was walking toward Carter when the referee stopped it. I was just as happy. What's the sense of letting a guy take shots at you?

Emile learned from that. He didn't make that mistake again. Then in 1966 he went after Dick Tiger's middleweight title. I had been telling Emile in the gym, "You can handle Tiger inside. You punch better. You punch quicker." After he gets the decision, with the crowd pushing us into the dressing room, he turns to me and says, "I was stronger than him." I said, "That's what I was trying to tell you for three months." He fought Tiger again a few years later when Tiger was a light heavyweight. No contest. Emile just played with him.

The middleweight fights Emile had that people remember best were the three with Nino Benvenuti in the old Garden, Shea Stadium, and the current Garden. He lost the first and third, but he had no business losing at all. The second, he really did a job on Benvenuti. He timed Benvenuti's jab and came in behind it. The third, I had a spy in Benvenuti's camp, Tommy Bethea, one of my fighters. Tommy told me, "This guy is shot. He can't fight much at all anymore." In every workout I kept telling Emile, "The first round is the most important round of this fight. You've got to go out and show this guy you're still the boss." But the night of the fight, the opening of the new Garden in 1968, he wore his tuxedo and hung it in the dressing room. The moral of that story is, his mind was on everything but the fight.

In the first round, Emile didn't throw a punch. The whole fight, he didn't do that much. The last round, he almost knocked Benvenuti out. He had him wobbling all over. But I was so mad about Emile's poor performance that I didn't care about the decision until I read the next day that the referee, Johnny LoBianco, had the fight seven rounds each going into the last round. Then he gave the last round to Benvenuti, which was ridiculous. Emile almost flattened Benvenuti in that last round. One of the other judges had it even in rounds and gave it to Benvenuti by one point. The other guy voted for Emile. So we sent the middleweight championship of the world over to Italy on the most questionable scoring you ever saw. But me being a perfectionist, I wasn't even thinking about the decision because I knew what Emile should've done to the guy and didn't.

Three years later, after Carlos Monzon knocked out Benvenuti for the title, Emile fought Monzon in Monte Carlo. All the newspapermen had Emile winning. When the bell rang ending the last round, Mickey Duff, who was there as a spectator, jumped into the ring, went to each of the three officials, and came over to us and said, "Griffith is the champion again."

In the corner, Emile and I kept waiting and waiting for them to check the scorecards and come up with the decision. Howard Cosell was doing the fight, and he finally yelled, "Gil, what's going on?" With that long delay, I knew what was going on. When they finally came up with a decision from the officials, they came up with Monzon winning by one point.

Every fight Emile had, I was in his corner, one hundred and

twelve as a pro, about sixty as an amateur. I never missed a round. His last fight was in 1977 with Alan Minter in Monte Carlo, his third straight loss. When we got home, I asked him to come to my house. We sat by the swimming pool in the back and I said, "Emile, remember the pact we made when you started? I told you, 'When it's the end of the trail, I'll tell you it's the end.' Now I'm telling you this is the end of the trail. I'm telling you to retire." He said, "Gil, you have to end my career with me fighting a big tall southpaw like Minter? Let me fight one more regular guy." I said, "Emile, no, there's no point in it. That's it. You're finished." He said, "Okay, that's the agreement we made." He picked up the phone and called his mother, Emelda. He said, "Mom, I'm not going to fight anymore." That was it.

From the time I first knew Emile, his mother was always around. Always trying to help. I couldn't blame her for that. Emile was her son. Like before the third Paret fight, he had a little cold. Fighters always have something wrong with them before a fight. But when his mother saw him sniffle, she said, "I can't let my boy fight like this." I told her, "Your boy never looked better in his life." I had to put her out of the Concord, where we were train-ing. She called me prejudiced. To her, I was always the worst guy in the world before a fight. After the fight, I was great.

Sometimes a fighter's family can create more problems for a trainer than the fighter does. When I had Jerry Quarry, his wife, Charlie, always found a way to drive him crazy. One time we were getting ready to break camp at the Concord to go to a midtown hotel for his fight with Ken Norton when Jerry tells me, "Charlie found a big dog. She wants to bring the dog to the hotel with us, but I don't want any goddam dog around." I said, "You're one hundred percent right." I get Charlie and tell her, "You can't bring the dog into the hotel." She said, "I want the dog." I said, "Your husband's got a big fight coming up. He doesn't want any hassle about the dog." She said, "I don't care. I want the dog." I said, "Okay," but I had a plan.

I went down and talked to the doorman at the Concord, a guy I'd known for years. I gave him a sawbuck and said, "You got to do me a favor." He said, "What's that?" I said, "When we're up eating breakfast tomorrow, come to our table and say, 'Did any-body find a dog? Some people nearby called to ask if anybody found their dog.' " That's how I got Charlie to leave the dog there.

Another time, Jerry's about to fight James J. Woody in Las Vegas. Only forty-five minutes before we're ready to leave the Thunderbird for the Convention Center, Jerry calls me and says, "I'm not fighting." I said, "What the hell are you talking about?" He said, "Charlie won't go to the fight and I'm not fighting unless she goes." I go over to their room and Charlie's sitting there crying. I said, "What's the problem?" she said, "I'm not going into the same arena with Jerry's sister because of what she called me." I said, "Charlie, this is a big arena. I'll sit you right in Jerry's corner and his sister will be sitting on the other side." She's still crying and in the background I can hear Jerry saying, "If she don't go, I don't go." I told her, "You won't be anywhere near her." She finally said, "I'll go."

About a week later I had Jerry in with Tony Doyle on the Ali-Norton card in the Forum. The day of the fight, Charlie calls me and says, "That sonofabitch!" I said, "What's the matter?" She said, "He promised me he wouldn't gamble while he was in Vegas, but now guys are calling me up and telling me he's got eight thousand dollars' worth of markers." I said, "Charlie, the fight's tonight. We'll settle this problem later. Just don't say anything to Jerry until after the fight." She says, "Okay." Now we're going to the fight and Charlie's picking us up in a big limo. As soon as we get in, she stares at Jerry and says, "You sonofabitch. You promised me you wouldn't gamble and you owe eight thousand dollars' worth of markers in Vegas." He goes completely ape. Then he goes sullen. And he's going to be fighting in about two hours.

I was already worried about this fight, because everybody kept telling me how good Tony Doyle looked in the gym. And if the Vegas markers weren't enough, I'm bandaging Jerry's hands when Big Dave Centi comes in and says, "Charlie don't like her seat." Jerry gets up to put on his robe and go out into the arena to argue with the usher, but I wink at Dave and tell him, "I want you to put Charlie in the first seat in the first row right in Jerry's corner, and if there's any problem, you come back and tell me." Jerry sat down and I finished bandaging his hands. P.S.—he knocked out Tony Doyle.

Sometimes the fighter himself is the problem. No matter what you tell him, he won't do it. I had Jorge Fernandez fighting Walter Seeley, who couldn't fight much. He'd just tap you. But he was a southpaw, so he confused a lot of guys. Day after day in the gym I told Jorge, "All you have to do is walk to your left and throw left hooks underneath. Even if you don't hit him, you're going to bring him into exchanges, and he can't exchange with you. You'll walk right through him." First round, Jorge does just what I tell him. No contest. Second round, Seeley's bouncing around and Jorge's bouncing around with him. One round, Jorge would do what he was told, the next round he wouldn't. In the corner I finally grab his left hand. I shake it and I yell, "Throw this goddam left hand. Throw this goddam left hand." Jorge looks up at me with his big innocent eyes and says, "Shhhh, he'll hear you."

Most fighters listen to you. Or try to listen to you. Like my first pro fighter, Ralph [Tiger] Jones. I was a kid training fighters in South Jamaica, Queens, the 103rd Precinct Police Athletic League gym, when he walked in off the streets. When he signed up for the Golden Gloves, they gave him a list of gyms. He just happened to walk into my gym and I started to work with him.

He wasn't a kid. He must've been eighteen, nineteen years old. Very strong, durable guy. Worked hard. Took to the training routine easily. Good guy. You'll find that most fighters are good guys. If they were wise guys, I got rid of them. Wise guys can't take the discipline. In the Golden Gloves quarterfinals, Ralph fought a serviceman. The guy's name was Clarence Franks, I'll never forget it. Ralph won from here to China, but they gave it to the serviceman. Maybe because he had a lot of guys rooting for him. Ralph wanted to quit right there, but I said, "Ralph, why should you quit? You know you can fight even if the judges don't know you can fight. You got a good future." The next year he lost in the open-class Golden Gloves, but you could see he was a professional-type fighter.

Ralph wanted to turn pro. That's when I made the deal with Bobby Melnyk to manage Ralph while I trained him. Ralph never was a champion. But he beat four guys who either had been champions or would be later: Ray Robinson, Kid Gavilan, Joey Giardello, and Johnny Bratton.

As a teenager Robinson had represented the Salem-Crescent Athletic Club, which turned out great amateur teams. Robinson was ahead of Ralph by about ten years, so all of the kids at the Salem-Crescent tried to imitate Robinson's style. Robinson and Willie Pep were the best fighters I ever saw. If I had to pick one, it'd be Robinson, because he was a bigger guy. He was a boxer-puncher with beautiful ring generalship who did a lot of feinting.

But when those Salem-Crescent kids who copied Robinson tried to feint Ralph, he punched right through the feints. Fancy Dans didn't bother him that much.

When they made Ralph with Robinson in 1955, I had just moved into my house in Malverne, Long Island, same house I still live in. The house cost fifteen-five, and I was making thirty-five hundred a year as a teacher. I was wondering how I was going to pay the mortgage. But a week later when Ralph Jones beat Ray Robinson, I thought I was safe for a while. I made maybe five hundred dollars, a lot of money then.

Looking back, most people think Ralph beat Robinson in Ray's first comeback fight, but it wasn't. It was Ray's second fight back, his first on national television. When we tried to get a rematch, the New York State Athletic Commission said that Ralph wasn't a fit opponent. In those days the Boxing Managers Guild ran everything. If I'd been the manager, there would've been hell to pay, but Bobby Melnyk was the manager. He accepted it and that was that. In those days the Boxing Managers Guild was a closed corporation. Even if you developed a fighter, like I did with Ralph, you couldn't manage him. If he was your own son, you couldn't manage him. You had to turn him over to a guild member. Then you'd work out a deal and he'd give you a percentage. When I turned Ralph over to Bobby Melnyk, he gave me ten percent as the trainer.

Strangely enough, I went first to Cus D'Amato, but Cus looked at Ralph and said, "What can I do with another black fighter? Go to Bobby Melnyk." Later on I developed a kid by the name of Eddie James who was a great amateur, the outstanding fighter in the New York Golden Gloves that year. Chris Dundee was our guild representative, so Angelo Dundee, who was Chris's younger brother, and I became partners with the fighter.

Soon after that, Angelo decided to move to Miami, where Chris was living, but Angelo and I always remained close. We had a lot of fighters who fought each other, like Emile Griffith and Luis Rodriguez. In Louisville in 1961 I had Alex Miteff fighting Cassius Clay, as he was known in those days. Howie Albert and myself had gone down there before Angelo got there. One night Howie and I went to a nightclub way out in the woods. To get there, you drove on dirt roads with no lights. All of a sudden you came to a big clearing and there was the nightclub with belly dancers.

The next day, Angelo came into town. I said, "We're taking you out tonight." He said, "No, it doesn't look right for you and me to be seen together." I said, "What are you talking about? We're not doing the fighting."

We pick Angelo up in a cab. He sits in the backseat, in the middle between Howie and me. Now we're driving and driving. Angelo is wondering where the hell we're going, he's looking out the window. By now we're in the middle of the woods. No lights, no nothing. Finally he said, "Where are you guys taking me?" I said, "Angelo, I didn't want to tell you this before, but we're kidnapping you. We're taking you across the state line to Indiana. You're going to be safe, but you're not going to be able to work with Clay in the fight."

Angelo couldn't believe it. He said, "Gil, all the years we know each other, you can't do this to me." I said, "Angelo, you're going to be in a nice cottage but you're not working the fight." You never heard a guy plead like Angelo was pleading. He kept saying, "No, no, you guys can't do this to me. I'd never do anything like this to you."

Just then the cab drives into the clearing in the woods and there's the nightclub. Angelo looks at us and laughs. But up until then, he was really shaky. Now we go inside to have dinner and a few drinks, but Angelo can't drink. You give him two drinks, he's shot. When the belly dancers came out, a guy named Murat was the leader of the little band playing music for the belly dancers. After two drinks, Angelo kept jumping up and yelling, "Murat the rat, Murat the rat." Now the guy gets up to describe the different instruments in the band. For one instrument, he said something like "This is the *coglione*, the Italian word for testicle." Then he snapped one of the strings on it and the string broke. Angelo jumped up and yelled, "He broke his cogliones." We finally calmed Angelo down and got him out of there.

The next night Miteff was landing a lot of body punches. But in the sixth round, Clay threw a right hand. Something like the right hand that knocked Sonny Liston out in Lewiston four years later. It just knocked Miteff cold. One right hand. Over his career, Muhammad Ali, as he came to be known, was not recognized as a puncher. But every once in a while every fighter gets off a perfect punch. That's what Miteff got hit with, a perfect punch.

It's funny how things work out. Even when Angelo and I were

working against each other with fighters all those years, even with him living in Miami and me living in New York, we always stayed good friends. One night in 1977 when I was the Garden match-maker I went to a cocktail party at Bob Arum's apartment. Angelo was there and we started talking boxing. Barry Frank, then the president of CBS Sports, heard us talking. Finally he said, "Could you two guys do this on television?" I said, "Sure." Angelo said, "Why not?" The next day we had a deal.

Angelo only did it for a couple of years, but I'm still doing it. I love it. I like to be around the fights. I like the fighters and the people. It's the same business with no pressure. It's not whether you win or lose. Your check is going to come every week.

In his understated manner, Eddie Futch *(left)* changed Joe Frazier's style.

Eddie Futch:

"Joe Louis's Punches Could Paralyze You"

———

Eddie Futch was trying to give Marlon Starling some advice. Suddenly the reigning world welterweight champion started to walk away in a huff. But the old trainer never raised his voice.

"Marlon," he said softly, "some good fighters listened."

Marlon Starling stopped, turned, and walked back to listen to what Eddie Futch was telling him.

Through the years some great fighters listened. And learned.

Eddie Futch is a familiar name in the boxing business now. He's worked with fifteen champions, including Joe Frazier and Larry Holmes. But for four decades he always needed other jobs to pay his bills. He toiled as a hotel waiter, a road laborer, a welder, a sheetmetal worker in an aircraft plant, and a distribution clerk in the Los Angeles Post Office, where he had to know the locale of every city and town in Texas.

"I think Texas had seven hundred and thirty-seven cities and towns then," he was saying now. "Big cities like Dallas and Houston and Amarillo were the distribution points for all the little towns. But no matter how well you knew where the towns were, you had to take a test every year. You had eight minutes to throw a hundred cards in the right cubicle. You had to get ninety-five percent correct. I did it in three minutes and I always got one hundred percent."

But he didn't do it the way the post-office instructor taught him, the way everybody there was supposed to do it.

"When I was first learning the scheme," he recalled, "my instructor told me I couldn't do it that way, that I had to learn it by straight memory. But I promised him that if he let me do it my way, I'd be the first one in the group to learn the scheme. My way was how I associated things in my own mind. I was the first in the group to learn the scheme."

As a trainer, Eddie Futch also has done it his way. From working with amateurs in the Brewster Center in Detroit, where he grew up with Joe Louis, to working with all his champions, he has always been himself.

"It's just like the post office," he said. "I have my prescribed system: the use of my fighter's strengths and the exploitation of his opponent's weaknesses. Then you put the pieces together."

Trim and soft-spoken, this nine-time great-grandfather lives in Las Vegas, Nevada, now, but he puts the pieces together for boxers all over the world. Born on August 9, 1911, he was an amateur boxer and one of Detroit's most respected amateur coaches before he began tutoring champions. In addition to Frazier, Holmes, and Starling, he's worked with Ken Norton, Michael Spinks, Trevor Berbick, Bob Foster, Virgil Hill, Alexis Arguello, Marvin Campbell, Mike McCallum, Don Jordan, Hedgemon Lewis, and Antonio Gomez.

"Arguello," he said of the Nicaraguan boxer who won the featherweight, superfeatherweight, and lightweight titles, "would take a battle plan and work it as good as anybody I ever had."

In the days before Arguello defended the WBC lightweight title against Ray (Boom-Boom) Mancini in Atlantic City, New Jersey, in 1981, Futch's plan was to thwart Mancini's aggressiveness with body shots.

"I told Alexis it wouldn't look like he was winning until the eighth round, but in the first round he had to start doing the things that would make him win," Futch said. "His jab wasn't going to catch Mancini early, because Mancini was quick enough to get inside his jab. So I told him to hit Mancini in the body every chance he could until Mancini starts to slow down. When he starts to slow down, I knew Alexis's jab would start working and the fight would be over."

It was over in the fourteenth round, Mancini's first defeat. "Alexis," he said, "had the good sense to listen to me."

===

Not long before Joe Louis died, I drove over to his house in Las Vegas to sit with him. He couldn't get out of bed, he couldn't even talk. But we had a full conversation. I'd say things and he'd nod his head. I'd been there about an hour when he turned over like he wanted to go to sleep. I got up and told his nurse, "He's tired. I think I'll leave now." She looked at Joe and said, "When I was a little girl my father used to take me to see newsreels of his fights. I just thought he was wonderful. And now here I am taking care of him." So I told her how Joe always wanted me to spar with him when we were growing up in Detroit even though I only weighed about 140 pounds.

In the ring I couldn't force Joe anywhere, but I could lead him if he was following me. I would go to the corner, then I would come out and make a circle quickly before he knew what I was doing.

I would feint the left hand into the body, watching him drop his right hand to parry the punch. The minute I saw him drop his right hand, I'd throw a quick left hook to the head, because he had nothing up there. His right hand was down. As I threw that quick left hook, I'd pivot and fall into the ropes and we'd both be against the ropes. He never could figure out how I landed that left hook and he never could get me. I'd do that two, three times in a workout and always get away with it.

But one day I feinted the left hand to the body and Joe didn't do anything. That right hand didn't come down. I feinted again and nothing happened.

I stepped back and said, "What are you doing?" He said, "I'm trying to see where you throw that damn flukey left hook from." I said, "What do you care? I can't hurt you." Then he said, "I want to see how you do it. Because if you can hit me with a left hook, somebody who can hurt me with a left hook can hit me." I said, "Joe, as long as I'm working with you, you'll never know how I do it."

Telling that story to Joe's nurse, I thought Joe was asleep. But when I got to the part about us talking about the left hook, I heard Joe chuckling.

Joe Louis was a remarkable man. I knew him in our boxing club at the Brewster Center when he was an unlettered amateur. But after he turned pro, he learned so much so quickly by keeping his mouth closed and his eyes and ears open. About a year after he turned pro, he came back to the club. I was amazed at the way he handled himself. Not only in boxing but in his attitude toward people, his responses. This was a different man altogether than the one that left a year earlier. He knew the right move to make, the right thing to say. All in a year's time.

I don't know anybody who disliked Joe Louis, but he deserved that respect. He was regal in his approach to being the heavy-weight champion of the world. He was like a king.

I remember once visiting his training camp in Pompton Lakes over in New Jersey, about an hour's drive from New York City. The townspeople there naturally took to him with open arms. But some of his sparring partners liked to dance, especially one guy. Joe was afraid that this fellow and some of the others might abuse the town's hospitality. So one day Joe told 'em, "When you fellows go into town, you're going to act like gentlemen. Or you've got me to answer to."

When I first met Joe at the Brewster Center, he was a light heavyweight with only one amateur fight, and he had lost that. They had overmatched him and put him in with the state cham-pion. He used to struggle to win our club championship, that's how many good fighters we had. After I won the club lightweight championship the second time, Joe asked me to spar with him. But it was never really meaningful until a few months before he turned pro in 1934.

One day when Joe wanted me to spar, I said, "You're too big for me. I know what you're after. You want speed. Get some of those middleweights. They're fast enough for you."

Joe said, "No, I can hit them with everything, but if I hit you with anything, I know I'm sharp." I said, "Joe, I don't intend to get hit with anything. Ever." He was persistent. I never knew any-body so persistent. If you had an apple, he'd beg and beg for a bit until you gave him a bite. So he always got me in the ring to spar with him. But I told myself, if he wants me to work with him,

I've got to know when those punches are coming. I've got to know the moves he makes before he punches, because he never telegraphs anything. The left hook came out of nowhere. Bang. If he hit you with a shot, you never saw the punch coming. You just saw a light in your head. Like a camera flash going off. Bang.

By studying Joe, that's when I first found that if you look, you can see things. Studying him, I picked up some things that maybe nobody else ever thought about. Things I've used working with fighters ever since.

Joe never threw a long punch. Always short punches. So I tried to stay outside the perimeter of those short punches. Another thing was that Joe did not throw a punch unless both of his feet were on the canvas. What I did, I stayed outside the perimeter, and when I moved to my left, Joe would turn to face me, then I'd move to my right and he'd turn back. But for him to move, he'd have to pick up his feet. So now I'd time it but it had to be split-second. I'd move left, then I'd move right. When he turned back, bing, I'd step inside that perimeter, throw my punches, and get out of there.

That's what Joe couldn't understand. How I could hit him and he didn't have a chance to counter. He had the quickest counter. If you threw a left hook, he'd counter with a left hook. But I'd catch him just as he picked up that foot to move. Bing, I'd hit him, and then I'm gone.

Not that I always escaped. One time Joe hit me with a left hook that knocked me out of the ring. I went through the two top ropes. Lucky for me, the ring at the club wasn't elevated. It was on the floor. But he could hit so hard. His hands were so quick. He never threw looping punches. He always threw good punches. Straight as an arrow.

But he wasn't the only one who ever hit me. One night I was fighting in a Polish club, a parish house. I'm matched with their local favorite, a kid named Frank Pomper. I'm in the dressing room when this little blond Polish kid about eleven years old comes in and asks me who I'm fighting. I said, "Frank Pomper," and he clucked his tongue and said, "Tsk, tsk, tsk. And you look like such a nice fellow too."

I soon found out what he meant. Could that kid bang. But one thing kept me in that fight. In the first round I hit him and he went down, but he grabbed me as he was going down. We wrestled each other to the canvas, but I'd felt that good solid right hand land before he pulled me down with him. I knew it was a knockdown and he knew it was a knockdown. But he got up and started hitting me with right hands. I was on the deck twice in that round. I was on the deck twice in the second round. When the bell rang, I was getting off the floor and my trainer said, "I'm going to stop it right here. He's just too powerful for you." But I said, "If you do, I'll never speak to you again. I'm not going to quit in the corner."

When the third round started, I got to the center of the ring before he did. When you get to within a step of your opponent, if you're walking to him, you're supposed to put your left foot forward and keep your right foot behind you. You don't pick up that right foot because then you're in range.

I told myself, if this guy picks up his right foot, I'm going to nail him. Sure enough, he picked up his right foot. Bang, down he went. He got up, but his heart wasn't in it. The fight lasted another minute. I stopped him. The fight lasted seven minutes and there were seven knockdowns. I was on the floor four times.

But what I didn't know at the time was that Joe Louis had been at the fight. The next day I'm in the gym loosening up to get rid of the soreness in my body when Joe walks in. He looked at me and said, "That was a great fight last night, but do you know why you were getting hit so many times with a right hand?" I said, "Joe, if I knew why I was getting hit so many times, I wouldn't have been getting hit." He said, "You were standing too square facing your opponent. You want to put that left foot forward and give the other guy less of a target." He turned my body and showed me what he meant. I didn't get hit with a right hand for a long, long time.

But in 1936, a couple of years after Joe showed me how not to get hit with a right hand, he got hit with about sixty right hands by Max Schmeling before he got stopped in the twelfth round of their first fight.

Right after that, Joe showed up in the club with bruises and swelling from all those right hands he took. In the ring, Thurston McKinney, who originally brought Joe to the gym, was sparring with somebody, acting cute. Joe Louis, our club's great graduate, yelled, "Thurston, you better keep your left hand up or you'll get tagged." Thurston yelled back, "You ought to know." But instead of Joe getting angry, he just laughed and said, "I sure do."

The year before, after Joe knocked out Max Baer, he came back to the gym and sent word that he wanted to spar with some of his ex-teammates. Young Johnson was a light heavyweight. Red House was a middleweight. Lonnie Wright and I were lightweights. He was going to pay us ten dollars a round, which was good money in those Depression years.

I showed up on time, but when somebody asked me if I was going to work with Joe, I said, "No." Why not? "Because every one of the guys he picked used to give him trouble in the gym, one way or another. Now that he's been a pro for more than a year, he wants to measure himself. He wants to see how far he's come. I'm not going to get in there because he's going to really be hitting people." But you're going to get ten dollars a round? I said, "Yeah, and I'd spend it all for doctor's bills."

The proof was when Joe boxed with Lonnie Wright, one of the greatest physical specimens I've ever seen. He had muscles on top of muscles. But the tipoff on what Joe wanted to do that day came when he cornered Lonnie. He was setting Lonnie up. Joe's trainer, Jack Blackburn, saw that he was going to hit Lonnie and yelled, "Let him out, Chappie. Let him out." Lonnie was frantic, but Blackburn walked along the ropes and yelled, "Let him out of there." Joe finally backed off.

Red House was next. Charley [Red] House, a good, good middleweight with a reddish face who could punch, box, a mean guy. Charley was a pro when Joe was still an amateur.

Joe was handling Red with some good moves that Blackburn had taught him. But another thing that made me leery that day was that Joe had brought a couple of ladies down to the gym. They were standing in the passageway outside the gym, looking through the window. Joe turned Red around so that Red's back was to the window and then I saw Joe wink at the ladies over Red's shoulder. As soon as I saw that wink, I thought, watch out. Red started to lead, but Joe slipped that lead and hit him with a left hook in the body. Red's reddish face turned blue.

Joe's punches could paralyze you, but Red didn't realize he had been hit that hard. When he tried to take a step and counterpunch, he fell on his face. He'd been hit in the solar plexus. He rolled over and started to call Joe every name under the sun. Joe just laughed, leaned down, and picked him up.

Young Johnson, the light heavyweight, was next, but Joe hit him a shot right away and knocked him stiff. Left hand. After everybody had walked out of the gym, I went over to Young Johnson and said, "How do you feel?" He said, "I feel okay, why shouldn't I?" I said, "Because you got knocked out." He said, "I didn't get knocked out." I said, "What do you remember?" He said, "I walked out of the ring and now I'm doing my exercises." I said, "No, no. Do you actually remember walking out of the ring? What's the last thing you remember?" He said, "The last thing I remember was sparring with Joe." I said, "He knocked you dead. You were out a couple of minutes. You don't remember walking out of the ring because we carried you out of the ring."

That's how hard Joe Louis could hit. Lucky for me, Joe never really unloaded on me, but having worked with Joe, I had an idea what Red House felt like after that shot to the solar plexus.

After an ordinary sparring session with somebody, when you went home you weren't sore. But after a workout with Joe, you were sore everywhere. Anywhere he hit you, you'd feel it. The next day you were as sore as if you'd been in a real fight. Even if he didn't hit you much, just blocking those shots was like being in an automobile accident. You didn't know how sore you were until you woke up the next morning. That happened to me after I went off the road in Arizona not long ago. I didn't realize my chest had hit the steering wheel until the next day when I had an occasion to cough. That's what getting hit by Joe Louis was like.

As hard as Joe could hit, he was a softie too. I never liked to bother Joe when I saw him because there were always so many other people around him. Wherever he was, he was mobbed.

One time when I took our Detroit Golden Gloves team to Chicago, where Joe was based, he was at ringside. I think he was the heavyweight champion by then and people were all around him, asking for his autograph. I caught his eye and nodded to him, but he motioned for me to come over. He said, "Eddie, what hotel you staying at?" I told him, and the next day Freddie Guinyard, who was Joe's right-hand man, came to the hotel with some spending money for each of my Golden Gloves fighters. I don't remember how much, maybe twenty dollars each, whatever. But in those years a twenty-dollar bill meant a lot to a kid. Joe was like that.

Years later, in 1955, I had a fine bantamweight, Billy Peacock, fighting in Houston. I sent Billy on ahead because I couldn't get to Houston until the day before the fight.

When my plane landed at the old Houston airport, I came down the steps. No jetways in those days. I was walking to the concourse when I noticed Joe and another fellow in a white Cadillac convertible parked by the fence. I called, "Hey, Joe," and he said, "Anybody meeting you?" I said, "No." He said, "Need a ride to the hotel?" I said, "Sure, I'd like to have a ride." I got in the backseat and we talked as they drove me to the hotel. Then they drove off. Joe was going to referee the fight the next night, and he said, "See you tomorrow."

I walked into the lobby, where Billy Peacock was waiting for me. Billy said, "Did you see Joe Louis?" I said, "He happened to be in a car sitting out there near the runway when we landed." Billy said, "He wasn't just sitting out there near the runway. He came in here asking where you were. When I told him what time your plane was arriving, he went out there to pick you up."

By that time, counting all the amateur kids I had coached at the Brewster Boxing Club, I had worked with at least two thousand fighters. I've worked with two or three hundred more since then. You have to work with every kid differently, because every kid is different. You have to apply a teaching technique that each individual understands. But as a trainer, I've always assessed my fighter's opponent with the same philosophy. Every fighter has strengths. That's why he's up there. But every fighter has weaknesses. My basic plan is for my fighter to avoid his opponent's strengths and exploit his weaknesses.

To begin with, I always have my fighters go out and jab. Especially if they're the clever boxer type. See how his opponent handles that jab. See what he does. See where he goes.

The jab was a big reason Muhammad Ali never figured out why he always had so much trouble with Ken Norton in their three fights. I thought Ken won all three. But he only got the decision in their first fight, the one in San Diego in 1973 when he broke Ali's jaw. Most people think that was the first time they were in a ring together, but a few years earlier they had sparred in Los Angeles when Ali was in exile. Whatever city Ali was in, he always had his boxing gear in the luggage compartment of his car. Whenever he stepped out of that car, people would gather. So the day he showed up at the Hoover Street Gym in Los Angeles, the gym filled up. Wall-to-wall people.

Three other heavyweights were working out, Scrap Iron Johnson, Howard Smith, and somebody whose name I've forgotten.

Ali boxed with each of those fellows, then somebody told him I had a young heavyweight, Ken Norton.

Ali didn't even know Norton's name. Ali looked at me and said, "How about working a round with your guy?" I said, "Okay." I took Norton aside and told him, "Don't try to be a wise guy. Just be smart. Just go out there and work along with him and try to learn something. If it gets rough in there, naturally take care of yourself. But just try to work along with him." The first round went like that, but Norton never was a smooth-looking fighter. He didn't have a classic style. Ali had looked him over pretty good. I guess he decided the kid can't fight much. So with this enthusiastic crowd there, Ali decided he's going to give 'em a show.

Near the end of the round, Ali stepped back and announced to Norton and the crowd, "Okay, boy, I'm through playing with you. I'm going to put something on you." Ali really starts punching, but Norton goes right with him. What a round that was, a wild round.

The thing was, Ali didn't think Norton could counter because Norton had been working along with him earlier. But when Ali started punching harder, Norton countered. Norton embarrassed him, and Ali didn't expect that. Ali didn't like that at all. The next day Ali walked into the gym screaming, "I want that Norton, where's that Norton?" But I had told Norton to stay in his street clothes.

Ali looked over and saw Norton standing around in his street clothes, then he looked at me and said, "Ain't he going to work today?" I said, "No." He said, "Why not?" I said, "Yesterday you came in here looking for a workout. Today you came in here looking for a fight. When this kid fights you, he's going to get paid. And paid well."

From that one-round workout I had determined that Norton had the style to lick Ali. He just didn't have experience yet. Norton's style was perfect. He was strong. He was awkward. And he was tall, as tall as Ali. Then I started putting their two styles together, thinking how Norton could avoid Ali's strengths while exploiting Ali's weaknesses.

Ali made a mistake that he was able to get away with most of the time because of his great reflexes. But it was very dangerous. The classic style is, when you jab, you carry your right hand high to parry the other fellow's jab or straight right hand. Ali carried his right hand out here to the side because he knew he could get away with it. Ali had that quick left hand that was more of a flick than a good jab. But it was so fast. If you tried to slip his jab and counterpunch, he was gone. If you tried to pull away and counterpunch, he was gone. If you tried to bob underneath, he was gone. Whatever you did, he was just too quick.

As soon as Norton started training to fight Ali in the San Diego Arena, I thought about what had happened in their one-round workout in the Hoover Street Gym. I told him, "You're not going to hit Ali by slipping or pulling back or dropping underneath or parrying. You have to hit him when he's punching. When he starts to jab, you punch with him. Keep you right hand high. His jab will pop into the middle of your glove and then your jab will come right down the pipe into the middle of his face. Every time he starts to punch, don't pull back, go forward toward him." That's what Norton did. That's what destroyed Ali's rhythm.

But there was another important factor: where Norton was in the ring when he went forward. I told him, "If you start from the center of the ring, it'll take you only three moves to get Ali on the ropes. Every time you jab, step in and make him jab again. Then do the same thing." With both of them being big heavyweights, I knew if Norton was in the center of the ring when he countered Ali's jab, those three moves would back Ali into the ropes.

When he got Ali on the ropes, I told him, "Don't do like all the other guys do. Don't throw your hook to the head. He'll pull back against the ropes and when you're off balance, he'll pepper you with counterpunches. When he's on the ropes, instead of going to the head with the left hook, start banging his body with both hands. I don't care whether you land or not. Make him, in order to protect his body, bring his elbows down and his head down. That gives you a shot to the head." Simple. So simple. But Ali could never figure it out. What he should've done was kept his right hand up high to parry Norton's job and countered with another jab. Once he parried Norton's jab, Norton's jab would go over his shoulder. He could jab right back. He could do anything he wanted because he had gotten rid of Norton's jab. But he never did. It was a basic move. But he'd done it the other way for so long he didn't know how to change.

Nobody seems to know for sure just when Norton broke Ali's jaw in that fight. Angelo Dundee always says the first round. But with all the shots Ali took, if his jaw had been broken that early, it would have been shattered by the time Norton got the twelve-round decision.

In my opinion, Ali's jaw was broken in the eleventh round with one very good right hand that Norton threw when he caught Ali on the ropes. I've always thought that was the punch. In watching the videotape, Ali's expression every time he got hit on the jaw was pretty normal until he got hit in the eleventh round. That fight will go down in boxing history as Ali going the distance in a valiant fight with a broken jaw, but I don't buy it. I'll always believe it happened in the eleventh round. Ali probably didn't have his mouthpiece clenched firmly. He liked to talk when he was fighting. He probably was in the midst of saying something to Norton when he got hit.

Norton made that first fight with Ali look so easy with his prescribed pattern, they were rematched for the Forum in Los Angeles six months later. When a fighter has a prescribed pattern, he follows it because it's new territory for him. But what usually happens in the rematch, instead of following the prescribed pattern, he thinks he can do it any way he wants to. He's going to have the same problems, but he's going to do it his way regardless of what you tell him.

In that second fight, Norton went out and suddenly decided to fight Ali like Joe Frazier had fought him two years earlier. Norton bobbed and weaved. The trouble was, Norton didn't know what to do from that position, so Ali won the first four rounds. I finally got Norton going in the fifth round and he started to come on. By the eleventh round I thought he was pulling even, maybe a little ahead. But then Ali, being the great con man he is, he knew that he had to win the last round. He marshaled his strength in the early part of the twelfth round, then he stole the fight with a garrison finish.

In their third fight at Yankee Stadium in 1976, Norton knew enough to follow the prescribed pattern. I've always thought that Norton won all three of his fights with Ali, and I thought he had a bigger margin at Yankee Stadium than in the other two. I gave him nine of the fifteen rounds. But on the judges' cards, it came down to the last round. Even I thought Ali won that round, because he was smart.

I wasn't in Norton's corner that night, I was sitting at ringside. By then I'd been Joe Frazier's manager for three years. I'd started working with Joe in 1966. Joe's manager, Yancey [Yank] Durham, and I were so close, Yank used to say, "If anything ever happens to me, I want you to take my fighters." I'd always tell him how absurd that was. I'd say, "If anything happens to you? I'm ten years older than you are." Which I was. That summer we were in London, where Joe went twelve rounds with Joe Bugner. The next day, Yank and I were waiting for the elevator on the fifteenth floor of the Hilton Hotel in London when he said it to me again. I told him, "You're out of your mind."

Eight weeks later, I was in California getting Norton ready for his second fight with Ali. Bobby Goodman, who's now the Madison Square Garden matchmaker, and I had gone over to Las Vegas to see Jerry Quarry fight. When we got back to our training camp at the Massacre Canyon resort the next morning, Bobby checked his messages. He was in the room next to mine. I could hear him talking on the telephone. The next thing I knew, he knocked on my door. When I opened it, he told me, "Yank had a stroke."

About an hour later Bobby told me Yank was on a life-support system. Later that night, after we heard that Yank had died at fifty-one, Joe Frazier called me. Joe said, "Yank's gone, Eddie. What are you going to do?" I said, "I've got Norton training for Ali, but he's got a day off coming. I'll be in Philadelphia tomorrow night." I sat down with Joe and Bruce Wright, the head of the Cloverlay syndicate behind Joe, and we worked out the deal by which I'd take over as manager. Two weeks later, right after the second Norton-Ali fight, I moved to Philadelphia. But from the first time I met Joe in 1966, he was the easiest fighter I've ever had. When you asked Joe to do something, he did it.

Back in 1966 I didn't know Joe, I didn't know Yank. But they knew me by reputation. Everybody in Philadelphia knew me from my trips there with good fighters. I took Lester Duncan and Big Boy Brown there. I took Bob Amos there—Bob beat Henry Hall, who boxed Archie Moore three times. I brought those kids to Philly and everybody there knew me and knew I always had good fighters who were always in good shape and who always performed well.

After I moved from Detroit to Los Angeles, every fighter who came from Philly was recommended to me. George Benton's manager had called me from Philly in 1963 and asked if George's fight with Johnny Smith was right for him. I told him, "This guy is our California middleweight and light heavyweight champion, a tall rangy guy who can punch with either hand, but George will handle him." At the time I had a good middleweight, Thell Torrance, and we wanted a shot at the California middleweight title, but they wouldn't give us a shot. So when George came out, I had Thell working as his sparring partner.

One day after his workout, George came to me and said, "Hey, the guy I'm fighting isn't as good as this sparring partner, is he?" I said, "No." He said, "If you'd told me yes, I'd have packed my bags and gone back to Philly." I said, "Thell would be fighting Johnny Smith if Johnny Smith would give us a shot. Does that make you feel better?" And George said, "That makes me feel better."

I told George it should take him only about three rounds to lick Smith, but before the second round George looked at me and said, "It's not going to take me three rounds, I'm going to get him this round." And he did. George was a good fighter, a good fighter. But he was just one of the kids from Philly that I worked with when they fought in California. So when Yank decided to bring Joe Frazier out it was only natural for Yank to call me even though we didn't know each other except by reputation.

From the minute they stepped off the plane in Los Angeles, we had a combination. Joe, Yank, and me. It was like we'd known each other forever.

Before Joe's first fight out there with Chuck Leslie, some of the California trainers were jealous that I was working with the Olympic champion. They were telling Yank things to make me look bad. In the dressing room Yank looked at me and said, "Some people tell me you put me in a bad fight." I said, "What did they tell you about it?" He said, "This guy is going to run. He's going to make Joe look bad." I said, "No, Yank, I'll tell you right now how the fight's going to go. I used to handle Chuck Leslie, and he's a pretty good fighter. Chuck Leslie is not a runner. But as strong as Joe is, as hard as Joe hits, yes, Chuck is going to run. But because he's not a runner, he doesn't know how to run. After a round or two, he's going to get hit with something that'll buzz him. Then he's going to stop and fight. When he stops and fights, he's going to get knocked out."

Well, when Joe knocked Chuck Leslie out in the third round,

Yank turned to me and said, "You must've written the script for this one. You're my man. I don't care what those other guys say."

But before Joe could take a shower, Mickey Davies, the matchmaker, told us, "The opponent we had for Memphis Al Jones next week has fallen out. Your guy only had three rounds' work tonight. What about taking that spot next week?" Yank pulled me aside and said, "What do you know about Memphis Al Jones?" I said, "I've never seen him, but I read where Jerry Quarry had him down in the first round and he got up and lasted the ten rounds. He weighed 201 pounds for that fight, so if he weighed 201 and was the kind of fighter who could stay with Quarry after getting knocked down he's got to be tall and thin and have a good left jab who'll pull away from Quarry's short left hook. I'd take the fight, Yank, and I'd send Joe after his body."

We didn't see Memphis Al Jones until the weigh-in. But as soon as he walked in, tall and thin, Yank burst out laughing. That night Joe knocked him out in the first round with a body shot. Never even hit him on the chin. Just a body shot.

After that, Joe stopped Billy Daniels in Philly, then he was lucky to get a ten-round decision over Oscar Bonavena in the Garden. Bonavena was a big strong awkward brawler from Argentina who knocked Joe down twice, and Joe also went down from a slip. All in the same round. The three-knockdown rule was in effect. If the referee had ruled it a knockdown instead of a slip, it would've been all over. But the problem was, Joe was standing up straight walking to his man.

That's when I told Yank, "We've got to have Joe start bobbing and weaving. We can't have him walking into these guys standing up straight like that." For his workouts, I got a rope and strung it diagonally across from one ring post to another ring post. Joe had to bob and weave under that rope.

Bobbing and weaving became his stock in trade. During Ali's exile Joe bobbed and weaved his way to an eleventh-round knockout of Buster Mathis for the New York heavyweight title. By the time Ali's exile ended in 1970, Joe was recognized as the champion by the World Boxing Association, but Ali was still recognized as the champion by the boxing public. When they signed to fight in the Garden on March 8, 1971, it was a natural. Each fighter had a claim to the heavyweight title. Each fighter was undefeated.

But for all of Ali's headlines, technically he was not the Greatest, at least not to me. Ali won with his intangibles. He had that great heart and a good chin. He had exceptional speed for a heavyweight. He was a gambler who got away with it because of his great reflexes. And he was an opportunist. If he got you at a disadvantage, he exploited it.

Ali had that great jab and a good right hand, but he was not a puncher. I used to get in more arguments about his punching ability. Everybody thought he was a knockout puncher because he had a lot of knockouts in his record. But most of his knockouts developed from an accumulation of punches. As it turned out, Ali fought Joe Frazier forty-one rounds and never had him down. Ali fought Ken Norton thirty-nine rounds and never had him down. Ali never threw body punches, and his left hook was more of a slap. His right hand was sharp. He never ducked a punch. He pulled back or sidestepped. But he had those intangibles. That great heart. That good chin. And that speed, that flash. Those were the things he won with.

In planning how Joe should fight him, I looked through those intangibles to the technical aspects. Ali didn't know how to throw an uppercut. He stood up straight and he dropped his right hand and threw what he considered to be an uppercut, but it really wasn't. Joe couldn't fight Ali the same way Norton would fight him two years later because Joe wasn't tall enough. If Joe stood up straight he'd give away the advantage of being a little guy. I wanted to increase that advantage by having Joe bob and weave to get inside instead of using his jab.

All that bobbing and weaving dropped Joe even lower so he could slip Ali's punches. It also made Joe an even smaller target.

Now with Joe bobbing and weaving down there, Ali had to throw his uppercut, but I knew he would throw it wrong. So I told Joe, "Every time you see Ali's right hand come down, that means he's going to throw an uppercut. But the minute he drops his right hand, throw your left hook, because he's got nothing up here to parry it." In the eleventh round, Joe had him wobbling around the ring. In the fifteenth round, Joe decked him with a perfect left hook. Ali got up quickly, because the punch hit him on the jaw. If it had hit him on the chin, that would've been it.

Joe got a unanimous fifteen-round decision. And he remained the undisputed champion until 1973, when he fought George Foreman in Jamaica. As soon as I got to Jamaica, I dreaded what might happen.

One of Joe's sparring partners there was Ken Norton, who was about three months away from fighting Ali for the first time. Ken had been his sparring partner for about two and a half years, but the first two workouts I watched Ken handle Joe easily. The first day I couldn't believe what I was seeing. The second day, I was convinced. I told Ken, "You're not working anymore. Stay and enjoy yourself." Then I said, "I can see what's going on from outside the ring. Tell me what you feel from inside the ring." Ken said, "Joe seems to have lost his drive."

That's when I put it all together. The whole scene. Jet-setters coming down to Jamaica from Philadelphia and New York in the wintertime. The weather's nice. It's a vacation for everybody. Especially Joe.

Joe loved to sing. He had his own rock band. Our hotel had a lounge adjacent to the swimming pool. Late one afternoon about a week before the fight I was sitting at the pool with my typewriter, knocking out some correspondence, when Joe walked up to me. You have no idea how hot it was, but Joe was all dressed up in a light tropical suit, shirt, and tie. He said, "I'm going over to the lounge just to relax for a few minutes. I'll be back soon." I said, "Whatever you do, don't go on that stage and start singing." I went back to typing some more letters, then I realized it's half an hour and he's still not back.

I went over to the lounge and Joe Frazier was up on the stage with a microphone belting out songs. He's perspiring so profusely, the perspiration is running down the lapels of his jacket. I was so mad. I grabbed that microphone out of his hand and pulled him off the stage.

Another time Joe was sitting by the pool in a pair of expensive slacks, just watching the festivities. Somebody said, "Joe, why don't you get in the pool?" He couldn't swim much. He didn't have a bathing suit. And he knew I didn't want him even trying to use a different set of muscles. But what did he do? He got a pair of scissors, cut those expensive slacks into shorts, and jumped in the pool.

I had told Yank, "I don't like what I see here. This isn't a training camp. This is just a great big party." That attitude lost the fight.

As big and strong as George Foreman was, I knew that if Joe got past five rounds with him, Joe had a great chance to beat him, because George would run out of gas. He'd already done that with Gregorio Peralta, but he got a ten-round decision. George was so tense, he would tire from losing all that nervous energy. He never relaxed. But you didn't want to trade punches with George early, because he hit so hard. So hard. I was really looking for Joe to get to him with a left hook, because George was a stand-up fighter, but George just pushed Joe away. George was so strong, he pushed Joe three, four steps away. I hadn't anticipated that. And as soon as George hit him, it didn't last long.

Joe also did something that night that I never saw him do before or after. I used to be amused at Joe's expression when he walked to the center of the ring for the referee's instructions. He kind of half-smiled, like he thought the other fighter was something good to eat. But in Jamaica, he tried to stare George down. That didn't work either.

Not long after Yank died later that year, Joe signed to fight Ali at the Garden early in 1974, but the fight almost occurred in a television studio. ABC wanted Joe and Ali to do a television show with Howard Cosell about a week before the fight. I didn't like the idea. Joe and Ali had been on two earlier shows together. The first time, I could see a little irritation in Joe at Ali's cracks. The second time, Joe got very angry at him, and I decided they wouldn't be on the same program again, period. But while I was away with another fighter, Cosell called Bruce Wright, who told him to call me. Cosell assured me, "I'll sit between the two fighters, I'll see to it that nothing happens." I said, "No, this show could wind up in a fight." Roone Arledge called me, and I said, "No." But when I got back to Philadelphia, I found out that Bruce had agreed to it.

I kept telling Bruce, "No, no, no," but ABC kept saying the show was scheduled and I kept saying, "I don't care about the schedule, Joe's not going." But finally, against my better judgment, I relented. I told Bruce, "I still don't think Joe should go, but just to show you that what Cosell told you is not going to work out, I'm going to let Joe go."

When we got to the ABC studio, instead of sitting in the middle, Cosell was sitting on the left with an empty seat in the middle. That's where Joe sat. Ali's brother, Rahaman, made some inflammatory remarks about Joe. Then during the interview Ali called Joe "ignorant." Joe exploded. Joe started after Rahaman first, then Ali went after Joe in order to protect his brother. That's when I got into it. By then chairs were falling all over the floor. It finally got broken up. To this day, some people still think that ruckus was a publicity stunt. Maybe because nobody got hurt. But anybody who was there will tell you that was no stunt. That was for real.

The next day Bruce apologized to me. He said, "I'll never interfere again." I said, "Always remember that I'm with Joe all the time. I knew Ali's wisecracks were getting to him. I knew he wasn't going to tolerate that crap anymore." As for Cosell, when I left the studio, I told him, "You lied to me. You told me you'd sit between them and you didn't."

I don't know if that ruckus affected the fighters or not. In the fight itself, the referee, Tony Perez, let Ali pull Joe by the back of the head one hundred and thirty-three times in twelve rounds. I know. I watched the replay of that fight at least ten times. I counted them. After the fifth round, I walked along the side of the ring over to where Tony Perez was standing in a neutral corner. I wanted everyone to see me. That's why I walked along the side of the ring between rounds. I said, "When are you going to stop Ali from pulling Joe in like that? When are you going to penalize him?" He said, "I'll do it." But he never did.

At the New York Boxing Writers Dinner a few months later, Tony took me aside. He told me he planned to apply for a referee's license in Pennsylvania. He wanted to know if I'd support his application. I said, "I'll oppose you, Tony." He said, "Why?" I said, "The way you handled the second Frazier-Ali fight, you were either incompetent or dishonest. Whatever it was, we don't need you in Pennsylvania." He just stared at me, so I told him, "You asked me and I told you. I went to you during the fight and complained about what Ali was doing, but you never did anything about it."

How a referee handles a fight is so important. That's why I had a head-to-head battle with Don King over the identity of the referee before Joe fought Ali for the third time in 1975 in Manila, what Ali labeled the Thrilla in Manila.

Don King kept trying to force a referee on me. He brought three referees to Manila. Two Americans, Zack Clayton and Jay Edson, and an Englishman, Harry Gibbs. With Don telling everybody he was Ali's promoter, I just didn't like the idea that all three of the referees there were Don King's guests. To me, they would be obligated to him. I didn't want to use any of them. As far as

Jay Edson was concerned, I would have used him under other circumstances. Jay is a good referee. But not with him there as Don King's guest. Not with him obligated to Don King.

The referee thing started months before we ever got to Manila. To give you an idea, when Joe started his light training, he and I were staying in an apartment in Philadelphia, the Society Hill Towers, up on the thirtieth floor. To get into the downstairs lobby, you needed a key. One day Joe's son, Marvis, who had a key to the downstairs lobby, and two of Marvis's cousins visited us. As they told us later, they had noticed this man hanging around outside the lobby, and when Marvis opened the door to the lobby, he followed them in. When they got into the elevator, he followed them in. When they got off on the thirtieth floor, he followed them off. When they walked down the hall to our apartment, he followed them. And when Marvis opened the door, he told Marvis, "I'd like to see your father."

Joe was in his bedroom and I was in mine. Marvis went in and told his father that a man named Zack Clayton had followed him upstairs and wanted to see him. Joe picked up his phone, we had different numbers, and called me right away. Joe told me, "Marvis is here and Zack Clayton followed him upstairs. I think he wants to be the referee in Manila." I said, "You tell Marvis to tell Clayton that you have nothing to do with the selection of the referee. Tell him that's my choice. And tell him I'm not here."

I didn't want Zack Clayton. He was a well-known referee. He had been the referee in Zaire when Ali got the title back with an eighth-round knockout of George Foreman. But there were certain things about Clayton's style as a referee that I didn't like. Some of the things he did were not what I considered to be in the best interests of boxing. I didn't know what the reasons or ramifications were, but I didn't want to be in a position where something like that could happen in a fight where I was involved. In my mind, that eliminated him.

Now the story gets complicated. Frank Rizzo, then the mayor of Philadelphia, used to come down to Joe Frazier's Gym every so often to talk about his plans for the community. He once told me, "If you ever need a favor, give me a ring at this number." He wrote down his private number. "Nobody picks this up but me."

Zack Clayton was a city employee, a firefighter I believe. When he was so persistent in trying to be the referee in Manila, I dialed

Frank Rizzo's private number. "One of your employees," I told him, "wants to moonlight as a referee in the Manila fight, but I don't want him over there." The next thing I knew, Clayton quit his job. If I didn't want him as the referee before, I certainly didn't want him now. Not after he'd quit a year-round job. But that didn't stop him. And it didn't stop Don King.

As so often happens when you're working with other fighters, you can't be everywhere at once. I was off with another fighter when Bruce Wright and Joe went up to Don King's office in New York to sign the contract for Manila, but I reminded them of the terms I had discussed with Don King. The money breakdown. The number of ringside tickets. The number of plane tickets and hotel rooms.

When I got back to Philadelphia, I went to Bruce's office to read the signed contract. Bruce hadn't noticed a clause about the referee. According to this clause, if the two camps disagreed on the referee, Don King would have the privilege of selecting the referee. Bruce and I hopped on the Amtrak, went up to New York, and walked into Don King's office. He gave us a big hello, then he said, "Everything all right?" I said, "No, everything's not all right." He said, "What's wrong?" I said, "That clause in the contract about you picking the referee if there's a disagreement." He said, "That's no problem, we'll take that out." He knew he didn't have a fight if he didn't take it out. He just thought he could slip it through. That's how badly he wanted the referee's spot for his man.

That was two shots fired already at us. The third shot was when I found out Don King had brought the three referees to Manila as his guests. That's when I told Luis Tabuena, the chairman of the Games and Amusement Board in Manila, that in working fights in the Philippines in other years, I always had been impressed by Filipino referees. I proposed that a Filipino referee should work this fight.

As soon as Don King heard my proposal, he argued that a Filipino referee would be too small to handle two big heavyweights. But when he said that, I said, "Harry Gibbs is six feet four inches tall and weighs two hundred and forty pounds. I've seen him referee in London on a number of occasions and I was always impressed. Here's a big hulk of a man who never puts his hands on the fighters. He commands them to obey his directions. If they don't, he penalizes them. But he never touches the fighters. He never struggles with them. Now a midget could do that. So don't tell me about a referee having to be a big man. All a referee has to be is a man who's the boss. If you don't believe me, ask Harry Gibbs. He's here." Don King couldn't refute that argument. Not with Harry Gibbs right there.

Around that same time, Ferdinand Marcos, then the President of the Philippines, invited five members of each camp to his office as a public-relations gesture. Marcos was obviously proud that the fight would be seen worldwide.

The next time I saw Luis Tabuena, I told him, "President Marcos knows this great event has put the Philippines in the world spotlight. If you don't have a referee who can control Ali, it'll make a farce out of this fight and embarrass your President and the Philippines worldwide." I told him how Tony Perez had let Ali pull Joe from behind one hundred and thirty-three times in their second fight, that the wrong referee had spoiled the quality of what could have been a great fight. Apparently I convinced him.

As I walked into the press conference at which Carlos Padilla, a Filipino, was announced as the referee, somebody I didn't even know told me he had overheard Don King talking about me. The man told me, "I heard Don King say, 'That damn Eddie Futch, he pulled the rug out from under me.'"

In the fight, Padilla did a good job. My plan for Joe was to stay low, bob and weave, work Ali's body, bring his hands down, then shift to the head. No different than the other two fights. Keep constant pressure on Ali, don't let him celebrate. Bang the body regardless of whether you got immediate results. Body shots wear down a fighter. Even if you get knocked down with a punch to the head, when you get up, you're usually as good as you were before. But body shots, you can't shake them off. The trauma to the vital organs just doesn't go away. The trauma is still there the next day.

As the fight progressed, I felt Joe was ahead, but Joe was getting hit. In the end, the difference was in the swelling in Joe's eyes.

In the tenth round I thought Ali was going to get out of there from the terrific body beating he was taking. But in the eleventh and twelfth rounds, the swelling in Joe's eyes was more pronounced. After the twelfth round Joe told me he couldn't see well from the crouch position. I told him, "Back out a little and stand up a little bit more." I was hoping that would enable him to see better out of his left eye. But when the thirteenth round began, Ali noticed Joe's change of position right away. Ali was always an opportunist.

That was Joe's worst round. He couldn't see the right hands coming. He got hit with a right hand that knocked his mouthpiece six rows back.

I was wavering about stopping the fight, but I decided to give Joe one more round. I was hoping maybe Ali will punch himself out, maybe he'll slow up. But in the fourteenth round Ali kept firing those bullets and Joe couldn't see them coming. I thought Joe might really get hurt. I started thinking, this man is a great father, he's got a family he loves and they're so close, I don't want him to wind up a vegetable and not see his kids grow up. Joe's a human being, he's not a machine. Remember now, I was watching Joe get hit in the late stages of a brutal fight with a terrific pace. Even though I thought Joe was ahead, I knew I couldn't let this go on. In the final seconds of the round I turned to George Benton in the corner.

I said, "George, when the bell rings, I'm going to stop this fight. Joe's taking too much." George said, "That's a good decision."

When Joe came back and sat down, I said, "What's with his right hand?" Joe said, "I can't see it. I can see the left but when I move away, I get hit with the right." I said, "I'm going to stop it, Joe. The fight's over." He bounced up and said, "Don't do that. I can finish." I just tapped him on the shoulder and said, "Sit down. The fight's over. This is the best thing to do." Then I turned to Carlos Padilla and I said, "That's all." Joe never said anything to me one way or another. So many other people told him that I shouldn't have stopped the fight, I thought perhaps Joe might have thought that. But if he did, he never complained to me about it.

It turned out that Ali was way ahead: 8–4–2 in rounds on Padilla's card, 8–4–2 and 8–3–3 on the two Filipino judges' cards. Unless Joe somehow knocked out Ali in the fifteenth round, he could not have won.

I didn't agree with that scoring. Neither did some of the writers at ringside. Some of them had given Joe as many as nine rounds.

But the way Joe was getting hit, the scorecards didn't matter. I've seen fighters who took a lot of punishment, they're not right for the rest of their lives. I've been unfortunate enough to have been at more boxing fatalities than any other living trainer. I was there when Davey Moore got killed. I was there when Talmadge Bussey got killed. I was there when Kid Dynamite got killed. I was there when Jimmy Doyle got killed.

Jimmy Doyle looked right into my eyes as he was being carried out of the Cleveland Arena on a stretcher after Ray Robinson knocked him out in 1947.

When Doyle got hurt by Artie Levine the year before, I was sitting on the aisle. When you walked into that arena, you were at the top row, then you walked down to your seat. When they brought Doyle up on a stretcher past my seat, he looked in my eyes. I knew him and he knew me. He couldn't say anything. He couldn't do anything. But his eyes told me he recognized me. And when they brought him up on a stretcher after the Robinson fight, I was sitting in almost the same seat. He looked in my eyes again. He died later that night.

I'd seen Doyle at the weigh-in. He was pasty-faced. He didn't have a healthy color. Before the fight, Whitey Lewis, the sports columnist of the *Cleveland Press*, had written an article that I've saved. Whitey didn't like the way Doyle looked. His last sentence was, "They'd better have a sawbones handy." It was so prophetic. I talked to Doyle at the weigh-in, but I didn't like what I saw, I didn't like what I heard.

About six months later I told Sam Baroudi that I'd try to be in Chicago when he fought Ezzard Charles. Sam and I were leaving New York together. I told him I had to go back to Detroit to check Lester Felton's hands, but I promised him that if I could get to Chicago, I'd be there. He told me, "If you come, bring Felton with you. And if you guys get there, come down to the dressing room and let me know. It'll make me feel better knowing there's somebody in the audience rooting for me." As it turned out, I not only couldn't get to Chicago for that fight, I didn't have time to turn on the radio.

The next morning a friend of mine said, "Too bad about that kid last night." I said, "What kid?" He said, "Baroudi." I said, "What happened?" He said, "He got killed."

I'll never forget the other circumstances surrounding that fight.

They found Baroudi's manager, Mike Miele, at the airport about to board a plane with the money after the fight while Baroudi's in the hospital dying. Miele didn't have the decency to stay at the hospital with him.

Another bitter memory for me was Talmadge Bussey's death. I wasn't Talmadge's manager, but I booked him. We had our passports and our tickets for a fight in Caracas, but they had a revolution in Venezuela and he took a fight with Luther Rawlings instead.

It was a savage fight. Talmadge went down just before the bell ended the eighth round and they dragged him to his corner. His father and his brothers were in the corner. When the referee came over, he told them they ought to stop the fight between rounds. But their family pride wouldn't let them. When the bell rang, they pushed him out. As soon as the bell rang, the referee had the authority to stop the fight, but he didn't do it. Talmadge got hit again and he later died. Then they passed a rule disallowing family members in the corner. Too much emotion involved. But it was too late to save Talmadge. I've always thought that the referee was just as responsible for Talmadge's death. That's always been a bitter memory for me. If it wasn't for the revolution, Talmadge wouldn't have fought Rawlings because he would've been in Caracas with me.

The closest any of my fighters ever came to a fatality was a kid named Billy Hatcher, a middleweight who looked like a smaller Ezzard Charles. His father and his uncle brought him to me. One night at the Arcadia Club in Detroit he got hit a shot and he went down. The moment he went down, the doctor was in the ring. The doctor told me, "This kid's in trouble. He's seriously hurt." We called an ambulance. I can still hear the doctor telling me, "We almost lost him in the ring." In the hospital it took him three days to come out of it. While he was there I asked his father and his uncle if he ever had any head injuries as a kid. They told me that when he was six years old he hit his head on the sidewalk. I said, "And you brought him to me to make a boxer out of him." He recovered. But he never boxed again.

Another time Hedgemon Lewis, who's now my assistant trainer, was getting hit by Indian Red Lopez in the last round of a welterweight title elimination. I thought Hedge was ahead on the cards, but Lopez had him backed against the ropes. Hedge couldn't get his hands up. I looked up at the ring clock and there were only thirty seconds to go. Lopez was firing with both hands. I knew Hedge was going to get hurt. I looked up again and there were fifteen seconds to go. Hedge was right above me in the corner. I jumped up, put my hands between Hedge and Lopez and stopped it.

All those memories were in the back of my mind in the Philippine Coliseum when Joe Frazier was getting hit. After fourteen hard rounds, a fighter's resistance has to decline. His body no longer could throw off the effects of that pounding. The fighters who get hurt most, as a rule, are the ones who stand there taking a lot of punishment. The ones who get hit and go down, their punishment's over. But the ones who take those shots just standing there, like Davey Moore and Duk Koo Kim, those are the ones who really get hurt. Those were the shots I didn't want Joe Frazier to take. To this day some people still say to me, "But there were only three minutes left." My answer has never changed. I tell them, "I'm not a timekeeper. I'm a handler of fighters."

Joe didn't fight again until the following June, against George Foreman in the Nassau Coliseum. As soon as Joe started training, I knew something was wrong. I told him some things I wanted him to do, but he wasn't doing them.

During one of Joe's workouts, he was against the ropes all the time. I thought I knew the answer, but in teaching George Benton to be a trainer, I wanted to see if he knew. I called George over from the other corner where he was handling the sparring partners. I said, "Why is Joe on the ropes all the time?" He said, "I don't know." I said, "You were a really good fighter, George, but near the end of your career, you were doing that. Why?" He said, "I was resting my legs." I said, "That's the reason Joe is doing it too." I knew that if Joe couldn't keep himself off the ropes in training he'd be in real trouble if he did that against a puncher like Foreman. You can block punches on the ropes, but if one gets through and you're hurt, you're gone.

In the first four rounds, Joe went to the ropes briefly and escaped. But in the fifth he went to the ropes and never got off them. Once he got hurt, I stopped it.

Immediately after that fight, Joe announced his retirement. But he never accepted it. He had a chance to fight Kallie Knoetze of South Africa. When he convinced me in the gym that he was in pretty good shape, I agreed to go along with it. But when he was hospitalized with hepatitis, that fight never came off. When he decided to make a comeback in 1981 against Jumbo Cummings, I told him, "I don't approve of it and I won't help you get ready for it." What a stepdown. Joe was a little miffed at me for a while, but when he had to struggle to get a draw with a fighter of that caliber, that killed him on the market.

By then I was working with Larry Holmes. Two years earlier, I happened to watch him train for Earnie Shavers, who was a tremendous puncher. I didn't like what I saw. Larry wasn't boxing his sparring partners. He was fighting them, slugging it out. After his workout, I stopped to talk to him.

I told him, "You're in great shape, Larry, but you're working wrong. Fighting your sparring partners isn't the way to get ready for Shavers." He said, "I can do that with these guys, but I don't intend to fight Shavers that way. I intend to box Shavers." I said, "But at some point in the fight you're going to do subconsciously what you're practicing here. If you do that with Shavers, you could be in trouble." As it turned out, Larry did just what I warned him he would do. He got knocked down by a right hand. He got up to stop Shavers in the eleventh round. But the minute he and Richie Giachetti had that argument early in 1981, he thought about hiring me. He had Don King call me.

Larry had a fixation about weight. He was lucky that it didn't cost him his biggest fight, the one with Gerry Cooney in 1982. Larry had won the title from Ken Norton in 1978 at about 213 pounds. He weighed in at 209 but by fight time he was around 213. Against Cooney four years later he still wanted to weigh 213.

The difference was, Larry was older and bigger. I told him, "If you put on one solid pound each year, you now should weigh about 217. After your sparring sessions, I check your weight every day. You should fight wherever your weight stops when you're in good shape." He was up around 219, 221 until the last week, then I brought him down to 217. I figured that with two days of rest, he would weigh 218, 219, a good weight for him. He worked well at that weight. And it was hot, it was June in Vegas, so two days before the fight I knocked off his roadwork. The fight was Friday, but I told him not to run Wednesday morning and Thursday morning.

But on Wednesday morning Larry got up and ran anyway in

all that heat. He wanted his weight to be 213. At the weigh-in on Thursday, when Larry was called to get on the scales, he kept his running suit on. Right away that told me that he had run and he didn't want me to know about it.

Sure enough, Larry weighed 212 ½ with his running suit on. His real weight was probably 210, 211. Too light. Much too light. I didn't say anything, because I knew there was nothing I could do about it now except try to compensate for it during the fight itself. I told him, "Stay in the center of the ring as much as possible and use that good jab. Look for your shot. Stay off the ropes and out of the corners. This kid's got a good left hook, especially to the body." I didn't want Larry hit in the body with shots that would take his legs away from him. So he does this in the first round. In the second he's going along and down goes Cooney near the end of the round.

In the corner, I told Larry, "Box, box, box. I don't want you to go out there and get in a fight with this big, strong kid in all this heat. I just want you to pull his teeth," meaning make him harmless. Jab and move and box. In all that heat I didn't want him to lose any more weight than necessary.

In the tenth round, just what I figured would happen and could happen did happen. Larry hurt Cooney, but Cooney fought back like a tiger. That was a great round. The best round of the fight. All that took a lot out of Cooney, but in the corner, I told Larry, "Just keep sticking. Keep moving and boxing." Then before the twelfth round I said, "Now go out and get him." I knew Cooney didn't have much left, but I didn't want Larry to get into a punchout because he was already down too low. With that heat sapping Larry's weight and strength, I didn't want Cooney to be able to come on and catch him at a disadvantage. Late in the thirteenth round Larry finished him off.

Later on, Larry admitted to me that he had run Wednesday morning. He had the same weight fixation against Tim Witherspoon, and it turned into a tough fight. When Larry tried to get his punches off, he couldn't. When your weight is too fine, you see the things you want to do, but you can't do them. You see punches coming that you can't get out of the way of. Just like you can't do things when you're too heavy. It works both ways.

It never occurred to me at the time, but I was already on a collision course with Larry and Michael Spinks. The night in 1981 when Eddie Mustafa Muhammad defended the WBA light heavyweight title against Michael in Vegas, I had a fighter on the show. The weigh-in was the previous midnight. Michael had already made the weight and gone to bed, but the champion had failed to make the 175-pound limit, and Michael's manager, Butch Lewis, was waiting for the champion to weigh in again when I walked in. Butch took me aside and said, "I'd like you to work with Michael in this fight." I said, "I don't even know Michael. I've never even met Michael. He doesn't know my terminology. I don't even know if he thinks I can help him or not. That's one of the things a fighter must believe. That you can help him." But he said, "I know you from when both of us were around Joe Frazier and I know you can help him. Would you please work with Michael as a personal favor to me?" I agreed, but I didn't meet Michael until two hours before the fight in the dressing room.

Now I'm thinking, how can I help this kid? I'd known one of his cornermen, Nelson Brison, since he was a boy, so I decided to talk to Nelson during every round and then Nelson can express my thoughts to Michael in the corner in his own terminology.

During the first round, I told Nelson what ought to be done. He went up and told Michael what we had discussed, but he forgot what I considered an important point. I reminded Nelson of that point and Michael heard me. At the end of the second round, the same thing. Nelson again forgot an important point. I reminded him again, and Michael heard me again. At the end of the third round, Michael sat down on the stool, looked at me, "I can understand you perfectly. Why don't you talk to me?" At that point, I took over the fight and I steered him to the championship. That night he must have thanked me seven different times. Every time I looked up, Michael was putting his arms around me and saying, "I want to thank you." That's how I started off with Michael Spinks, but when he decided to step up and challenge Larry Holmes for the heavyweight title, I had to decide what I would do. I certainly couldn't be in both corners. The day the fight was signed, the writers asked me which fighter I would work with, and I said, "Neither one."

Larry jumped on me, arguing that I had worked with him longer. I told him, "Only three months longer. And you already were the champion. Michael was the challenger, so I helped him win the title."

My argument was that both men, each of whom had never lost a professional fight, were going for a special place in boxing history. Larry, who was 48–0 at the time, wanted to be the heavyweight champion who retired undefeated with more wins than Rocky Marciano, who had a 49–0 record. Michael wanted to be the first light heavyweight champion to step up and win the heavyweight title. In all good conscience, I didn't think it was fair for me to be a party to the defeat of either man. I didn't even go to their first fight. I went up to Reno and watched it on television. I thought Michael won that one and their rematch.

I also thought Michael had a good chance against Mike Tyson, mostly because of how Michael fought Larry in their rematch. Michael stayed away from him in the first few rounds. Larry came out furious, he even threw Michael down one time. But pretty soon Larry started slowing down and Michael came on.

That was my plan for Michael in the Tyson fight. Use his jab. Stay away. But two mistakes disrupted the plan. After the New Jersey commission had approved the taping of the wrist area on each of Tyson's gloves, Butch Lewis complained that there was too much of a lump from the knotted laces under the tape on the left glove. Butch was trying to annoy Tyson, and when the hassle got hot, they sent for me. I said, "It looks all right to me. Let's go." But by then Tyson was steaming. Butch had made a big mistake. If we were going against a real boxer type, that would've been all right. You want a boxer to lose his cool. But against Tyson, a fellow whose tremendous energy is all bottled up and ready to explode anyway, it was a big mistake to get him angry, a big mistake. The last thing I said to Michael before the bell rang was, "Box. Make him miss. Move. Frustrate him. Stay away from him for at least five rounds." But when Michael went out and planted his feet, that was the second mistake that disrupted the plan.

For a couple of weeks before the fight, I'd heard that some people in our camp were telling Michael to go out there and make Tyson respect him. To show Tyson that he can punch. To get Tyson's respect. It didn't work. Ninety-one seconds later, the fight was over. But it really was over when Michael planted his feet to trade punches with Tyson.

That's human nature. And that's boxing. But at least Michael Spinks decided to retire right then and there. Too many boxers never retire when they should. I've always thought that Muhammad Ali should have retired after he regained the title from George Foreman in Zaire. After that, Ali didn't want to pay the price anymore. He didn't want to train the way he needed to train. As our bodies get older, we need to take better care of them, not less care. Ali's sparring sessions were a joke. He'd get in the ring and he'd back up against the ropes and let the sparring partners beat on his arms and elbow. He'd take shots to the body and the kidneys and whatnot. He did that because he didn't want to exert himself. And after Zaire he had several hard fights with Chuck Wepner, Ron Lyle, Joe Bugner, Joe Frazier, Jimmy Young, Ken Norton. Hard fights where he couldn't throw off the effects of the punishment because he wasn't in condition.

But there's never been anybody in boxing quite like Muhammad Ali. Not long ago there was a reception at City Hall in New York City honoring Ali, Joe Frazier, George Foreman, and Larry Holmes. Joe and I had been there awhile when Ali walked in with George and Larry. As soon as Ali spotted me he walked over and whispered, "You always gave me trouble."

In the corner, Richie Giachetti instructed Larry Holmes.

Richie Giachetti:

"Don King's Hair Was Normal Then"

On the worn and weathered west side of Cleveland, the intersection of Lorain Avenue and West 104th Street is known as Giachetti's Corner. On one side is Richie Giachetti's bar, Round 15. Across the street is the Giachetti Athletic Club, where framed photos of Larry Holmes, Muhammad Ali, Roberto Duran, and Sylvester Stallone are among dozens on the walls of Giachetti's office. Sitting at the desk he was talking loudly, as he often does. Then the phone rang.

"Giachetti's," he said softly. "Yes, we do have boxing. . . . You sign up. . . . It's twenty-five dollars a month, that's just for the gym dues and the facilities. . . . We train the guys for nothing. . . . Three times a week. . . . When they get better, we put 'em on a different schedule. . . . Yes, ma'am. . . . But basically Mondays, Wednesdays, and Fridays. . . . 10326 Lorain Avenue. . . . There's a big sign, Giachetti's Athletic Club, you can't miss it. . . . We're nine to nine, but Sundays we close at two o'clock. . . . Thank you."

He put down the phone and smiled. "Some kid's mother wants him to start boxing. You never know. He might be my next champion."

Through the years, Richie Giachetti has worked with several world champions: Larry Holmes, Aaron Pryor, Esteban de Jesus, Greg Page, Julian Jackson, and Johnny Verderosa. For a short time he also was around James (Buster) Douglas, and he was installed as Mike Tyson's trainer after Tyson was dethroned by Douglas.

"Me and my twin brother, Bobby, that's us in those pictures there, the two blond kids. We were both Golden Gloves champions. I was a welterweight, he was a lightweight. They called us the Golden Twins."

His twin brother helps him train boxers in their neat wood-paneled gym, but Richie is the boss. Wearing a bulging black sweatshirt and black sweat pants, he's a heavyweight now. His curly hair is dark. So is his mustache. Across the left side of his face, slanting from below the inside corner of his eye to below his cheekbone, is a long scar.

"Right here in the bar across the street," he said, "this guy asks, 'Who's the toughest guy in here?' Somebody pointed at me. This guy comes over, takes a glass, and shoves it in my face. I hit him. The guy pulls a knife and tries to stick me. I don't know how, but I took the knife off him and stuck him three times with it."

Richie was in surgery more than seven hours. The area around his eye was numb for years. But somehow he didn't lose any vision.

"I swear to God, I didn't know this man," he said. "I heard stories that he died in the hospital later. The cops who wrote up the report talked to witnesses. It was justifiable."

In a brawl about five years earlier in the same bar he was stabbed in the ribs with an ice pick.

"At that time there were no blacks around here, but some black friends of mine had come over to the bar," he said. "Some guy said, 'What are these niggers doing here?' I said, 'They're friends of mine.' That started it. The doctor told me the ice pick went just underneath my heart and touched my lung but didn't puncture it. He told me if I was a normal person I would've been dead. My muscle tone saved me."

Born on April 20, 1940, younger than his twin by half an hour, Richie Giachetti grew up with two other brothers and a sister in Uniontown, Pennsylvania, as a high school linebacker and an amateur boxer.

"After one day in the coal mines, I knew it wasn't for me," he said. "I moved to Cleveland, where my mother was, and started fixing cars. I was always good with my hands."

Before he started training boxers, mostly those under the wing of promoter Don King, he was the proprietor of an auto-body shop and a transmission shop that were behind his gym and his bar. In those years he competed on the stock-car circuit.

"Stock cars was great," he said. "It was just like boxing. Get out and fight, man. One time somebody asked Richard Petty, 'Do you know those Giachetti brothers from Cleveland?' He said, 'No, but I know them Spaghetti brothers.' "

—

Back when Don King was known as the king of the numbers racket here in Cleveland, he really wasn't. He'd walk around saying he was the king of the numbers and the other guys who were really bigger would go along with it to keep the heat off themselves. Don got bigger than them because he was so flamboyant and the other guys wanted to play low profile. Don liked to play high profile.

I didn't know Don when he went to the can for manslaughter. I just knew of him as a numbers guy. I heard all the stories from other black guys. They called him the best numbers player ever around here. He played the numbers more than he took the action. And he win. Don is a master mathematician. He don't need a phone book. He has every phone number in his head. He just rattles 'em off.

The first time I met Don was right after he got out of the can. My attorney Clarence Rogers got us together to put on a Muhammad Ali exhibition for Forest City Hospital, a black hospital. August 28, 1972, that's the poster over there on the wall. I got the four guys Ali fought. Terry Daniels four rounds. Vic Brown, Amos Johnson, and Earnie Shavers each two rounds. When Don walked into my attorney's office that day, I thought he was a farmer. He had overalls on with the cuffs rolled up. He and his wife, Henrietta, had a farm out in Windsor, Ohio. Still do. But his hair was normal then. Not standing straight up like it is now. He had a nice Afro. He used to have a guy come out every week to cut his hair.

Ali got ten thousand dollars for that show, I took fifteen hundred in expenses, and we made eighty-seven thousand for the hospital. That's how Don got in boxing. He was thinking about going into entertainment, but he figured out that boxing was entertainment. He said, "Let's get in the boxing business." So we bought Earnie Shavers from his managers, Dean Chance and Blackie Gennaro.

I needed a mouthpiece, and Don King was the best. He was Shavers's manager and I was the trainer. We made a good team. We were all family. I was around from day one. Working with Shavers is how I met Larry Holmes and helped him win the heavyweight title. Me and Larry later split up when the FBI was investigating Don King, but then we got back together again. And after Larry lost to Mike Tyson, I trained James [Buster] Douglas for a year and a half when nobody wanted him. Douglas went to Bob Arum, to Mike Trainer, to the Duvas, nobody wanted him. I helped negotiate his contract with Don King. Everybody else said he was nothing, but I told Donald, "No, the kid's got quality." Donald said, "But he quit in the Tony Tucker fight." I said, "Douglas just has to be pushed. And he's got a jab."

My thing is, you jab. All my fighters, if they're good fighters or mediocre fighters, they all have a good jab, because I have 'em stepping with the jab. Stepping forward so there's power in the jab, like Larry Holmes did. That's why Larry was so effective. Stepping with the jab makes it a punch. As soon as Douglas knocked out Tyson, everybody else wanted to take credit for Douglas, but they couldn't, because James Douglas didn't step with the jab until I started working with him.

Most guys jab, then they throw the right hand and wonder why guys slip the right hand. But they're not stepping with the jab. When they don't step with it, the jab and the right hand aren't coming together. The jab is the binder. The right hand is the catcher. Some guys do it naturally, but other guys don't step with their jab. Carl [Truth] Williams jabs good, but he don't step with his jab. That's why you can get to him. Because he's not doing anything to keep you away.

Even aggressive fighters like Mike Tyson, if you back them up with the jab, they don't know what to do because they've never been backed up before. That's what happened to Tyson in Tokyo, he got backed up and he didn't know what to do. The biggest bully in the world wasn't the bully anymore. I was there with King and I wanted Tyson to win, because when I was training Douglas, his manager, John Johnson, didn't want to pay me. They wanted to give me twenty-five thousand dollars to help him get the million-three for the Tyson fight, but I wanted a contract. I told John Johnson, "Why should you get a million-three and I get twenty-five thousand? I'm not going to prostitute myself." It ain't like I'm rich. I need the money. But I figured, at this stage of the game, I was turning fifty years old, I know what I can do. I'm the last of the great trainers. Very few guys around can do what I can do.

John Johnson would call my house ten times a day. I kept telling him, "You got a good fighter here, but you got to pay people." I worked three of Douglas's fights. Before the one with Mike Williams, I looked at the tapes and seen Williams go back on his heels. His uncle who's a trainer, J. D. McCauley, and John Johnson didn't see shit on the tapes. I looked at the tapes and when I seen Williams go back on his heels, I knew all Douglas had to do was step with the jab. I knew that fight would be easy, and it was. I was the hero then. I was the greatest thing since peanut butter and jelly.

I also knew Douglas liked me, so I told them, "It's all about money." Angelo Dundee called me and said, "Richie, take whatever you can get." But I said, "I'm different than you, Angelo, I'm not a cornerman. I have to be around the fighter. I have to believe in the fighter. I have to see what the fighter does. How am I going to give the fighter instructions if I don't see how he trains? You got to be with him. You got to be involved with him. You got to know what his habits are. Like when Marlon Starling wanted me to train him, I told him, "I got to get into your head." He said, "Nobody gets into my head. I don't tell nobody what I'm thinking." I said, "Then I can't train you."

But before I left Buster Douglas I told him, "If you fight Tyson, you got a good shot at beating him because of your jab. And your jab will meet Mike Tyson with authority." Which it did. I have no animosity because of John Johnson. I made my choice and I'm going to live with it. I hope Buster makes a hundred million dollars, because on the plane back from Tokyo, he came over to me and said, "Richie, you showed me a lot. Thank you." And I said, "Thank you." No matter what John Johnson thinks, Buster and I know that I was a part of that man being world heavyweight champion.

After the Tokyo fight John Johnson said, "See, I showed you."

I said, "Showed me what? What did you per se show me? Buster showed me, not you." I reminded Johnson that I liked the fighter before he got the fighter. Back when I was with Tiger Eye Promotions with Sylvester Stallone, I told Stallone, "Douglas will be champion someday. He's got the qualities and the tools." Stallone wanted white fighters, so he didn't want Douglas, but I knew Douglas had the talent. I have a good eye for boxers. Like great football coaches and great basketball managers, you got to be able to pick the talent or you're not going to be great. I believe one thing: If you come to Richie Giachetti, you're going into another dimension in the boxing world. I'm taking you one more step farther than what other trainers can take you, because I have the experience and the knowledge. It's like I tell young fighters: "I've been to the mountain. If you pay attention, I can take you to the mountain." Just like I took Larry Holmes to the mountain.

I used Larry as a sparring partner for Shavers after he had been turned down by five trainers. Cus D'Amato, Angelo Dundee, Gil Clancy, Eddie Futch, and Archie Moore. None of 'em thought Larry would make it. Maybe they thought he was too arrogant, which he was. And he wasn't in real good shape. For two rounds, he'd fight his ass off, then he'd tire out. But I just knew that if I got Larry running in the morning, if I got him in good shape, if I got him stepping with his jab, I just knew he could be a good fighter.

From way back, my Uncle Johnny taught me about the jab. He told me from day one, boxing starts with the jab. Me and my twin brother, Bob, beat guys because of the jab. In the Golden Gloves I beat a big monster kid, stronger than hell, with the jab. Everybody always said that the tradition of the Giachettis was the jab. I got Larry stepping with the jab. I seen things in Larry nobody else did. But Larry was so arrogant, Ernie Butler wanted to get him beat. Ernie was a nice old man in Easton, Pennsylvania, who had trained Larry, but Ernie wasn't aggressive. Larry wouldn't listen to him. Ernie told me, "Larry needs to be taught a lesson." I said, "Why?" Ernie said, "He's too cocky." I said, "But that's the great thing about him." Ernie and a lot of other people thought Larry's arrogance was a negative but I turned it into a positive.

In those days, Larry was getting two hundred or four hundred dollars a fight, then two thousand or twenty-five hundred. When he was one of Ali's sparring partners, he got fifteen hundred a week. Ali paid good. Before the Thrilla in Manila, he used Larry as a sparring partner, then Larry knocked Rodney Bobick out on the undercard.

No matter how good a young fighter is, sooner or later he has to step up in class to find out just how good he is. Larry stepped up the next year against Roy Williams on the Ali–Jimmy Young undercard at the Capital Centre in Landover, Maryland. Larry didn't want to fight Roy Williams. Larry told me, "He's too big, I'm not ready for him." I said, "Larry, when you were in Ali's camp, you sparred many a round with Roy Williams and you beat him up. If you beat him in the gym, you can beat him in the ring. But you got to want to beat him. You're going to be showcased in this fight. This is the time in your life when you have to be tested." He looked at me and said, "Richie, if you believe it, I'll do it." He went out and won a ten-round decision despite a broken right hand.

One of the early rounds Larry broke the bone behind the base of his right forefinger. In the corner he told me, "My hand's broken." I said, "Don't worry about it. Just stick and move. Just throw your left hand." I grabbed his right glove near the little finger and said, "Does it hurt over here?" He said, "No." I said, "If you throw your right hand, punch with the outside of your hand. But don't favor it. Don't let him know. If something happens, I'll stop the fight. But we're not going to stop the fight just because your hand's broken." Williams and his corner didn't realize Larry's right hand was broken until the tenth round. By then Larry had just kept sticking and moving. I knew he was ahead. I could always judge how a fight is going.

Most cornermen don't know if their fighter is winning or losing. I can name you ten trainers who always think their guy is ahead. Bullshit, he's not ahead. But they're so wrapped up in the fight, they don't know. That's one of the things you have to learn. Johnny Dunn in Boston once told me, "You got to pay attention to the rounds, you got to know if your fighter's winning." I just don't look at it one way.

The night Larry fought Ken Norton in 1978 at Caesars Palace, I knew he had to win the fifteenth round. In the corner I told him, "If you win this round, you'll be the champion. This is what we trained for. You got to show off. You got to shine. If you want the title, you got to fight like you never fought before." Some boxing people will tell you that was the best round they ever saw anywhere anytime. When it was over, Larry Holmes was the WBC heavyweight champion. I was mentally drained. It was like I went fifteen rounds with him. It was like every punch he took, I felt. It was like that in every big fight.

I once told him, "Larry, I am your reminder. I can't fight for you, but I can tell you what you're doing wrong and remind you what you should be doing." That was my success.

People say, "How do you keep your ego from getting bigger than the fighter's?" I say, "As long as you praise the fighter, as long as you make the fighter bigger than you, then you become big. But if you become bigger than the fighter, then the fighter don't want you." Every fighter I go to, the first meeting I have with him, I tell him, "I've had world champions. I want to do it again. I love the thrill. To make me big, to make me money, is for you to win. If you listen and pay attention and we work as a team, we'll become big together. Then it'll be another notch in my belt because you made me big." But even though Larry kept winning, when he was getting ready to defend the title against Earnie Shavers at Caesars Palace, Don King threw Ray Arcel and Freddie Brown in with us. I said, "What do we need them for?" Don said, "You got to have names." I said, "You want 'em, I'll take 'em."

Freddie came in about a week before the fight, Ray arrived a few days before the fight. So when we had our meeting, I told them what I wanted Larry to do. Stick and move. Lateral movement. In and out. Don't clinch. Stay away from Earnie's big right hand.

As soon as I said that, Ray said, "No, you're wrong." I said, "What do you mean, no?" Ray said, "Larry's got to hate Shavers more." I said, "When we go into the ring, Larry would beat up his own mother if he had to." Ray said, "He's not talking bad about Shavers," and then he said, "I think Larry should go to the body more." I said, "Go to the body, huh? Well, Mr. Arcel, I have high respect for you, but if you go to the body, Mr. Arcel, what do you give away?" He said, "Your head." But now he got mad and said, "What do you think, that I don't know boxing? I've been in boxing seventy years." I said, "Mr. Arcel, what does Earnie Shavers do better than anybody else in boxing?" He got mad again and said, "Don't you think I know? He's the best puncher there is." I said, "Case closed. The meeting's over. I don't want to hear anything more out of you guys." I couldn't say anything about that to the newspapermen at the time, because it would have been sour grapes. Ray Arcel is a great name. I can tell you that story now because it's true. But back then, I had to keep my mouth shut. I had to be humble.

I don't know what Ray Arcel's theory is about a fighter getting up from a knockdown, but I know that my theory might have saved Larry Holmes from losing the title to Shavers that night. Old-timers used to tell fighters, "If you get knocked down, stay on one knee until the count of eight. Get your breath and then get up." But my idea is for the fighter to get to his feet as soon as he can.

If you stay down until the count of eight, then try to get up, at eight there's only two seconds left. Now if you stumble and you look weary, you'll be counted out. It's over. But if you get up, shake your head, get the cobwebs out, give your legs time to steady themselves, you'll get your balance faster. When you stay down, you're not dizzy. But as soon as you get up, your balance might be shaky. So the sooner you get up, the better. It's like a doctor told me, the brain is the greatest computer there is, but when you're down, the brain doesn't have to compute because it's stable. But the sooner you stand up, the sooner it starts computing again, the sooner you got your balance.

All the old-timers still tell their fighters to stay down until eight, but I say get up. Douglas almost lost in Tokyo because he stayed down too long. George Foreman stayed down too long in Zaire because Archie Moore was signaling for him to stay down and take the count. That's the old way. And the wrong way.

So when Larry got knocked down by Shavers late in the seventh round, he was up by the count of five, shaking his head and hopping up and down to clear the cobwebs. In the corner I was yelling, "Keep your composure." Larry knew what I meant, because we'd talked about it. See, when a guy gets hit, his natural reaction is to hit back, to get even. That's what you do in the street. If you get hit in the street, you want to hit the guy harder. Some old-time fighters, they hit back like they were in the street. Jake LaMotta, Rocky Graziano. They'd get into a toe-to-toe brawl. But that's a mistake. When you get knocked down or get wobbled in the ring, you don't fire back. You hold on until your head clears. You keep your composure. You get yourself together, then you fire back. That's what Larry did. He got himself together, then he stopped Shavers in the eleventh.

But as good as Larry was, when he fought Muhammad Ali in 1980, I thought it was a no-win situation. If he didn't knock Ali out, he was a bum. And if he ever lost, he was done. He might win the battle but he could not win the war. Not against a legend.

To distract the tension, I had Caesars Palace make up a drawing of Porky Pig and put Ali's face on it. Fat as a pig. That's how fat Ali was when he started training. That's where I got the idea. Then I realized that Black Muslims don't like pork. Perfect. When I presented the drawing to Ali at a press conference a few days before the fight, he told me, "You got me." But by then I had a real worry. The day before, Larry got cut over his left eye sparring with Jody Ballard. Larry was wearing a headgear, like he always did when he sparred, so nobody seen it happen but me, because I was standing up on the apron of the ring.

When I seen Larry cut, I didn't stop the sparring session right then. That would've been a dead giveaway. When he came back to the corner, I wiped his face off with a towel like I always did. I rolled the towel to hide the little bit of blood on it. I told him, "You're cut, but just go out again and get off a quick flurry of punches. I'll stop it and we'll get the hell out of here."

Larry loved to finish sparring that way. He went out, moved around a little, then got off a fast flurry. I yelled, "That's all. You're in great shape, champ. You're going to kick Ali's butt. That's all." He climbed through the ropes and ran to the dressing room. Of all the writers there, only Dick Young suspected anything. He must've seen the blood on the towel. Dick hurried over to me and said, "Let me see that towel." I said, "You think Ali's going to win. Get the hell out of here." I kept going to the dressing room. We stopped the bleeding. I had Larry put on dark glasses and a hat. I told him, "If anybody asks you to take off the glasses, take your hat off first. But when you take the glasses off, tilt your head back so your eyelids go up. Then tell them to look at your pretty face." It worked. Nobody noticed. It wasn't much of a cut. It only needed three stitches. But there was no need to get the commission all excited.

In the fight, the cut opened in the second round, but I stopped the blood. It was never a problem. Ali was the problem. He wouldn't go down.

If you remember the fight, I kept yelling, "In the center. In the center." I wanted Larry to fight him in the center of the ring. But what Ali would do was retreat to the ropes. Ali was taking punishment, but Ali took the best punch in boxing. On the ropes Larry couldn't get clean shots at him. Unless you clean-shot Ali while he was boxing, like Joe Frazier did in their first fight, you couldn't knock Ali down. When you're boxing, you can get caught with a clean shot. But on the ropes Ali just took every punch thrown at him. Larry kept coming back to the corner and saying, "He won't fall. I'm hitting him with everything but he won't fall." After a while, Ali wasn't even throwing punches. Around the ninth round I hollered, "Stop the fight. Stop the fight." The referee, Richard Green, wouldn't stop it. But when Ali didn't answer the bell for the eleventh round, that was it.

At the press conference the next day, Larry handled it well. I told him to praise Ali, to tell everybody Ali was his idol. Larry also said that he didn't want to fight Ali, that the money forced the fight. Larry came out of a no-win situation with a win, but I didn't.

Before the Ali fight, the FBI was trying to get Don King any way it could. Joe Spinelli was the FBI agent who was after him. His informant was José Torres, once the light heavyweight champion and later the chairman of the New York State Athletic Commission. Torres was feeding information to Spinelli that Richie Giachetti was the guy, that if you want to get Don King, you got to get Richie Giachetti first. I'd been through this with Donald a few years before when he put on a heavyweight tournament for the ABC network that turned out to be a scandal. Some fighters had false records. But when the investigators questioned me for six and a half hours, I came out the cleanest guy in the whole thing. I told them I was managing Holmes and that I worked other corners but I never falsified records like some guys did and I never cut any other fighter's purse like some guys did. I brought other fighters into the tournament, but I never took a piece of 'em.

People like to say that Don King knew all about it, but Donald just told the people working on the tournament: "You do what you got to do and I'll do what I got to do. What I don't know about ain't going to hurt me because I ain't involved in it." He really didn't know what was going on per se. He just told them to put the tournament together.

Donald's the best tightrope walker going. The FBI never filed any charges. But when Spinelli was after him later on, Donald knew that I ain't never gonna talk. What the FBI did was play off it. When they started coming at me and Larry Holmes before the Ali fight, I told them, "This is a big fight for us. You back off Larry, and after the fight, I'll talk to you." When the fight was over, I talked to 'em, but I didn't tell 'em nothing. They were so far off base, I had to laugh at what they were looking for: fixed fights, kickbacks, payoffs. The kickbacks and payoffs were right in front of their eyes, but they couldn't see it and I wasn't going to tell them.

One of the FBI agents said, "Now we're going to come after you. We know you're connected." When I started laughing, he said, "We know you used to be an enforcer for the union." I said, "I'm glad you know all this shit."

Way back I was sort of an enforcer for Babe Triscaro's truck drivers in Cleveland, but I knew the FBI could never connect me. Babe had been a good fighter, so if there was a wildcat strike, he'd hire fighters to walk around and scare the guys who were picketing into going back to work. Yeah, I'd do that. I'd hire other fighters at a hundred dollars a day to do it with me. Hey, a good fight is a good fight. Just your presence scared those guys into going back to work. But one day when they brought the guns out and told me to get the truck drivers back to work, I said, "I'm not getting paid enough to get involved with guns." I never did nothing illegal in my life. Like when I had the body shop, tough guys would come to me and want to paint cars and do things but I just never got into it.

I was accused a lot because I knew all the mobsters downtown. I played cards and shot dice. Back in Uniontown, that's what I was brought up on. Stud poker, blackjack, dice. I didn't take no shit on the street. I kicked a lot of ass. I stood up for my rights. But I wasn't connected to organized crime. I ain't no gangster and never was. Far from it. I'm a hardworking guy.

Yeah, I knew some tough guys. I taught them how to box. Joey Kovach and Keith Ritzon, who turned out to be notorious killers. Trigger guys. They were in dope and gambling. I just knew those guys from boxing. I wasn't involved with what they did. I knew I was clean. That's why I defied Spinelli when he came to see me. You only know your own soul. So if I wasn't clean, I knew they'd get me. But when Spinelli said, "I'm gonna burn you—I know you're in organized crime," I said, "You don't know shit," and I laughed at him. But as soon as I laughed, I knew I'd pissed him off. You don't tell FBI people off. By now Larry was about ten days away from the Trevor Berbick fight in Vegas when they subpoena me. But when Larry hears about the subpoena, he tells me, "If you leave, you're fired." Now, if you get a subpoena from the United States government, you better show up. I went back to Cleveland for the subpoena, but when I called Larry, he said, "Don't bother coming back to Vegas for the fight. You're fired."

I never was hurt more in my life. I didn't even watch the fight on television. Two days later Larry called me and said, "Come to Easton and let's straighten this out." But what I didn't like was that I'd heard that Larry's lawyer there, Charley Spaziani, didn't want me around anymore. I did all the sacrificing and Spaziani made more money with Larry than I did. When the big money come, I wasn't there. Everybody thinks I'm set, but I didn't make the money people think I made.

Larry wanted me back, but my lawyer told me, "Don't go, wait." And when I didn't go to see Larry right away, we got into another argument and now he don't want me back. I was whipped. I was a dead puppy. I didn't know what to do. For two years I didn't do nothing. I was in limbo. I didn't have any good fighters. I was penalized there too. Like when me and Don King had Michael Dokes, Don told me, "Give up Dokes. I want to give Dokes to my son Carl." I said, "Dokes is my fighter. He's a potential champion. I'm not giving him up for nothing." At the time Larry had just become champion and he told me, "You'll never leave me. Give up Dokes." So me and King settled on a price—when Dokes fights for the heavyweight title, I was to get forty thousand dollars. But in 1982 when he knocked out Mike Weaver for the WBA title, I never got nothing. I was on the outside then.

That same year, before Larry fought Gerry Cooney, one of Cooney's managers, Dennis Rappaport, asked me, "How'd you like a hundred thousand dollars to work Gerry's corner?" I said, "Nah, I really ain't that way." He said, "Think about it." The next day Rappaport told me that Cooney's trainer, Victor Vallee, was for it, that I would be the decoy. I said, "I'm no decoy." Then he upped the price to two hundred and fifty thousand, but I said, "If I don't have no input, I wouldn't do it. And furthermore I want a contract." I knew if Cooney won, he'd be the first billion-dollar fighter. If that happened, I wanted three percent of the gross. Not net. The gross. I had Rappaport thinking about it. He and Cooney's other manager then, Mike Jones, were known as the Whacko Twins, but Rappaport was a businessman. He was trying to work every angle to get the title.

The more I thought about Rappaport's offer to work with Cooney, the more I thought, I can't do that. As bad as Larry and King were screwing me, I still couldn't do that.

Larry won in the thirteenth round when Victor Vallee jumped into the ring to save Cooney from really getting hurt. That night Eddie Futch was in Larry's corner and Eddie stayed there until Larry signed to defend his IBF title against Michael Spinks, who Eddie also trained. Eddie decided not to work with either fighter, so Larry asked me to come back. But that wasn't the whole story. In his fight with Bonecrusher Smith, his corner was chaos. But even before that Larry told me, "Eddie don't motivate me. Eddie don't holler. Eddie mumbles. I can't hear what he's telling me to do. But if I get rid of him, the writers will get on me. The writers like Eddie." I said, "You got rid of me but now you can't get rid of Eddie." He said, "Don't worry, Richie, you'll be around." He gave me a little money to keep me going. And little by little, he asked me how to fight this guy and that guy. We started getting back together. In his Truth Williams fight, he was overtrained, but I hollered from the corner. He knew my voice and he listened. Then it fell into place when Eddie had to make a decision between working with Larry or Michael Spinks.

I was back with Larry, back with my fighter, my heavyweight champion. Another win would tie the 49–0 record that Rocky Marciano retired with. But about five days before the fight, Larry complained that his neck hurt. He couldn't throw the right hand. I figured it was a pinched nerve, and it was. But the doctor Keith Klevin brought in told Larry, "If you get hit on it, you could be paralyzed for life."

Keith was a physiotherapist in Vegas who had been around Larry ever since he rehabilitated Larry's left biceps before the Ken Norton fight. But as soon as I could get Keith alone, I said, "You don't let a doctor tell a fighter that he might be paralyzed. You don't let anybody tell the fighter nothing until you get two or three opinions." So we brought in some other doctors. They told us that Larry could fight with the pinched nerve, that the chances of him being paralyzed if he got hit there were the same as the chances of him getting killed by a car if he crossed the street. But the doubt was in Larry's mind.

In the fight, Larry wasn't himself. I was yelling, "Throw the right hand. Throw the right hand." He kept hesitating. What played on him was this doctor telling him he might be paralyzed. When he went back to Easton, another doctor told him it was nothing serious, that there was no way he could've been paralyzed. But the doubt was there. Larry lost a unanimous fifteen-round decision. Then he lost a lot more when he criticized Rocky Marciano in the press conference afterwards. He lost all the respect he had earned over the years.

Sitting next to him, I couldn't believe what I was hearing. Looking out at the writers and cameras, Larry was saying, "I'm thirty-five fighting young men and he was twenty-five fighting old men. To be technical, Rocky Marciano couldn't carry my jockstrap." I tried to shut him up. I nudged him and whispered, "You're out of hand. You got to be humble." He pushed me away. Then he seemed to realize that maybe I was right. He tried to apologize, saying, "Rocky was one of the greatest fighters of all time. For anyone to accomplish forty-nine victories, even if they were all bums, is some kind of record. If I didn't think he was a great fighter, his pictures wouldn't be on the walls of my motel near Easton." But after what he said about Rocky earlier, it was too late to apologize.

I understood how people felt. When I was a kid growing up in Uniontown me and some other guys used to drive eight hours to Grossinger's in the Catskills to see the great Marciano train in the hangar near the little airstrip. I always watched his trainer Charlie Goldman just as much. Charlie was out of a movie, a little old guy with a cigar and a black derby. But he was the boss. If he had Marciano sparring or hitting the heavy bag, you could hear Charlie saying, "Work hard. Work hard. Punch. Punch." Years later, when I trained Larry Holmes at Grossinger's, we worked in the ski lodge down the hill from the hangar and the airstrip. To me it was an honor just to be in the same hotel where Charlie Goldman trained Rocky Marciano for all his big fights.

As if rapping Marciano wasn't bad enough, just before the rematch with Spinks early the next year, Larry popped off about

how the Vegas boxing judges drank before fights and took payoffs. Duane Ford, the chairman of the Nevada commission, or-
dered Larry to apologize at a prefight press conference. So now
Larry had just about everybody against him: all the boxing fans
who knew anything about Rocky Marciano and all the Vegas judges.

Anyhow, in the rematch with Spinks, I thought we were winning the fight big. After the tenth round I looked over at the guy
I had telling me how the judges were voting on their scorecards.
He signaled to me that through ten rounds the fight was dead
even. I always had somebody giving me the cards. I can't mention
who the guy was, but I always made sure I was informed where
we were at. I don't think it's illegal. I think it's just something
where I'm doing what the other guy isn't. But when I found out
we were dead even going into the eleventh round, I pulled the
microphone out of our corner so nobody would hear me when I
whispered into Larry's ear that it was dead even. I told him, "You
got to go. You should be ahead but they got us even. You got to
win these last rounds." In the fourteenth round Larry got Spinks
in trouble but let him off the hook. In the corner I said, "Why
didn't you finish him?" He said, "I was scared of running out of
gas." Again, the case of a fighter thinking too much. Now I told
him, "You got to win the last round." And he did. I thought he
won at least ten rounds.

Spinks's promoter, Butch Lewis, even thought Larry won. When
the fight ended and I jumped into the ring, I happened to be
near Butch when he turned to Spinks and said, "You blew this
fight." You know what Spinks's reaction was: "I did everything I
could do."

Two of the three judges had Spinks ahead, so he got a split
decision. Larry didn't lose that fight in the ring. He lost it with his
mouth. What he said about Marciano and what he said about how
Vegas judges drink before fights and take payoffs. Judges never
forget. One of the Vegas judges who penciled Larry out of the
Spinks rematch also penciled me out when I had Sanderline Williams going against Iran Barkley in Atlantic City two years later.
To him, I was still Richie Giachetti and I was still Larry Holmes's
guy. He gave the last two rounds to Barkley, who got a split decision. Vegas and Atlantic City are the capitals of boxing now but
they have some of the worst judges.

Boxing commissions always talk about the integrity of their judges
and referees. That's bullshit. Personalities come into judging. If

Larry didn't knock Gerry Cooney out, they had Larry penciled
out. They wanted the white boy to win. That was the most racial
fight in the history of boxing. That was worse than with Joe Louis
and Max Schmeling.

Two years after the second Spinks fight, Larry came back to
fight Mike Tyson for the title. Larry got in good physical shape,
but mentally he wasn't prepared. All the years we were together
he never questioned me about gloves, about anything like that.
He always left all that to me. But that night a good friend of ours,
Saoul Mamby, once the junior welterweight champion, visited us
in the dressing room. Saoul picked up Larry's gloves and said,
"Richie, these are ten-ounce gloves." I said, "Saoul, we've been
fighting with ten-ounce gloves for five years. Heavyweights fight
with ten-ounce gloves." Saoul said, "I fight with eight-ounce gloves."
I said, "You're a welterweight." But then Larry said, "What the
hell's wrong with the gloves?" I said, "Nothing's wrong with the
gloves." But he still thinks something's wrong.

All this bullshit is happening fifteen minutes before we go out.
Just when I get Larry calmed down, his brother Jake comes in
and says, "They're not taking us out the right way." Larry gets all
upset again. I had to go out and check. But what the hell's the
difference which way we go to the ring? Here's a fighter who was
the world heavyweight champion, who had twenty-two title defenses, who never worried about anything, now he's worried about
all these little things he always left to me.

Strategically, our thing for that fight was, let's get past five rounds
and then come on, because Tyson fades. In Tyson's other fights,
he always faded just like he faded against Buster Douglas. But in
our corner everybody was talking at once. I never had that before.
You're not supposed to have that. I was always the one guy who
talked to Larry in the corner. If anybody else had anything to say,
they told me and I told him. But now Lee Black and Syd Martin,
who were never in our corner before, were hollering so much I
yelled, "Shut up," but Larry said, "I want to hear 'em talk." I said,
"Oh, you want to hear 'em talk." They're telling Larry, "Hook.
Hook." I said, "Tyson can be hit with a hook, but Larry, your style
is to jab. Forget the hook. Why would you change what you won
the title with, what made you one of the greatest fighters ever?
Jab. Jab." So after Larry got in the fight, he started fighting on
instinct, fighting like he always did, stepping with that jab.

But then Larry started waiting instead of jabbing. When he

waited, sooner or later he had to get hit. When he got hit with Tyson's right hand, he just stood there. Larry Holmes never stood in front of anybody before in his life. When he stood there in front of Tyson, that was the beginning of the end.

I never thought I'd be training Tyson about two years later. But for a trainer to get Tyson's respect, he's got to relate back to old fighters, because he's studied so many of 'em. He's seen 'em all in old fight films. Like one time he come up to me and said, "Who do you think would win, Sugar Ray Robinson or Carlos Monzon?" I said, "Monzon would knock Robinson out." He said, "Goddammit, Richie, you're right. You're the only one who agrees with me." We both thought that Monzon was taller, had a good jab, could drop the right hand in after the jab, and had good movement. Robinson had all that and he was fancy too, but he had to get off on you. Jake LaMotta and all those other guys were brawlers. They had no finesse. That's why Robinson outclassed all those guys, because he was a boxer-puncher, but Monzon would have knocked his ass out.

Talking with Tyson that time, I said, "If you asked me who's the greatest fighter of all time, I'd say Sugar Ray Robinson, but certain styles beat certain styles." Against certain fighters, some fighters just can't do the things they do against other fighters. Robinson was my idol. Nobody can compare with him. But that doesn't mean he was unbeatable.

Working with boxing champions, working with movie stars like Sylvester Stallone, you got to know how to deal with ultra egos. The first time Stallone come around, me and Larry Holmes was in New Orleans in 1978 for the second Ali–Leon Spinks fight. He's wearing a green tank top and he says, "I'm Sly." I said, "So what?" He says, "I'm Sly. I'm Rocky. I want to see Larry." I said, "I know who you are, but so what?" Another time he wanted to get into Ali's dressing room, but I said, "I can't let you in here." The next year, when Larry and me were honored as fighter of the year and trainer of the year at the Boxing Writers Dinner in New York, he was there and we started to be real good friends. Then in 1982 he started Tiger Eye Promotions and hired me. He wanted white fighters, but I told him they're just not there.

One day Sly told me the fighters were complaining I was too rough on them. I said, "If they're coming to you to complain, I'm doing my job. You're the real live Rocky and you want to find another real live Rocky who can fight. But most of these guys don't want to be fighters. They're just hoping to be a movie star like you."

I still consider myself to be Sly's friend. I worked with the man for four years. I lived in his Hollywood mansion for two years. When he got married to Brigitte Nielsen, I was one of only ten people invited to the ceremony. There's the picture on the wall. When he did *Rocky III* and *Rocky IV*, me and him choreographed all his fight scenes. The early *Rocky* movies, he'd go from one end of the ring to the other throwing five left hooks. I told him, "No, a fighter can't throw four or five left hooks in a row. He can only throw two." It's easy to choreograph punches, because there's no actual punches thrown. Nobody ever gets hit. All the punches are pulled.

I got fired from *Rocky V* when Tyson's manager of record, Bill Cayton, threatened to pull his fighter Tommy Morrison from the film if I stayed. Cayton didn't like me because he was battling with Don King over Tyson and he knew I had been around Donald all these years.

In those years when the FBI was investigating Donald, some people think Donald put a hit out on me. I don't know about that, but I do know that two guys showed up in Cleveland to see me. One said, "You're Italian. You don't talk. Why would you talk to the FBI?" I said, "What are you talking about? You don't even know the whole story." I don't know if Donald sent those guys or what. For all I know, they might have been FBI guys. But I know this. During all that bullshit, my buddy Keith Ritzon, one of the guys I trained who turned out to be a notorious killer, Keith came up to me and said, "Richie, your problems are all over. I'll take care of King for you."

I said, "Get the hell out of here. I'll take care of this myself." I didn't know until afterwards that Keith Ritzon was supposed to have killed something like seven guys. He couldn't care less about killing somebody else. Don King don't know I saved his life.

Index

5/29/91